JOURNEY BEYOND WORDS

To mike —
Peace + blessings
on the journey —

Brent
11-21-97

MIRACLES STUDIES

is a term suggested

by the

Foundation for Inner Peace,

and which may be used

to designate materials

which provide information

about and/or interpretation of

A COURSE IN MIRACLES.

Such materials pertain to,

but should not

be confused with,

the original

Course.

JOURNEY BEYOND WORDS

A Companion
to
The Workbook
of
The Course

received by
Brent A. Haskell, Ph.D., D.O.

A MIRACLES STUDIES *Book*

 DeVorss *Publications*

ISBN: 0-87516-670-9

Library of Congress Card Catalog No.: 94-70459

The ideas represented herein are the personal interpretations and understanding of the author, and are not necessarily endorsed by the copyright and trademark holder of *A Course in Miracles*.

DeVorss & Company, *Publisher*
Box 550
Marina del Rey, CA 90294

Printed in the United States of America

TABLE OF CONTENTS

PREFACE

The Jeshua Tapes are a series of channeled auditory tapes which were received by me between January 1, 1990 and January 2, 1991. *Journey Beyond Words* is an edited version of the transcript of those tapes.

During the year the Tapes were received, I was personally doing the daily lessons of the Workbook of *A Course in Miracles*. It is clear from the material that the Tapes were designed to complement *A Course in Miracles*, specifically the Workbook. The source, who identifies himself as Jeshua, speaks of himself as the author of the Course. The reader, of course, may decide for himself whether he believes that to be true, or whether it matters. As always, that which each of us accepts as true for himself is independent of any labels we may attach to it. Simply stated, truth speaks for itself.

Although I had been through the Workbook a number of times, and have been a devoted student of the Course since 1986, I was continually amazed by the insights which were afforded our study group as we supplemented our endeavors with the Tapes. In spite of the fact that I had read the entire Course a number of times, I was repeatedly surprised at how the meaning of the Course came forward with previously unsurpassed clarity. It is my belief that many readers will have a similar experience as they use this book in conjunction with *A Course in Miracles*.

A Course in Miracles is a complete work and stands beyond any need for supplementation or clarification of its contents. Any reason for additional material would presumably be based on a decision to vary the format and language in which the contents are presented. In that vein, the auditory format may become beneficial to many. In addition, the language of the Tapes is somewhat less "philosophical" than much of the Course seems to be. The different tone of the language may make the material easier for many persons to experience.

In any event, being the channel for this material has been without question the most significant event in my life. I believe that one of my primary reasons for living this lifetime is to participate in the reception and dissemination of the Jeshua material. I offer this book for what it is, one more of the aids we are bringing into our lives as we inexorably progress toward knowing the truth of what we really are, which is the Son of God.

The section entitled The World of *A Course in Miracles* is designed to serve as an introduction to the principles of the Course for those readers who may be less familiar with the Course than others. The section also serves to introduce some of the significant concepts that appear in the Tapes, as well as in the Course itself. It is based on material received from Jeshua, but it would be inappropriate to state him as the direct author of those pages.

All the material in the forty-nine chapters which make up the core of the book came directly from Jeshua. The editing is only for the purpose of readability. It is my intent and belief that the basic content and meaning of the material has been unchanged.

Appendix I is a suggested outline which a student of the Course may wish to follow as he uses the material in conjunction with the Daily Lessons.

Appendix II is a list of direct quotations or close paraphrases from *A Course in Miracles*. I extend my gratitude to the Foundation for Inner Peace, which holds the copyright and trademark on the Course, for allowing those references.

My appreciation and gratitude go out to Fran Dailey, who participated in our study group during the year I received the Tapes. My deep appreciation also goes to the members of our current *Course in Miracles* study group: Ronda Campbell, Marvel Clark, Kathy Day, Janet Fix, Mary Ellen Lind, Perry Weigel, Linda and Pat Wilson, and my wife Marsha. Their contributions to my personal growth, both spoken and unspoken, have been deeply appreciated. Special thanks to Mary Ellen for taking time to proofread much of the material. I remain extremely grateful to Marvel for the many hours she has spent in proofreading, offering suggestions and guidance in many ways, and above all for being my beloved friend. Lastly I am most appreciative of my beloved wife, Marsha. She has been a great source of personal support during and after the time I was receiving this material, as well as a fellow student of the Course, and my best friend.

Brent A. Haskell, Ph.D., D.O.

WHAT IS *A COURSE IN MIRACLES*?
And How Does *Journey Beyond Words* Relate to It?

A Course in Miracles was first published in 1976. Since that time approximately one million copies have been printed. The Course, which states its own purpose to be that of a teaching device, is comprised of three sections, The Text, The Workbook, and the Manual for Teachers. The Text is primarily theoretical, and describes the thought system upon which the message of the Course is based. The Workbook consists of 365 Daily Lessons, which may be used on a daily basis over one full year. There is, however, no pressure on the student to strictly adhere to a one-a-day format, only the suggestion that the student not do more than one lesson in a given day. The Workbook emphasizes the experience of the Course through application, and applications are often suggested in the Lessons. The Manual for Teachers has a question-and-answer format, and appears designed to answer many of the common questions which may arise during the student's learning. It also includes a Clarification of Terms, which explains a number of terms from within the framework of the Course.

The story of how the Course came to be is both inspiring and fascinating. The story has been admirably told by Robert Skutch in a book entitled *Journey Without Distance*, which is available from bookstores, or from the Foundation for Inner Peace, publishers of the Course.

A Course in Miracles came into being as a collaborative venture between Helen Schucman, William Thetford, and a Voice which spoke through Helen. Helen's function was to receive the material from the Voice and write it down. Bill's function was, in part, to type the material from the "dictation" Helen had taken. There was no doubt on the part of Helen and Bill that this was a mutual project which they were involved in together.

The Course was preceded by an experience in which Bill, after one too many frustrating staff meetings, became overwhelmed with an inner realization that "there must be another way" for us to relate to each other. Helen, as if guided, agreed to help him find it. What *A Course in Miracles* became is "another way," another way of seeing and experiencing ourselves, our relationships, the world, and life itself.

The Course suggests that there does exist a universal experience (might we call it Truth?) which we all, of necessity, will one day share. It also states that a universal theology is not possible, which is to say that there must exist different, yet valid, pathways to that Truth. The Course is one of those pathways.

The universal experience described in the Course is one which includes the awareness that we all are One with God and with each other, and which also creates for us a life of peace, love, joy, and freedom. If there is within you, as there was within Bill Thetford, a quiet longing for "another way," rest assured that the pathway is there awaiting you. And it may be *A Course in Miracles*.

In the section entitled "The World of *A Course in Miracles*," I have attempted to encapsulate the message of the Course as I understand it, and as I find it expressed in *Journey Beyond Words*. The reader may also refer to the Preface of the Course itself, wherein is contained a synoptical discussion of what the Course says.

Insofar as Jeshua refers to himself as the author of the Course, we are wont to ask certain questions. Whence the name Jeshua? Why the need for more material from the same source? If it is the same author, should this material be treated as more of the original *A Course in Miracles*, or as it states itself to be, a discussion of the original Course?

Historically, one of the names used for Jesus has been Jeshua (sometimes Yeshua). Since the Course implies that Jesus is the Voice that Helen heard, the two names can be seen as compatible.

Over the years, I have met many persons who aspired to experience the message of the Course, but who, as one friend put it, "couldn't get past the language." This simply meant that the terminology, the wording, the metaphors, were not conducive to their desire for peace. Persons who have reviewed the material I received from Jeshua have often told me that they felt more love in the words of Jeshua than in the words of the Course. That surprised me because I personally have never found anything but love in the Course. However, it remains that there may be a place for the same message, but in a different format. I personally have found that the Jeshua material has greatly clarified my understanding of the Course, as have many persons who have read it. To that end, there may be many like myself who will benefit from its presence in their lives.

The Jeshua discussions of values and valuing serve to amplify what is already in the Course. However, a clear understanding of what valuing means (from Jeshua) has significantly clarified my understanding of much of the Course. The emphasis on valuing, in my opinion, is one of the reasons for this additional material being given.

The Foundation for Inner Peace has a goal, with which I concur, which is to ensure that any reader not become confused about what is THE *A Course in Miracles* (meaning the original Course), and what is discussion, or interpretation, of it. As Jeshua states at the beginning of each tape, this material is a discussion of *A Course in Miracles*. In that regard, this book, in my opinion, consists of material which is designed to accompany the Course and serve as an adjunct to it.

To that end, one point needs to be made. There are many references by Jeshua to "the Course" and also to "this Course." Those references should be understood as references to *A Course in Miracles*, and not as implying that this material is THE original Course.

The reader will note that this work has been designated a MIRACLES STUDIES book. MIRACLES STUDIES is a term suggested by the Foundation for Inner Peace, and which may be used to designate materials which provide information about, and/or interpretations of, *A Course in Miracles*. Such materials pertain to, but should not be confused with, the original Course. The hope is that this designation will eliminate the above-mentioned confusion.

The Jeshua material uses language and metaphors which are not exactly the same as the Course, which I presume is for good reason. However, its goal, like the Course itself, is to guide us to the universal experience. And as the Course suggests, and the Jeshua material continually emphasizes, that experience lies beyond the words. The goal of both the Course and the Jeshua material is to allow us to open to the awareness of God, which lies deep within.

It may be for some that *Journey Beyond Words* will stand alone. For others *A Course in Miracles* will suffice full well. And for others still, the two may function together to provide yet "another way" to the life of peace we all seek, and which is God's inviolable promise to us all.

PROLOGUE:
THE WORLD OF A COURSE IN MIRACLES

As you begin to experience *A Course in Miracles*, you will find yourself entering a new world. Contained within its pages are the tools that will allow you to see the world in a completely different light. This new world you will discover is a world of unchangeable love, a world of unshakable peace, a world of childlike joy, and a world of absolute freedom. This love, this peace, this joy, and this freedom are so great that they extend even beyond what we can comprehend with our thinking minds. The new world of *A Course in Miracles* already exists deep within you, where it has always been, and shall always remain. And all it takes to enter that world is your own willingness to reconsider, to challenge, every belief you now hold.

When your body dies, YOU do not die. The ultimate reality of what you are does not lie in your body, but in the Spirit that continues to exist after you die. Most of you reading these words already believe that is true. The real You, which is created in the image of God, is Spirit. It is that Spirit which is part of God, and which shares with Him His creative power. One of the fundamental messages of *A Course in Miracles* is that this Spirit, which IS the reality of what you are, is alive and well right now, even though you seem to currently exist as your body. Your Spirit does not cease to exercise its creative power, it does not leave for distant parts of the universe, simply because you right now seem to be walking around in your body. Because Spirit is alive and well RIGHT NOW, and because it IS your source of creative power, your Spirit is active in this world, NOW. As such, it is your Spirit that determines what you experience, and what seems to happen to you. The physical world is controlled by the creative power of Spirit, and not the other way around. That awareness suddenly turns the world upside down, as you come to realize that everything in your life has its source in the creative power of your Spirit. That awareness shall become for you a source of great peace, and great joy.

In a word, the world of *A Course in Miracles* is a world of freedom. That is all. If you understood freedom in its entirety, freedom as it truly is, no further words would be necessary. You are free. That is all.

Your real nature is Spirit. And as Spirit you are free. Spirit lives without limitation. It is not limited by space or time. You could only say that Spirit exists everywhere, forever and ever, without beginning and without end. It is in this sense that we are created in the image of God, Who likewise is Spirit. Soon, as the Course spells them out for you, you begin to realize the implications of being Spirit, and of being totally free.

Spirit is as free as an idea. In that sense It is completely safe and beyond attack, for what can harm an idea? Spirit is beyond being threatened by anything. It is completely safe in God's world. There is no external circumstance which can alter the nature of your Spirit. In the words of the Course, you are invulnerable.

Just as you are invulnerable, so is God Himself. A being who is invulnerable NEVER has any reason to fear the attack of another being. Indeed, a being who is truly invulnerable is incapable of even sensing that an attack is present. As a Being possessed of infinite strength, God is completely beyond being attacked, threatened, or offended by ANYTHING His Son might choose to experience. Because that is so, God naturally extends to His Son absolute freedom to be and to experience whatever he can imagine. The extension to another of such complete freedom is what you shall come to know as love. Such love is only possible when seen through the eyes of Spirit.

As a Being of Spirit, created by God in His own image, you possess other attributes which we find delineated in the Course. Your mind is part of God's Mind. This makes you holy, because you are part of God. This also means that the strength of God is within you, that the Love of God is part of your being, that the vision which can and does see the truth about Life is within your mind. It also means that you, as Spirit, and as part of God, are always sustained and protected by the Love of God. There is within each of us the desire to be cared for, protected, and loved. The God of *A Course in Miracles* blesses us with just those gifts, raised to perfection, and extended without exception of any kind.

As we struggle and toil through this earthly life, it is far from obvious that the preceding paragraphs are true. That is because we view this world through eyes which do not see the truth. We make our interpretations of what this world is based upon the thoughts within our brains. The Course refers to those thoughts as the "thoughts we think we think," but which are not our real thoughts. In order to experience the world of *A Course in Miracles* we must be willing to consider the notion that the thoughts of the brain do not bring evidence of what is true. In fact, we must open to the awareness that it is not even possible to discover our true nature so long as we insist upon functioning within the thought system of this world.

The world of *A Course in Miracles* is to be found beyond your thoughts. The thoughts of this world, the thoughts of the brain, take the form of perception. Perceptions are always formed in response to an experience which is born in the creative part of your mind and then projected onto the screen of space and time. Your perceptions are thoughts formed after the fact, about an experience born in your mind. *A Course in Miracles* states this by saying that you see only the past, and that your earthly mind is occupied only with past thoughts. Perceptions, since they are after the fact, do not have creative power. As such, the Course states, they have no meaning.

The sum total of our perceptions forms what is basically a filter through which we see the physical world, including ourselves. Insofar as our perceptual framework has its basis IN this world, we are constrained to believe that this world is reality, and that our own reality exists within it (i.e. you believe that your body is what you really are). The message of *A Course in Miracles* is that our real nature is Spirit, that we are not bodies, and that the perceptual framework of this world does not and cannot tell us what we are. It is in that sense that the thoughts "we think we think" are meaningless, for they do not tell us the truth about our Selves.

There does exist, however, a perceptual framework which comes very close to informing us of what our real nature is. The Course refers to this framework as True Perception. True Perception is quite fascinating, for it is not something that you "figure out." It is not a reward that comes after years of studying and contemplating a complicated thought system. In fact, the Course states quite emphatically that there is nothing for you to DO that shall achieve for you the end result, which is the peace of God. The pathway to True Perception and the world of peace lies in your willingness to open to the simple truth that your true nature IS Spirit, and that it is not to be found within this world of bodies and space and time. And when once you open to the possibility that truth and peace lie beyond this world, you will find that they exist within you, and have always been there.

Beyond the level of our bodies, beyond the level of our brain's thoughts, there is the level of mind. It is there that all creative activity takes place. If you desire to experience anything, or to change your current experience in any way, you must do so by functioning at the level of mind. You touch the level of mind by doing your best to silence the thoughts of your brain. You do not bring with you the interpretations and judgments which this world has taught you. You do not bring with you stigmas of guilt from the past. You do not bring with you fear of the future. Indeed, you already know through your own experience that you are the closest to being fully alive when you simply EXPERIENCE your life, when you lose yourself in what you are doing, so that there are no thoughts of past, future, or consequence. We all know that this is so, whether we refer to playing the piano, hitting a golf ball, or enjoying a sunset. The level of mind is akin to that state in which you are free of your thoughts, and are simply being alive. It is at that level that you encounter your creative reality. The Course has a goal of helping us learn to live our lives at that level of mind.

What we learn in *A Course in Miracles* is that when we leave the busyness of our thoughts behind, and choose to listen, we can hear the Voice of God. That Voice is always there in the silence of our minds, quietly awaiting the day when we open ourselves to Its presence. That Voice will teach you of a new world, a world in which there is nothing but love, a world of peace, and joy, and freedom beyond what your thoughts can comprehend.

What will you discover as you enter the world of *A Course in Miracles*? You will discover that your true nature exists as Spirit, as an idea in the Mind of God. As such, you are part of God and can never, under ANY circumstances, be separated from Him. As part of God, you have been endowed with the creative power of the universe. There is essentially nothing which you cannot do as you exercise that power. Furthermore, it is God's Will that you use that power without limit or restriction, for the purpose of creating joy, which automatically extends to all of Creation.

You will learn, however, that creation always extends itself in one direction (outward). The creation cannot turn tail and alter his creator. This means that you, the Son of God, cannot reverse the direction of creation, that you cannot change God or what He has created. The only limitation on your absolute freedom to create is that you cannot change God or what He has created, which includes your Self. You are as God created you, and MUST remain so. You are locked safe and secure in the arms of God, always to remain so, and there is no power in the universe that can do or imagine anything to change that fact.

I have already alluded to the fact that we are invulnerable. This, in application, means that there exists no power in Creation which can do anything to us against our will. Since our creative power lies within, it also follows directly that we must be the creators of whatever we experience. The Course states quite directly that no happenings can come to the Son of God (us) except by his own choice. As you come to experience this truth within the world of *A Course in Miracles*, it will be for you a doorway to rejoicing and to freedom.

As you realize that you are the creator of your own life, to the last detail, and that all experience arises within you, then what disappears is all tendency or desire to blame your brothers for the circumstances of your life. What then disappears with that awareness is your anger. Without struggle and without effort, anger disappears from your life. And in its place appears peace.

Since every being, in his invulnerability, creates the circumstances of his own life, it follows just as surely that you can never do anything to hurt another. With this awareness, guilt dissolves into nothingness. And as the cause for guilt, sin has dissolved with it. The Course repeats over and over that the Son of God (you) is absolutely without sin. Your freedom and your invulnerability make sin impossible. Such is the love, such is the wisdom of God.

Within the world of *A Course in Miracles* you will also discover that God is One. God is All That Is, and nothing exists but what is part of God, and is God. This includes you and me, and every brother who walks this earth with us. At the level of Spirit, at the level of mind, at the level of our reality, we are all One, created thusly by God, always to remain so. Within this world, you soon come to realize that all of Life is one grand, splendid harmony of existence, and which is an expression of our God-given creative power in action.

As you realize that you are truly One with your world, there will come a new vision of your brothers and this world we share. As you look upon each aspect of your life as but an aspect of your Self, you will automatically approach it with a compassion and a gentleness you had not known before. As the Course suggests, you will walk this world in quiet gratitude, and you will be peaceful as you recognize each experience in your life as a form of your own gift to yourself. You will find that same gratitude and gentleness caressing your eyelids while you sleep in quiet peace.

Always one must ask about the seeming tragedy in this earthly life. What about the violence, the killing, illness, death, the sadness and the tears? The Course helps us realize that all of it stems from fear. There is no man who strikes out at his world, except that he be screaming at his own fear and his own pain. Fear has its source in the mistaken belief that this world IS what we are, and is our reality. Insofar as we believe that we are bodies, separate and alone in the presence of other bodies, constrained to be the victim of circumstance, and cursed with the inevitability of death, we must live in fear.

The process whereby we identify ourselves with this world is called valuing. The Course tells us directly not to value anything which will not last forever. This means, quite simply, for us not to become confused about our real nature. We are Spirit. Our reality is not our body. When we believe that our body, or this world, IS what we are, we are valuing it. Furthermore, our belief that we ARE our body, which we know will one day pass away, must lead to the fear of that day when we (our body) shall die. Thus we create the fear of death. The fear of death, indeed fear itself, could not have arisen if we had not valued this world by equating it with what we are.

The Course states that nothing in this world is worth valuing. Nothing in this world is or can be the reality of what you are. Therefore, the loss of nothing in this world is to be feared. In the world of *A Course in Miracles* there is no fear. You simply realize that what you are is the Son of God, eternal, incapable of dying, absolutely safe, absolutely loved, and absolutely free. You then realize, as the Course says, that there is NOTHING to fear.

The Course tells us not to value this world. It is important to realize that not to value does not mean not to love. In fact, just the opposite is true. It is not possible to truly love another being unless you do not value the relationship. The reason becomes clear when you realize that love is freedom, as we learn in the Course. If you value a relationship with someone else, then you have made that person part of who you are, and you NEED that person. Whenever you need someone, you automatically resist any changes in that person which affect your relationship. In essence, you desire to deny freedom to the person you claim to love. It is not possible to truly love another unless you grant that person complete freedom. God knows that, and created us totally free.

As you do not value, you do not need, and you are only then able to allow complete freedom to another. Only by allowing real freedom can you truly love. And because we are One, it is only by GIVING such freedom and love that you can RECEIVE that same freedom and love into your own life. The love of *A Course in Miracles* brings you freedom and joy, and without effort casts fear totally out of your life. In the absence of fear, you will see beyond what the world calls tragedy.

As you look at the seeming tragedies of the world with the vision of the Course, what you see is beings who have valued this world, and are acting out their fears as they try to experience the impossible dream that they could be what they are not, that they could be separate from God and from each other. Beyond the fears, what you see is beings created free by God, who are totally loved, absolutely safe, and who cannot separate themselves from the loving arms of God, even though they may try to imagine it otherwise. Nothing in this world is worth valuing because none of it can have any effect on the real beauty of what they are. For they are the Son of God, and shall always remain so.

As you begin to experience *A Course in Miracles*, you will find yourself entering a new world. It is a world of freedom, where all beings are so free that they literally choose and create every detail of their lives. In the invulnerability of that freedom, there cannot exist blame, or anger, or guilt, or sin. All that exists is the Love of God, which all beings share equally and fully.

It is a world of oneness and harmony, in which all beings honor and rejoice in the creations of every other being. It is a world in which everything is in harmony with the Will of God, which is nothing more than the total freedom to create and to be. It is a world in which God's only plan for our lives is the joyful expression of that freedom with which He has endowed us.

Above all, it is a world of joy. God's Will is for you to be co-creator with Him in this grand adventure called Life. You have within you the power of God, which makes you invulnerable. Because you are invulnerable, you are totally safe in God's world. Because you are completely safe, you are free to experience whatever you will. Within the context of such freedom, joy becomes inevitable. And that joy IS the Will of God for us all.

The most beautiful aspect of the message of *A Course in Miracles* is its promise that every being in God's Creation will one day return to the full awareness of his true nature. It is not possible for anyone to remain in fear and darkness indefinitely. As you grow into the experience of love and freedom, never doubt that you are but taking the journey home. And home is the place where you shall dwell forever in peace, freedom, joy, and a love which is beyond the measure of anything you can comprehend.

And so we start our journey beyond words . . .

A Course in Miracles

INTRODUCTION

Greetings. I am Jeshua. I have come to discuss with you
A Course in Miracles. (1)

Even as you begin,
Be aware that it is possible
For you to be misled by its name.

In your world,
When you hear the word "course," you think of learning.
But you are not here to learn.
You are here to experience.
And you will find, with great joy,
That there is a dramatic difference between the two.

Learning is nothing more
Than a process undertaken by your brain.
But experience goes beyond the "learning" of your brain.
It goes beyond your thinking, beyond your analyzing,
To the very core of your being,
Wherein lies the true nature of what you are,
Which is the Son of God.

Hear me well.
If you undertake this Course
As an exercise in academic learning,
As the study of ideas to be mastered,
You will fail.
And in your failing, you will miss this Course,
And its miracles,
Entirely.

Your entry into this Course is your choice
To experience,
To live,
And to become.

The purpose of this Course is absolute peace.
Within peace there is the total absence of conflict.

Within peace there is never doubt, only total certainty.
Within peace there is never questioning.
Because there is never quesioning, there is never fear.
And because there is never fear,
There is only room for love.

Love is freedom. Nothing more.
To the extent that you allow freedom to your brother,
You shall receive, in the exact same measure, freedom,
Which is love.

If you, in your thinking, would restrict your brother,
Thus to deny him freedom, thus to deny him love,
Then you must deny yourself that selfsame freedom and love.

In the absence of your freedom,
In the absence of love,
You will experience conflict,
And you will not be at peace.

Again, I tell you,
This Course is nothing more than a pathway
Which shall lead you to the experience of total peace.
Such peace is not something you can think about,
Nor something you can debate.
Indeed, if you ever find yourself wondering
Whether you are at peace,
I promise you,
You are not.

As you approach the daily lessons,
The first two-thirds, as I have told you,
Are for the purpose of breaking down, if you will,
The ghosts you bring with you.

These ghosts, beloved masters of your lives,
Are the thinking, the concepts, the thoughts,
The patterns of behavior,
Generated from within your mind,
Which imprison you in this world of illusion,
And keep you from the peace of which I speak.

So bear in mind,
We are not trying to take anything away from you,

Rather to help you dissolve barriers,
Barriers to the state of peace.

As we help you to break down these walls,
You will realize, first in thoughts,
But then, and this is the essence,
You shall EXPERIENCE the truth we bring.
You will experience it with knowing and certainty,
At the deepest level of your being,
Far beyond the thoughts themselves.

In the knowing, in the certainty, in the experiencing,
The barriers will truly dissolve.
And you shall be free.

You are here to learn to live,
Not to learn to think.
Indeed, you will discover with great rejoicing
That your thinking, in great measure,
Is what keeps you from being truly alive.

Ponder for a moment your idea of anything.
That idea, that thought, is but an interpretation.
It is a choice you make,
A choice which defines for you
That which you seem to be experiencing.

I have come to tell you, and hear this well,
That what you perceive, what you interpret,
Which is based upon your thoughts,
Has nothing whatsoever to do with reality.
This is a description of the major barrier
Which separates you from your peace.

In order for you to have a thought about something,
It is absolutely essential
That the thought be preceded by an experience.
Without the experience itself, the thought could not be born.

So it is that your thoughts are always interpretations,
Based not upon this moment,
But upon experiences you have had in what you call the past.

Love is freedom.
Recall those words.

Say them over and over and over again,
Until the day comes
When you shall experience them as your reality.

Every thought, every opinion,
Every interpretation which enters your mind
Is based upon what you perceive as the past.
Therefore, when you perceive anything,
What you are doing is saying,
"I am choosing to demand, insofar as I am able,
That this entity, this aspect of Creation,
Which by its nature exists in a state of freedom—
I am choosing to demand that this being
NOT BE FREE."

For when you, in your thinking,
Choose to interpret, based upon the past,
What another being IS,
And then believe that interpretation to be reality,
You have made yourself the enemy of that being's freedom.

For you are saying,
"I choose to demand, for my purposes,
That you be as you WERE,
Indeed, not even as you were, but as I PERCEIVED you were.
And now, this moment, you do not exist.
For you are, I tell you, what you WERE."

Do you see that this is the absence of love,
And the absence of freedom?
And if you wanted to be vicious,
You could even call it hatred.

Hear me well.
When you form an opinion of any aspect of Creation,
INCLUDING YOURSELF,
It is but your wish to rob the universe, and yourself,
Of freedom, and therefore, of love.

Thus *A Course in Miracles* says, "I see only the past." (L 7)
And, "I am never upset for the reason I think." (L 5)

Deep within you there is total peace.
There is the absence of conflict.

There is a wellspring of complete freedom, which is love,
And which must be synonymous with vibrant joy.
That is your right, that is your inheritance,
As the Son of God.
And nothing can take it away from you.

In your thinking,
You can choose to imagine that you do not have it.
Which is exactly what you have done.

Thus the purpose of all the initial lessons
Is to help you to experience the realization
That the absence of peace,
The presence of conflict,
The absence of love,
The absence of freedom,
All stem only from your imagination,
And ultimately, from your thinking,
Which must be of the past,
And which is your desire to deny freedom
To the entire universe, and to yourself.

You have come into this world, onto this earth,
To imagine what it would be like to live in a state of separation.
But deep within you is the knowing
That you are not separate from any aspect of Creation,
And can never be.

So at the deepest level of your truth,
You realize that your goal must be to overcome
That which you have come here to experience.

And that you SHALL do.
The doing shall require of you
That you be willing to challenge every value,
Every thought, every notion which you hold.

Do not fear. Rather rejoice.
For your willingness shall be the doorway
That opens unto love, and joy, and freedom.

I tell you, as you open your being to this *Course in Miracles*,
The barriers will dissolve,
And the world will take on new meaning.

Your life will blossom, and grow,
And expand into an eternity of immense joy,
Into a world of light,
And into an unfathomable beauty of which I cannot speak.
For truly, your minds cannot comprehend
The measure of that which is your right,
And your inheritance,
As the Son of God.

Blessings upon you all. That is all.

WHAT IS MEANING?

Greetings again. I am Jeshua. I have come this day
To further, with you, my discussion of
A Course in Miracles.

I will comment further today about your thinking.
Perhaps it shall seem redundant to you
That I speak again and again of your thinking.
However, I cannot overemphasize the importance
Of your awareness about your thoughts and your thinking.

One of the lessons said, "I see nothing as it is now." (L 9)
And another said, "My thoughts do not mean anything." (L 10)

Indeed, what keeps you from seeing anything as it is now
Is your thinking.
For your thoughts confine you to the past.
But more so,
Your thoughts are the result of the hidden desire NOT to see,
To be separate FROM . . .

As an aside, if I were to speak to you of the Original Sin,
That which separates you from the awareness of God,
And which creates the false belief
That you can be separate from anything,
That Original Sin would be your thinking.

Nevertheless, do not judge yourself to be bad, or evil.
For the thinking is, in large measure,
What the experience of this world is all about.
Simply be open to what I say to you.

Try never to lose sight of the fact that your thoughts,
As thoughts, cannot mean anything.
Do not be disheartened by that.
For it is a statement of great joy, and great love,
Which shall bring to you great peace,
When once you come to experience it within your heart.

How can your thoughts be "meaningless"?
How can anything have "meaning"?

Meaning is that which applies only to truth.
Truth merely IS.
Truth is not, and cannot be,
Subject to any kind of interpretation.
Truth cannot be, and is not, affected by one's reaction.
Truth must be, and always is,
Independent of that which you call time.
And truth has meaning.

So when I say a thing is meaningless,
I simply mean that it is not of truth.

If a thing is meaningless,
You will find that it is subject to interpretation.
Indeed, you may use this as a measure of truth.
If that which you perceive in your world
Is subject to interpretation,
It cannot be of truth.
And therefore, it cannot have meaning.

So that which is meaningless
Is that which has been engendered
By your thoughts and your thinking.

Remember, there is only love.
Love is freedom. Love is joy.
And the three are the same.
Love is freedom is joy is freedom is love.
They are the same.

The purpose of this Course is peace.
To be at peace is to experience freedom,
And to experience the joy of being free.
And you shall, indeed, know that as love.

As I have said in the Text,
There are but two emotions,
Love, and its opposite, fear. (2)
Fear always arises from your thinking,
From your interpretations, and your reactions.

This is so because by the very act of thinking
You are denying the meaning and the truth of what you are.

For you cannot ever separate yourself
From the deepest truth of your being,
Which is that you ARE truth,
And meaning is all that you can know.

In your thinking,
You seek to deny the deepest truth of what you are.
Thus you generate statements which must harbor conflict.
Such statements are meaningless,
And must, by their very nature, make you afraid.

One of the lessons spoke about
Your being in competition with God. (3)
It said you might feel resistance to that idea.
Indeed, you probably shall.
But, think of it this way—
In your thinking you are generating a world
Which is subject to interpretation.
You are creating your own world, AS YOU PERCEIVE IT.
And every other person's world seems to be as he, or she,
Perceives it for himself, or herself.
By this you shall know that such worlds are meaningless.

In your thinking,
As you choose to cling to that which cannot have meaning,
Are you not trying to create a world, an image,
A life for yourself,
Which is SEPARATE FROM . . . ?

It matters not separate from what.
SEPARATE FROM . . . is enough.

Then, as you attempt, simply by virtue of your thinking,
To create a world for yourself,
Are you not trying to deny the world
Which God has already created?
Are you not attempting to compete with God?

It is very easy to perceive these early lessons as negative.
Indeed, it can seem quite frightening

When someone keeps saying to you,
"Do not think."

For you wonder,
"If I do not think, what will become of me?"
You may feel that in the absence of your thinking
You would surely die.

Nothing is further from the truth.
Always, you are totally safe in God's world.

If I say to you,
"Your thinking is what separates you;
Your thinking is what causes your pain and your fear,"
There must be something lying beyond the thinking
Which shall bring you to the peace, to the freedom,
And to the love of which I speak.

Beyond your thinking lies vision,
That which I shall call awareness.
Awareness is a state in which you do not think.
But it is far from emptiness.
It is a place from which you shall truly SEE,
And not with your eyes,
But with the innermost depths of that which you are,
Which is the Son of God.

What is this awareness?
What is this vision of which I speak?
Awareness is a state of BEING,
A state of pure freedom, and therefore, of love and joy.
Awareness is unfettered by your interpretations,
Unfettered by your reactions,
And above all, unfettered by your desire to limit it
Because you want it to be like the past.

Indeed, your thinking is your request
That things be like SOMETHING,
So you can feel secure, so you can feel safe.
And all you have for it to be like
Is the past.

Even if your past seems frightening and miserable,
Do you not often still cling to it?

Truly, most of you do,
For reason that the past is a place you seem to understand,
Where you know, at least, who you are.

I tell you, the goal of this Course
Is to move you to a state of awareness, and of vision,
Where you can experience things exactly as they are NOW.
RIGHT NOW.

That state is free of the past.
Indeed, I tell you in truth,
The moment that precedes, that did precede this moment,
Is totally independent of this moment now.

In fact, every moment in your time
Is totally independent of any other.
There is no flow of cause and effect within your time.
Only your thinking would make it seem so.
And that is but a reflection of your fear.

"Tell me of this fear," you might say.
"Why do I seem to fear a place in which I would not think,
In which I would simply be aware?"

This is the key to the answer—
In *A Course in Miracles* I speak of the ego.
I speak of it almost as your enemy,
As a thing to be fought against,
A thing which tries to separate you,
Which is constantly in battle with you
In its attempt to keep you from vision and awareness.

Well, this ego you have is nothing more
Than the collection of thoughts you have about who you are.
Now, this is the hard part.
Your thoughts don't mean anything,
Because they are always based on the past.
So it follows that your ego,
Your identity as you know it,
That which you perceive yourself to BE,
Is meaningless.
Hear me well.

This seems extremely frightening as you think about it.
For I have just said that your ego,
Your identity and the thoughts which define it for you,
Your existence as you know it,
Has no meaning.
And for the most of you who yet feel
That your thinking is somehow an integral part of what you are,
It can indeed be frightening for me to say,
Albeit with great love,
"It's OK, you just don't exist."

What we are doing in this Course
Is helping you to allow yourself
To move past the point where your thinking matters.
That will be vision; that will be true awareness;
And that shall be your freedom.

So do not be frightened as you read lessons
Which seem to say, as you probe them,
That you don't exist.
All it means is that your collection of thoughts,
Your collection of interpretations,
Your collection of reactions to an imagined past,
All which have caused you to believe that you exist
Somehow separate from others—
All of that has no meaning.

If anything is frightening,
Is it not the fear of being totally alone?
So think of it this way—
Your ego, the "I" that you are,
Is just a collection of thoughts which has no meaning,
Which has no purpose, really,
Except to cause you to believe that you are totally alone.
Now is it understandable that this should frighten you?

So much of your life is about figuring out
How you can keep from being alone.
Can you get even a hint of the joy that shall come to you
As you evolve past your imagined aloneness
To a world of unlimited freedom,
Which is totally shared,
Free of time,
Free of interpretation,

Free of conflict,
And free of any worry about what you are?

What you really are,
Far past the little collection of meaningless thoughts,
Is the Son of God.
You are the truth of Reality.
You are the Ultimate Meaning associated with all of existence.
You are the Son of God.
And you cannot possibly be meaningless.

So do not fear when I say, "You don't exist."
All I am referring to
Is a little collection of meaningless thoughts.
While beyond those thoughts and the fear they bring with them
Is the real you,
The ultimate meaning of all that is.

As you have read in the Text,
Forgiveness is of great importance in this Course.
Indeed, in one sense, forgiveness is all this Course is about.

Within the context of what I have said this day,
I will help you to see what forgiveness is.
Your forgiveness is nothing more than the realization,
First applied to the world you see outside yourself,
And then applied to the world within,
That all of your thinking, all of your interpreting,
Even all of that which you call yourself,
Has no meaning,
And is just a thing of fear.

In your forgiveness, you will come to see every other being
As but the same as your Self, as your brother.
You will then look beyond, as meaningless,
Everything his thinking seems to create,
All his fears,
And all his reactions to those fears.

You will then come to realize within yourself
That everything you look upon with regret,
Everything you would want to make you special,
Everything that would SEPARATE you,

Is what you will go beyond.
And in so doing, you will forgive yourself.

Hear me well.
Forgiveness is not a thing you offer
When another has done something to you,
Or even for something you have done to yourself.
Forgiveness is just the awareness, beyond your thoughts,
Of the meaninglessness of all that seems to cause you pain.

You shall see it first in your brother.
Then you shall see it in yourself.
And then you will be free.

Blessings upon you all. That is all.

THOUGHTS AS IMAGES

Greetings again. I am Jeshua. I have come this day
To further, with you, my discussion of
A Course in Miracles.

I wish to help you experience Lesson #15
From *A Course in Miracles*,
"My thoughts are images that I have made." (L 15)

We have said previously
That your thoughts do not mean anything.
I told you that meaning can only be associated with truth.
We spoke of thoughts,
And how they are but interpretations and reactions
To things you think you have seen in the past.
Indeed, without an image of the past,
We could not think anything.
Remember these words.

Everything you think you see, when you say "see,"
You associate with what you call the seeing of your eyes.
And I tell you, that is not seeing at all.
It is but an image you have made.

I have asked you, with this lesson,
To look around you, and to say,
"This room is an image I have made."
"This body is an image I have made." And so on—
I asked you to apply that statement
To everything you think you see.
I have come today to tell you, to clarify for you,
That this, indeed, is not seeing at all.

With your eyes you do not see.
All you are doing is working with an image you have made.
That image is a creation based upon what you call the past.
The past is an image based on a belief in what you call time.
And even time itself is an image you have made.

I tell you, time does not exist.
Time is not of truth. And therefore time has no meaning.
In order for you to see with real vision
What this Course is teaching you,
You will need not to see the past.
You will need to free yourself
Of every association you have made
With what you call the past.
For the past has nothing to do with the way things are NOW.
And that is why you see nothing as it is NOW.

NOW is freedom.
It is movement; it is change.
NOW is never a static thing.
NOW cannot be labeled.
NOW can only be experienced in the absence of time,
Or, as you might put it, in the fullness of this moment.

NOW can only exist
When there is no association with what you call the past,
With that which you call the future,
Or with what you call time.

So it is that you have thoughts you think you think.
And because you THINK those thoughts,
You also think you SEE what those thoughts are about.
However, you are experiencing images.
If you wish, you could even use the word "mirage," instead.

You all understand mirages.
You may not have experienced them,
But you've probably, at least, seen them in your movies.
A mirage is an image that seems to appear,
A trick played by light.
And when you get close to it,
It's not there.
Your thoughts, I tell you, are mirages.
And what will make them disappear
Is your getting close to the truth of what you are.

Now, all of light, as you experience light,
Is a form of energy.
The entire cosmos is energy.
The energy of which your world is made is very dense.

The energy of what you call matter is extremely dense.
The light you see with your eyes is less dense,
Though not very much less.

But the light of real vision is not dense at all.
The light of real vision cannot be contained.
The light of real vision cannot be brought down to a point
Where it can become dense enough, sluggish enough,
For you to see it with what you call your eyes.

Do not fear for this. Rather rejoice.
For you are coming to an awareness
That there is a reality
Beyond the thoughts you think you think.

Pause for a moment, and reflect.
I have said to you that
All of your conflict,
All of your fear,
All of your grief,
All of your pain,
Is but because of your thinking.
And so it follows that
All of your conflict,
All of your fear,
All of your grief,
All of your pain,
Is nothing more than an image you have created,
Or a mirage.

You are the Son of God.
Your inheritance is every gift that God has to give.
And the gifts of God can not be anything other than
An expression of love,
And freedom,
And joy.
Indeed, if you ever experience anything other than
The childlike bliss of total freedom,
A joy that reverberates through your being,
Then know that your experience is not of God,
That you have created an image, or a mirage,
Which you think you think,
And which you think you see.

True, you can imagine that you are in pain.
You can imagine that you are upset.
But such can never be of God.
For God, truly,
Does not even know
Of pain, or grief, or fear.

For truth simply IS.
And just as the light of real vision
Cannot be brought down to the dense level
That would allow your physical eyes to see it—
By the same token, the freedom and joy that is God
Cannot be brought down to a level
Where it can even imagine
Pain, and grief, and fear.

For pain, and grief, and fear are but the mirages,
The images you have created,
And which you in your thinking
Believe to be real.
Again, I tell you, they are not.

That knowledge shall become your freedom,
Shall become your joy.
For again I tell you,
Beyond your thinking,
Beyond the thoughts you think you think,
Beyond that which you think you see,
It is not emptiness.
It is awareness.
And awareness is rich,
And full,
And free,
And joyful,
And dynamic,
Changing, and growing.

It is beyond interpretation.
So you cannot call it good;
You cannot call it bad.
You cannot call it safe;
You cannot call it risky.
You cannot call it anything.

For as you do, as you would label it,
You are thinking,
And thus are creating that same dense form
That becomes within your being
An image,
Or a mirage.

It is most important you not forget—
One of the major mirages you must deal with
Is the one you call yourself.
You will move beyond those thoughts
Which seem to tell you of what you are,
Beyond those thoughts
Which seem to define you as a separate being.
For in truth, you are not separate.
You are One.
In truth, you are God.
You are the Son of God.
You are freedom. You are joy.
And all of that is love.
And you cannot BE other than that.

In your awareness you will become,
As I said thousands of years ago,
Like a little child.
A little child does not analyze or process before he experiences.
He simply moves through life from one experience to another,
Without fear, without thought of time,
Without thought of consequence,
Without analyzing whether a particular experience
Is good or bad.
He merely experiences.

I tell you,
Even when a little child cries,
He is not interpreting it as bad.
He is simply crying,
And being with his experience.
And your awareness,
Which you shall come to through this Course,
Will bring you to such a state.

What always happens when you hear words like these
Is that you begin to form images, mirages.

Thoughts come, which you think you think.
And they ask questions which you think you ask.
"How can I function in the world?
How can I go to my job?
How can I find enough food?
How can I stay warm?
How can I take care of my obligations?"

I tell you now, although in preliminary form,
You truly do not have to worry about any of those things.
For as you experience this *Course in Miracles*,
You will move to a state of being, to a state of awareness
Which is free of all those concerns, and all those fears.

You will read lessons in the Workbook which say
That the Holy Spirit will guide you
Through every aspect of your existence.
Everything you need in order to exist will be given to you,
Or you will know exactly where and how to find it,
Without conflict, and without concern.
If you need a word, it will be given you.
And there will be no fear,
No doubts and no conflict.

Pause this moment, if you will, and allow yourself,
Within your thoughts,
To begin to imagine that you can, indeed,
Live on this earth just as I did,
Functioning on a daily basis—
Eating, sleeping, drinking,
Talking, communicating,
And eventually, if you choose, dying.
Allow yourself to imagine
That you shall function on all those levels
Without a moment of doubt,
Without a moment of conflict,
Without a moment of concern
About how everything will be provided.

That shall be so because
In your awareness you shall be free of your interpretations,
Of the thoughts you think you think,
Of the images, of the mirages.

And in that freedom,
Everything which your being imagines is instantly yours.
For such is the power you have as the Son of God.

Indeed, you are already expressing that power in your life.
Every single thing which you experience
Has evolved out of your awareness.
The grief, the pain, and the conflict
Which you seem to experience
Are but your choice.
They all arise out of your thinking and your interpretations.
They are simply the mirages you think you see.
But already, always,
You are the Son of God.
And that cannot change.

The goal of this Course is to allow you
To evolve past the images you have made,
Past the thoughts you think you think,
To a point of reality, to a point of truth
Which is independent of time, the past, and the future,
Which is independent of interpretation,
And independent, therefore, of conflict.

In this moment do your best to pause
And imagine as freely as you can,
A life of no conflict,
A life of total peace and total freedom.
Try to imagine the ability to move through life with total safety,
Never having to wonder,
Never having to doubt,
Never having conflict of any kind.

For as you imagine thusly,
You shall be touching upon the reality of what you are,
Which is the Son of God.
And you shall be touching upon Love,
Which is the creative power of the universe,
And which is God.

Blessings upon you all. That is all.

THOUGHTS ARE NOT NEUTRAL

Greetings again. I am Jeshua. I have come this day
To further, with you, my discussion of
A Course in Miracles.

If you could imagine that you hated someone,
That you wanted for him
The worst that life could possibly bring,
What you would wish for that person
Is for him to be
Totally alone.
You would wish for him to be separated from all other beings,
And to be apart from love.
You understand, I am sure.

If you wanted for another person
Love, and joy,
Or if you wanted the same for yourself,
You would wish for that person, or for yourself,
To be joined,
To know sharing and togetherness.

For you know that sharing is completeness,
That it is what leads to happiness and peace.
And, although your perception is misguided,
Such joining, such sharing,
Is what most of you are seeking here,
In this sojourn upon your earth.

One of the lessons said,
"The world I see is a form of vengeance." (L 22)

Ponder, for a moment, your perceived world of separateness,
Separate bodies, people hating others, competing with others,
Persons wanting to be special above others.
All of this is based on a desire
To be SEPARATE FROM . . . ,
Whether it is for you to be separate from another,
Or for another to be separate from you.

And I already said that if you really hated someone,
You would want him to be separate and alone.

Now does the lesson make sense?
Insofar as you even think of, or imagine, a world of separation,
Whether you see yourself as separate,
Or another being as separate,
You may call it vengeance,
You could call it hatred,
Or anger, or fear.
It is all the same.

And I tell you, in the reality of the Kingdom of God,
There exists but One Mind.
All of that which you perceive as different minds
Is joined as One.
There is only total harmony and total peace.
In the Kingdom of God
There cannot exist vengeance,
Or hatred,
Or separation,
Or fear.

And anything which does not exist
In the Kingdom of God
Cannot be real.
Rejoice over this fact.

As you progress further in the lessons,
You will hear often,
''This is not real.''
''This does not exist.''
''This cannot mean anything.''

It can be very frustrating, indeed,
For me to tell you that a thing is not real,
Or does not exist, or has no meaning—
Especially when you perceive it
As being so very real for you.

Again I tell you,
Anything which is based on a desire for,
Or a belief in, separateness, or specialness,
Or exclusion, or aloneness,

Is not of God—
And more so, cannot be of God.

And all that exists in Creation itself
Is that which God has created,
Is that which God IS.
So anything at all which seems to yield
An imagined separation in any form,
Truly, cannot exist.

It can, indeed, be terribly frustrating for someone to say,
"All of that on which you base your life does not exist,
For it is not real."
Do not be frightened by this notion.
Rather rejoice.
For the truth of what I have just said
Is the key that shall unlock the door
To your freedom, and your joy,
To your peace,
And to love.

Some of the lessons for this week
Have been about your thoughts—
That you have no neutral thoughts, (L 16)
That you are not alone in the effects of your seeing, (L 18)
That you want to see things differently. (L 21)
All of them have been about your thinking, and your thoughts.
That seems strange, does it not,
When we spent the first lessons telling you
That your thoughts don't mean anything,
That your thoughts aren't even real.

I am fully aware that you have chosen
To spend this sojourn upon your earth,
That you have assumed the illusion of bodies and form.
I am also aware that an integral part of that illusion of form
Is the illusion of your thoughts.
It would be very difficult, too difficult for most of you,
For me to begin with the command,
"Stop thinking"—
Even though that IS your goal,
And I HAVE told you to do just that.

However, I have stated that this is a Course in mind training.
And you will become aware,

As you progress through the lessons,
That you are, in fact, thinking.
Do not dismay.
For the lessons are geared
To train your mind
To let go of that selfsame thinking
Which you currently use.

But do not lose sight of the fact that you WILL, ultimately,
Free yourself of the illusion of a separate mind
Which harbors separate thoughts.
Then shall be yours
The peace of Oneness,
And the joy that is born out of experience
Unhindered by the judgment of thought.

It is true that your thoughts are not real,
That they do not mean anything.
They are but images you have made.
However, in this illusion of human form
Which you have chosen,
Your thoughts and your brain are, for now,
One of the best avenues you have
To the true perception
Which lies beyond your thoughts,
And to the knowledge
Which shall only be yours
After you have long since left this earth and human form.

So we will use your thoughts as a pathway
To the deepest truth of your being,
To the knowledge that you ARE the Son of God,
To the knowledge that you ARE free,
That you ARE only love,
And only joy.

I have said,
"You have no neutral thoughts." (L 16)
"You see no neutral things." (L 17)
This is so because
Everything you see is the result of your own choice.
Everything you experience is the product of your thoughts.
Every thought you have either brings you to peace, or to war.
Each thought either brings you closer
To the realization of the truth

That all minds are joined as One,
Or it leads you further astray, toward the illusion
That you can be separate one from another,
Which you cannot.

I admonish you, therefore,
To use your thinking to be aware of all your thoughts.
And any time you find a thought carrying with it
Upset, or frustration, or anger, or fear,
Be assured that you are choosing to support the illusion
That you are separate,
That you can be different.

What I tell you now, you will hear often in the Course—
"What is the same can not be different." (4)
The same means Oneness.
For all of you are One.
You are all the same.

In you thinking,
You shall become aware of the thoughts that lead you to peace.
They are the thoughts which remind you that all is one,
That you are One,
That you are the same.
They are the thoughts which lead you
To the realization that there cannot be a difference
Between the desire, the truth, of your heart,
And the desire, the truth, of another heart.
This applies to every heart, every soul,
Every aspect of the Son of God.
For the Son of God is One.

And when I say
You are the Son of God,
Then you ARE One,
And you ARE the same.
All other beings are part of that Oneness.
Hear me well.

Perhaps you can begin to perceive, even now,
That in your Oneness,
You are not, and can not, be alone
In the effects of your thinking.
For even now, when you think a thought,

The energy of that thought instantly becomes part of
The whole of Creation.

And even though your consciousness may not be aware,
There are no private thoughts. (5)
Every thought you think,
Be it of separation,
Or be it of peace and love,
Is known by the entire Sonship.
And for you,
This means it is known by every person on this earth.

You cannot feel anger at another without, at the level of truth,
That other being knowing it.
And you cannot feel anger at another without,
At the level of truth,
That anger being at yourself.

We shall discuss these things many times,
Seemingly over and over again.
This is a Course in mind training,
A Course that shall allow you to let go of the illusion
That you are separate from any other being.
For you are not.

Within your untrained mind
You always see a world of separation,
Of individual beings different one from another.
But as you begin to realize that you are the same,
It will cease to be a world of vengeance,
And shall become a world of peace,
A world of joy.

At the deepest level of your being you already know
That your true desire is for peace, and love,
And oneness.
And, except in the illusion of your thoughts,
That is already true.
God created you thusly,
And you cannot be otherwise.

You are free to imagine it otherwise.
But nothing more than the frailty of your imaginings
Which, ultimately, do not exist,

Can separate you from the Oneness
And from the Love that is God.

So begin, even now, insofar as it brings you peace,
To watch your thoughts.
Do not struggle with them.
Do not fight them.
Do not despair at them.
Do not rejoice in them.
Merely let them be,
And watch them.

When you have thoughts
Which create in you a sense of oneness,
An awareness that none of you is special,
That none of you is different,
Be of good cheer.
And allow that experience to flow through you.

When you have thoughts that speak of upset, however slight,
Of anger, or of fear, or of attack of any kind,
Realize that these are the thoughts
Which shall dissipate before this Course
As fog before the morning sun.

Insofar as you can replace the thoughts of fear
With thoughts of love and of oneness,
Then do it.
If it happens not easily,
Do not despair.
And never make yourself wrong.
Merely allow yourself to be.

Do not forget that eventually
Your thinking will joyfully pass away,
As it takes you away from
The illusion of separation.

And without the illusion of separation
All is One,
All is the same,
All is God.
And that is naught but Love.

Blessings upon you all. That is all.

YOU ARE INVULNERABLE

Greetings again. I am Jeshua. I have come this day
To further, with you, my discussion of
A Course in Miracles.

One of your lessons currently says,
"God is in everything I see." (L 29)
The reason for this is very clear.
In essence, you are God.
As I say so often in *A Course in Miracles*,
You are the Son of God. (6)
Indeed, in the truth of what you are as His Son,
You are part of God,
And, therefore, part of All That Is.

I say "Son" in the singular
Because the "Sons" of God do not exist.
For you are One.
And what you are in your collective Oneness
Is THE Son of God.
It is your essence,
In your totality and your Oneness,
Which makes you THE Son of God.

All other beings whom you perceive as separate from yourself
Are, in truth, but aspects, or facets of that Oneness,
Which is, indeed, but your Self.
This truth pertains not only to living beings,
But to that which you consider inanimate—
The tables, and chairs, and cars,
The things which seem without life—
Also to the trees, and flowers,
Those things which seem to be living.
They are all the same.
All of it is but part of
That which you call yourself.

God is in everything you see.
Because, in truth, everything you see

Is seen through the eyes of God.
For God is what you are.

It is not exactly true that you are completely God.
For God is the Creator,
And we, including myself, are the created, the creations.
It is our inheritance to be One with God,
To be co-creators of All That Is.
'Tis a fine point of difference
Between the Creator and His creations.
And for purposes of your living
On this earth, in this world,
You ARE God.

So everything you see is, in fact, a creation of your own.
And you ARE the God of that creation.
As the Son of God,
You ARE the Spirit of God, yourself.
All of that which you see is God,
And, indeed, IS God.
For everything is One.
So it must be that
That which you see IS your Self.

This point shall be made over and over again,
Until you go far beyond the limited understanding of words.
The words shall become unnecessary.
And what remains shall be
A realization, an awareness,
Simply EXPERIENCE.
And then you will be free.

One of the lessons said that you could escape the world you see
By giving up your attack thoughts. (L 23)
And one of the others said your attack thoughts
Are attacking your own invulnerability. (L 26)

Hear me well.
You are, in fact, invulnerable.
Over that you have no choice.
There is nothing you can do
To change the fact that you are invulnerable.
There is NOTHING outside yourself
That can have any effect, of any kind,

Upon you, or your experience,
Or your awareness.

Even if you actively resist,
And would oppose these words I say,
You cannot change the fact that you are invulnerable.
For you ARE the Son of God,
And the creator of the entire world you see.
Over this you have no choice.

Every aspect of your world,
Everything you might call good,
Everything you might call bad,
Every upset you feel,
Every joy,
All of it MUST be created by you.
And nothing,
No one,
No being,
Can alter that fact.

This truth applies directly
To every relationship in which you find yourself.
If it ever seems to you that someone separate from yourself
Is CAUSING you to feel anything,
Be it anger, or hatred, or upset, or joy,
You are mistaken.
For you then are asking that you BE vulnerable.
And I tell you again,
It cannot be so.

Every time you experience joy,
Know that it is your own creation,
And that you have chosen it for yourself.
Every time you experience frustration,
Or anger, or grief, or sadness,
Or any of that which you perceive as negative,
Be fully aware that you have chosen it for yourself,
And indeed, have cherished it,
And delighted in it.
For if you had not done so,
It could not be,
And you could not experience it.

Were I to repeat these last few sentences
Over and over and over again,
Until at last you EXPERIENCED them as truth,
Then you would be done with *A Course in Miracles,*
And you would be free.
That knowing, in itself, would be enough.

For in your knowing that you choose, that you create,
That you delight in everything which you experience—
In your knowing of that truth
You become free.

Freedom in your relationships
Shall come from that same knowing
That each being is not only himself,
But is also you.
All dynamics of all relationships
Are but mutual choices within the Oneness,
Which is both of you,
Or the three of you,
Or the four of you,
Or the billions of you.

Your invulnerability knows no limits.
If suddenly you found yourself the only living being on earth,
It would still be so.
And if the wind blew,
It would be your creation, and your choice.
If you are walking along and the wind blows your hat off,
It could not have happened had you not chosen it.
For such is your invulnerability.

And so it is with everything you perceive—
If your car does not run,
If an appliance stops,
If it rains, if the sun shines,
If flowers grow in your garden,
Whether your garden grows well or not—
Hear me well,
Always, you are invulnerable.

You are the sole creator of everything in your existence.
But because you are One,
Everything in existence harmonizes

Instantaneously, fully, totally,
With that which you create.

What, then, does it mean to attack?
To attack means to believe that somehow
You are NOT invulnerable.
If you think, even for a moment,
In any circumstance or relationship,
That something can happen TO you,
And NOT by your own choice,
Then you believe that you can be the victim of something.
For you believe it is possible for something to happen TO YOU.

That belief implies separateness, does it not?
The only way anything can HAPPEN TO YOU
Is if there exists a something DIFFERENT FROM YOU
Which can make it happen.
And in your invulnerability
That cannot be.

In that moment of attack upon yourself,
You have chosen to believe
That you are separate, one from another.
And such a belief in separateness
Is what forms the building blocks of this world.
This world, if you will, is but a game you are playing
In order to see what it's like to be alone.

Be still for a moment,
And ponder what it's like to be totally alone.
It will take you that long, a moment,
To realize that it does not contain joy.
And if it does not contain joy,
It cannot be of God.

If you would discover the world of joy,
If you would escape the troubles and fears of this world,
All you need do is escape from the belief in separation.
All you need do is realize, beyond your thinking,
That separation cannot be,
That all is One,
And that nothing can BE in your life
Except by your choice, your delight,
And your creation.

If you would discover that world, begin here,
Albeit it within your thinking—
In every circumstance,
Bring with you this idea, which says,
"I am invulnerable. I have chosen
Every last detail of my life."
In every circumstance in which you find yourself believing
There is someone or something outside of you
Which can do something TO you,
Be it joyful, or be it negative,
Draw yourself up short, and say,
"Wait. I am God, and I am invulnerable.
This could not be here in my life had I not chosen it
Out of my own delight,
And out of my own love."

Do this as often as you can,
As often as your Spirit will allow.
For the more you do so,
The more you will find yourself free.

One of the lessons said,
"Above all else, I want to see." (L 27)
Do not forget, from your earlier lessons,
That seeing is not something you do with your eyes.
Your eyes are idols of separation.
Your eyes are part of this illusion you call your body,
Whose very nature epitomizes separation.
So seeing is not of your eyes.
Seeing is of the depth of your being, of your experience.
And when the lesson says,
"Above all else, I want to see,"
What it means is,
"Above all else, I want to experience this world
In my Oneness, in my invulnerability."

As you see this world, not with your eyes,
You WILL see it as your own creation.
You will see your own invulnerability,
Your own godliness.
You will see beauty, and peace, and joy.
For that is what you are.
And that is what you will know.

So as you move toward true vision,
Beyond the seeing of this world,
You will say,
"Above all else I want to see things differently." (L 28)
Be aware that what you want, in your invulnerability,
Is to see the world as your own creation,
And as part of the Oneness of All That Is.

One of the first steps you take in learning to SEE
Is to realize, as one of the lessons said,
That you don't understand what anything is for. (7)
Because as you try to think and analyze,
And use the physical senses,
It will not be possible for you to SEE.

Indeed, if you wish to go beyond your senses
To true vision, and true perception,
You will need to give up the notion
That you can truly experience your world through your senses.
And, even if hard for you to believe,
The thinking that your brain does
Is a product of your senses.
This is to say,
Your thoughts are of the physical world and of the senses.
And they will pass away,
At such time as your body passes away.

If you desire, then, to go beyond your senses,
And therefore, beyond your thoughts, unto freedom,
You must realize that your thoughts
Are not telling you the truth,
That your senses are not perceiving the truth.
You must realize, ultimately,
That your senses are not perceiving
What is real.

Insofar as you, heretofore,
Have experienced your world through your senses,
Then, indeed, you do not understand what anything is for.
You do not understand its nature, or its purpose.
You, really, don't even understand
Why you have created it so.

Do not be upset by this.
It is so easy to interpret these words as negative.
But what they open for you
Is the gateway to freedom.

You are the Son of God.
You are invulnerable.
There can never be, on this earth, or in any world,
Anything in your experience which you, as the Son of God,
Have not brought to yourself as your own creation.

Substitute that thought for the thought
That things in your world can HAPPEN TO YOU,
With you as the victim.
And simply ask yourself,
Which of the two speaks of freedom.
And in an instant,
You will know.

So do not be disheartened.
Realize that I am speaking to you of freedom.
As you allow this freedom and this joy to enter your life,
It will involve letting go of the old beliefs, and the old patterns.
But as you follow this Course,
You will let them dissolve easily and freely.
And always, in their place,
You will find nothing but love.

You shall never be alone.
You will never find yourself in a void.
You will never have to deal with fear.
Such is the love I bring to you.
For such is the message of *A Course in Miracles*.

Blessings upon you all. That is all.

SEEING THE TRUTH

Greetings again. I am Jeshua. I have come this day
To further, with you, my discussion of
A Course in Miracles.

One of the things you may have experienced this past week
Is confusion.
For the first time, perhaps,
You have directly met the idea that truly,
God is in your mind.

God is, indeed, in your mind.
That is akin to what I said before
That truly, you are God.
Once again, everything you see,
Everything you experience
Is a creation of your Self.
If God is in your mind,
And if you are God,
Then everything you see and experience
Is, likewise, a creation of God.
This must be so.
For God is all that exists.

There is no opposite to God.
There CAN BE no opposite to God.
There can be no conflict within God.
And, I tell you,
There can be no conflict within you.
This is so because, truly,
You are God,
And God is in your mind.

You can imagine many things.
For you do have the power to imagine.
You can even imagine what seems to be conflict.
You can imagine that you are upset.
You can imagine that you are angry.

While, in truth, you are not,
And cannot be.

When you have said,
"Above all else I want to see things differently," (L 28)
The experience of those words
Is merely the realization within yourself
Of the truth of what I have just said.
Within all that you experience is God.
Within everything you see is the experience of
Your Oneness with God.
And when you see things differently,
That is what you will see,
And that is what you will experience.

To the extent that it is not clear to you
That what you experience always arises
From your Oneness with God,
From your Oneness with all things,
Then what you are experiencing is an illusion.
That experience also must be a product of your thoughts.
It therefore has no meaning.
Furthermore, it doesn't even really exist.

Hear me well.
This statement will be made over and over again.
Even that which you perceive to be your self is an illusion.
As you hear these words,
Allow yourself to experience whatever you will.
But allow yourself to EXPERIENCE something.
For, as we have said,
A Course in Miracles is not about learning
Academic, abstract thought patterns.
It is a Course in experiencing the truth of what you are,
Which is the truth of what God is,
Which is THE truth of the entire universe.
And that truth shall be found, not in your thinking,
But in that which you experience.

So as I speak to you, and tell you,
"Your thought, your concept of what you are,
Doesn't really exist,"
Allow yourself to feel something.
For the feeling, in back of the thoughts, in back of the words,

Is what touches reality.
When you hear these words which suggest that
Your thoughts (about what you are) have no meaning,
If you can begin to feel even a hint of peace,
Or release, or freedom,
Then, I tell you,
You have advanced a thousand years
Toward experiencing the truth of what you are.

If you do not feel such peace, do not be upset.
You cannot fail.
You cannot err in this quest.
You may take sideroads.
You can elect diversions, but you cannot fail.
Never make yourself wrong.
Always accept yourself for exactly where you are.
And realize that where you ARE
Lies not in your thinking,
But in that which you are experiencing.

One of the lessons said,
"My holiness envelops everything I see." (L 36)
You are holy because God is in your mind.
Everything you experience is a product of your own holiness,
Of your own godliness.
Such is the power given you by God.
Whatever you experience
IS what you have chosen to experience.
And nothing, not God Himself, can take that away from you.
You have the power to feel and to experience
Anything you wish.
And you are in total control of that.
Just as God creates a world
And beings within that world,
So do we, and you,
Create worlds of our own.

Your world is what you experience, what you feel.
It cannot be otherwise.
You are, in fact, the God of your own experience,
The God of your own universe.
And everything you experience
Is a product of your own godlikeness,
Your own holiness.

You can even imagine that you are experiencing
Things which are not of truth,
And which ultimately do not exist.
For you have the power to imagine such,
And to believe it real.
Nothing can take that away from you.
Such is your holiness.
Such is your power as the Son of God.

The other side of that is that
You are totally in command of everything you feel.
One of the lessons said,
"I could see peace instead of this." (L 34)
Nothing could be more true.
I cannot overemphasize that you, in your holiness,
Choose, solely of yourself,
To experience whatever it is you wish.
Hear me again. And hear me well.
If you experience pain,
It is because you have chosen it,
And have delighted in it.
If you experience anger, or frustration, or grief,
It is only because you, as the God of your own being,
Have chosen it, and created it.
If you choose peace,
It is, likewise, because you have chosen it,
And have created it.

I will say again, and cannot overemphasize,
What causes the absence of peace,
What causes you to seem to be upset,
What causes the illusion of separation,
Is always your thoughts.
And your thoughts are your reactions, your interpretations,
Which are based on your belief in
Time and space and physicalness,
And which are based on your imagination that it is real.
Always it is your thoughts.

One of the previous lessons had said that
You do not understand what anything is for. (7)
Now do you see?
The goal of that lesson was to allow you
To open to whatever experience is present,

Without the interpretation,
Without the judgment,
Without the confusion of your thoughts.
It is then that you will find peace and freedom.

Everything that you call the past, all your memories,
Are comprised of thought.
That is why we shall often emphasize the Holy Instant,
Which is totally free of the past,
Free of concepts, and of thoughts,
Free of interpretation, and of wishes,
Free of all the things which generate your pain.
Likewise, the Holy Instant is free of everything
Which creates guilt, and the lack of freedom.

If you are truly God,
And your holiness envelops everything you see,
How does it happen that you all seem to see the same world?
Hear me well. You don't.
There are the common things
Which you do seem to experience together,
Like the snowfall, the rain, the wind.
But I tell you,
Even a snowflake, the rain, the wind,
Events which two of you seem to observe at the same time—
They are truly different events for each of you.

In any circumstance you experience only and totally
That which your own mind has created.
The fact that two of you, or more, or a city full of you,
Can seem to experience the common things at the same time
Is merely a demonstration of the fact that all minds are joined.
Indeed, not just joined, but One.
And when you think you see a snowflake,
All of humanity is part of that experience.

Now, hear me well again.
The major purpose of this world is forgiveness.
In your forgiveness, you become free,
And you set the world free with you.
For, in your reality, in your vision, in your true seeing,
You will know that the snowflake, the rain, the wind,
And your body itself,
Are but illusion.

And then you shall choose, in your holiness,
Not to be affected by the illusions.
That is what I was demonstrating
When I did things like walk upon the water.

When you see a snowflake,
All of humanity experiences it with you.
But more importantly,
When you choose not to be affected by the illusion,
All of humanity is part of the freedom that you experience.

So when you forgive the illusion,
When you free yourself of it,
You truly have become the saviour of the Son of God.
As I say in this Course, you are saviour. (8)
And indeed, your brother is saviour.
He is your saviour.
For in your forgiveness of him,
You find your forgiveness of yourself.

Remember, forgiveness is the awareness
That your thoughts, your interpretations,
Truly do not have meaning, and ultimately do not exist.
This applies to any kind of behavior you choose to experience,
That which you call good, that which you call bad.
It applies to everything experienced
With what you call your body,
From sickness, to health, to snowstorms,
To walking on water.

When you, in your holiness, experience with true perception
The realization that your brother's thoughts
Are, in fact, only thoughts, and have no meaning,
Then you shall set him free.
For your experience is part of his own.
But you also free yourself,
Because his experience is part of yours.

Your inner world and your outer world are the same.
As you read often in the Text,
An idea, a thought that you have, cannot leave its source. (9)
Anything which you create within your own consciousness
Becomes for you, on this earth, a form of thought, an idea.

Those thoughts, those ideas,
Are the building blocks of the world you see.

What seems to be out there, your outer world,
Cannot exist independent of the thought that gives it birth.
The EFFECT of the thought is what you seem to experience.
The cause is always the idea, the thought,
The experience which gave it birth.
And what seems to be out there cannot exist
Without the thought, the idea, the experience,
Being present within your Self.

Your thoughts, therefore, are the creators of your outside world,
And are, therefore, the representations of your outside world,
And are, therefore, your outside world itself.
When you see something outside,
It is not outside.
Nothing can be outside yourself.
We will be saying,
Do not seek outside yourself, (10)
For there is nothing there.

So when you say,
"My holiness envelops everything I see," (L 36)
Realize that, in your godliness,
That which you experience, that which you think, your ideas,
Are the creators of what seems to be your outside world.
But there exists no difference, no separation between the two.
It is not possible for you to experience anything
Separate from the ideas,
Separate from the experience within your mind.

And if anything you seem to experience in your outside world
Is not to your liking,
You must look within to discover and to change it.
To look outside, to believe something IS outside,
Is to believe that what you see could be separated
From the idea that gave it birth.
And I tell you,
That is absolutely impossible.

Never look outside yourself.
If you could do so,

Then the Oneness, the unification that is God,
Could not exist.
For it would imply that things could exist
Which are apart from God Himself.
Thus there would be within the world, duality.
Thus there could be within the universe, conflict.
And in the presence of conflict,
There could not be peace.
But the nature of God is Oneness and Unity,
The absence of conflict,
And the absolute presence of peace.

So take these ideas I express to you,
And allow yourself to feel what you can of their truth.
Do not be overly concerned, right now,
With WHAT you shall feel.
Just remember that the goal of this Course
Lies in your experience and your feelings,
Beyond the ideas and the words we use.

And remember, once again, with peace and great happiness,
Your holiness envelops everything you see.
For you are the God of your own universe.
And you are One with the God of all,
One with me,
One with all beings,
One with the God who created us in His likeness.
Nothing can be in your life but what you have chosen,
But what you have cherished.
And in your knowing of that truth,
You will be free.

Blessings upon you all. That is all.

HOLINESS

Greetings again. I am Jeshua. I have come this day
To further, with you, my discussion of
A Course in Miracles.

Today I wish to discuss with you,
And to help clarify for you,
Your holiness.

Pause for a moment,
And imagine that you are God.
Imagine that you are the Creator of All That Is.
Imagine that you are the source, the giver of all Life,
That nothing happens without you,
Without your choice, without your wish,
Without your thought.
Just try to imagine that you are God.

And in your imagining ask yourself,
What would I need?
What could I possibly ask of another being,
To make me more complete than I am?
Ask yourself,
Could anything, or anyone, else
Deprive me of anything?
If you were God, and you wanted to experience something,
What would you do?
I believe your answer must be,
You would simply think it within your mind,
And it would be.

Then try to imagine, if you were God,
That something, or someone,
Could oppose you, could be your opposite.
You would realize,
Ah, I am the source of All That Is;
There is no opposite;
There can be no opposite.

Even the thought of an opposite wouldn't really exist.
For I would BE God.

Then try to imagine, if you were God,
Needing someone else to love you.
And remember, as God,
You are the source, you are the completion,
You are the completeness of All That Is.

Then imagine, perhaps a bit differently,
If you were God,
Wanting to extend, wanting to give,
Wanting to send out that which you are,
Which you would call Love.
You might imagine it being joyful
To take the wholeness of what you are,
To take that which truly is your Self,
Realizing it as Love,
And extending it to a universe of your own creation.
That could be joy; that could be fullness;
For that would be the extension and expansion of your Self.

If you were God,
Extending your Self could not make you greater.
For you already are All That Is.
You would not NEED to extend your Self
(Which we are calling Love)
For some purpose.
For you could not be incomplete.
You would only extend your Self (Love)
Out of simple joy,
The joy of experience, the joy of life.

Try for a moment, if you can, to imagine,
Beyond your thinking,
What it would be like to be God.
Try to BE in that place
Where you are complete, where you are whole,
Where it is impossible to need anything,
Where it is impossible to find anything outside your Self,
Because you know that you are the source.
You ARE All That Is.

Then imagine what it might be like to extend your Self (Love)
Into the creation of what you might call things,
Which are thoughts or beings which exist WITHIN you,
And yet THROUGH you, and as PART OF you,
And which can never be separate from that which IS you.
Try for this moment, if you can,
To imagine that you are God . . .

Hear me well, this day.
For in these words can be found
The essence of *A Course in Miracles*.
AS YOU TRY TO IMAGINE THAT YOU ARE GOD,
KNOW THAT YOU ARE.

You are One with All That Is.
God is your source,
But you are One with that source.
The completeness that is God is you.
God cannot need anything outside of Himself,
Because there IS nothing outside of Him.
And although you can, in your thinking,
Imagine yourself having needs,
In truth, there is nothing you can need.
There is nothing that could complete you more
Than you are already completed.
For you are the Son of God.

And that IS your holiness.
One of the lessons for this week said,
"My holiness is my salvation." (L 39)
When you know the truth of that within your being,
When you EXPERIENCE that truth,
Without conflict, without thought,
Without analysis, without struggle,
At the level of your BEING,
You will be free.
And you will no longer need
Anything like *A Course in Miracles*.

You are the God of your life.
Of your own life, YOU ARE All That Is.
Nothing in this life can exist outside of your Self.
Of all that you experience
There is nothing that is not WITHIN you.

Being the God of your life,
If you desire, if you choose to experience anything,
Just as with God Himself,
All you need do is create it within your mind,
AND IT IS.
Hear me well.
What I am describing to you is exactly the way your life is.
There exists no thing IN your life
Which is not your own creation.
There is no imagined ABSENCE of any thing in your life
Which is not, likewise, by your own creation.

This is true, and applies
To any possessions you can imagine,
To any physical amenities,
To the way they funcion, whether they work well,
Whether you find them pleasing or not.
It applies to what you call money.
It applies to that which you call health.

It applies, as well, to what you call relationships.
In your holiness, you are the God of your own relationships.
This includes relationships with your fellow humans,
With animals, domestic and wild,
With plants and trees,
With inanimate objects, the sand and the rocks.
It includes the very stars
Which you consider to be years of your light speed away.
Every last experience of any kind,
From a conversation with another person,
To sharing what you call love,
To seeing a tree,
To stubbing your toe on a rock,
To looking at a star—
All of it is an expression of your holiness,
And of your creative power as the Son of God.

Of your life, you are God.
Hear this well.
Of your life, you ARE God.
And your goal in this Course
Is to come to the point
Where it could not occur to your thinking
That something could happen,

That you could experience anything
Other than by your own willful choice.
You are very holy.
The power of God is expressing Itself through you
With every thought and with every feeling.
Every relationship you seem to experience,
With beings, with plants, with things,
Is a relationship with your Self,
Which is a relationship with God.
For you are, indeed, God.

Of your life, you are God.
You are, indeed, very holy.
And your holiness envelops everything you see.
The mere fact that you see at all
Is an expression of your holiness.
Were you not very holy,
Were you not the God of your creation,
Your life would be a void.

Your holiness blesses the world.
And you, as the Son of God, are blessed in return.
Everything you choose to experience is of God;
And you are blessed by whatever you choose.
You are blessed by your joy.
You are blessed by your pain.
Because, as the God of your life,
You would not have chosen your pain
Unless it brought you great joy.
Hear me well.
You would not have chosen your pain
Unless it brought you great joy.

And what brings you pain?
The thoughts that seem to tell you it is pain.
That is all.
For as we have said, from the very first lessons,
It is your thoughts, creations of the past,
That deprive you of experiencing this moment,
And your godliness.
It is your thoughts that separate you from that which IS.
It is your thoughts that separate you from your SELF.
Truly, without your thoughts,
That which you have called your pain,

And which you have created for your joy,
Would, indeed, BE your joy.

We have spoken during these lessons
About vision, about seeing.
"God is my strength. Vision is His gift." (L 42)
"God is my source. I cannot see apart from Him." (L 43)
Remember again, that vision, the gift of God,
Is beyond your eyes, beyond your senses.
Vision is experience.
Vision is being.

God is your source.
You are very holy.
In your holiness, you are the God of your own life.
And you experience that life in your Oneness with God.
Apart from God, you cannot see.
Apart from Him, you will but imagine your apartness.
Apart from your holiness,
You will imagine that you are separate,
That beings are different from you.
You will imagine that they are not your own creations.
You will imagine that your pain is pain.
You will imagine that things can happen to you
From outside yourself, not by your own choice.

None of this is seeing.
None of this is vision.
And without your imaginings,
Without the thoughts that separate you,
You will know your Oneness with God, with your Source.
You will know, in your holiness,
That all of life is your own creation.

You will experience it free of the past,
Free of the stories you make up to interpret it.
You will realize that your body,
Even that which you call your personality, your self,
Is just one of the stories you have made up.
And instead of the image of a body,
Instead of the image of a tree,
Instead of the image of a star, or a rock,
You will experience something very different.

You will experience a shimmering light that flows
And moves in a dynamic pattern, mesmerizing your self,
Flowing in and out of that which you are,
Expanding, growing, diminishing,
Ever changing.
And with that you shall experience your joy.

In one of the lessons I said,
When you start to have vision,
You will see little edges of light. (11)
That is true.
In your transition, you eventually will see,
Not bodies, not trees and stars,
But patterns of light,
Not light you see with your eyes,
But light you experience.
And it shall begin with the little edges of light.

Let me admonish you not to set a time schedule,
Not to pressure yourself to be at a certain point.
For insofar as you TRY to do this Course,
You are thinking,
And you are separating yourself
From the goal of your own holiness.

If you were God, you would never struggle
With whether what you were doing
Was right or not.
And you ARE God.
So never say to yourself that you SHOULD, by now,
Be seeing the little edges of light.
Simply be where you are,
In that which you call NOW.
Be there freely, in your holiness.
And that shall save you years and years of your time.

For every time you say ''I should,''
And every time you imagine
Having to TRY to accomplish something,
You are believing in time.
And time is the great mode of separation.
And separated, apart from God,
You cannot see.

Rejoice in what I have told you today.
This is not a message of discouragement.
It is not a message of chastisement.
It is a message of great love,
Of hope, and of beauty.

I have used these words in order
To bring to you a vision of what you are,
And of the time when you shall truly SEE.
Such is your right; such is your inheritance.
It cannot be taken from you.
For God Himself has deemed it be yours,
And there is no opposite to God.

Be not concerned with your imaginings.
That is all they are.
Be not concerned with your thinking.
For it is just the imaginings.
Do not be discouraged that you imagine,
And that you think.
Rather, rejoice in the creative power
Of what your imaginings and your thoughts can do.
Let them teach you the extent to which you are God.

God is in your mind.
You are very holy.
Your holiness is your salvation.
Every aspect of your life is a product of your own holiness.
And the God Who has made you One with Him
Is your source and your strength.
He has ordained that the vision of which I speak is yours.
Indeed, except for your imaginings
That you are apart from Him,
It is yours already.
And I tell you,
It is coming much sooner than you think.

Blessings upon you all. That is all.

THE LOVE OF GOD

Greetings again. I am Jeshua. I have come this day
To further, with you, my discussion of
A Course in Miracles.

This is most important.
That which I am saying to you this day,
You already know.
Before we even begin,
Allow that feeling, that thought, to penetrate your being.
What I shall say is already yours.
What I shall say IS your Self.
Beyond the words, beyond the perceptions,
Beyond the thoughts which the words generate,
You know all of this.

Your lesson said,
"I am sustained by the Love of God." (L 50)
I would discuss with you
The Love of God.

The Love of God ACTUALLY IS God Itself.
I have said God "Itself,"
For God is neither male nor female,
Just as you are male or female only in your imagination,
While in your reality you are neither.

When God gives you love,
He gives that which is, which was, which always shall be.
For God, when He gives you love,
Gives you Himself.
When you receive that Love,
When you receive God Itself,
You become God.
This you already know.
Hear me well.

Allow yourself, if you can, to feel this within your being,
Beyond the thoughts, beyond the words.
God loves you.

That Love is God's giving Itself to you, unto your being.
That is why you are sustained by the Love of God.
For as God gives you His Love,
He gives you Himself,
And you BECOME God.

If you are, indeed, God,
Which, as the Son of God, you are,
Then you are, of course,
Sustained, protected, eternal.
The word we have used is "invulnerable."

I tell you again,
You are in constant receipt of the Love of God,
Which is God Himself.
And there is nothing you can do about that.
As the Son of God,
You have the power of all Creation within you,
WITHIN YOU.
There is nothing you can do to change that.
You have WITHIN YOUR BEING the invulnerablity
And the power of the universe.

You HAVE within you the power of the universe.
But there is one thing you cannot change.
You do not have the freedom, or the power,
To separate yourself from the Love of God,
Which IS God Himself,
Or from the strength of God which sustains you,
Or from the thoughts of God deep within your mind,
Of from the Light of God with which you will truly SEE
When you experience vision.
There is nothing you can do to separate yourself
From all of that, which is your reality.

As the Son of God,
You have the freedom to IMAGINE anything you wish.
Indeed, that is what this lifetime,
This earth, this entire world, represents:
Your imaginings.
God has given you freedom,
Freedom even to imagine yourself separate from Him,
Just as you have done,

Even to imagine yourself separate from others,
As you have done.
Such imaginings are the essence of this world.
And that is why it is a world of illusion.

Do not be deceived.
You do not have the power to separate yourself from God,
Whether you like it or not.
The Love of God is within you, is sustaining you, all the time.
The Light of God with which you will see is always there.
The eternal Thoughts of God are always there.
That you cannot change.

Ah, yes, you are free to imagine.
You are free to imagine that you are separated,
That you are isolated.
You are free to imagine that you are unloved,
In the form of sickness, and poverty, and deformity,
And anger, and pain, even death.
You are free to imagine all of this,
And to believe that it is real.
But you cannot change the fact
That none of it is true.

In this Course, we talk about perception, and true perception.
Be aware that perception is of thought, and will pass away.
All of your perceptions, all of your thoughts
Which would make you believe, or would foster the belief,
That you are separated or isolated
Are not of reality.
They are illusions.
They are shadows and mists which will pass away.

The true perception shall also pass away.
However, your true perception will come to be based upon
That which I have been telling you this day—
The fact that God is within you and sustains you;
That God thinks with you, and through you;
That God's mind is, indeed, within your mind;
That the Light of true Vision is within you;
That this world, all of it, all of its perceptions and its thoughts,
Is but a grand illusion, and has no meaning,
Except that it be your imaginings.

In your true perception
You will come to see this world   ˎ
As the illusion it is, as imaginings.
When you do, you will simply let it go;
And you shall be free.
It cannot happen otherwise.
Over this you have no choice.

You may cling to the imaginings, to the false perception,
For a while longer, if you wish.
Insofar as you are enjoying your playing
With all these perceptions,
God has made you free to do just that.
You have even imagined time
In order to allow yourself "time" to do so.
But time, too, shall pass away.
Over that, also, you have no choice.

It is your invulnerability,
Yours because you are the recipient of the Love of God,
Which makes this true.
For in receiving the Love of God,
You are the recipient of God Himself.
And your goal in this Course
Is to feel that truth within your being.
For that shall lead you
To the understanding of love and forgiveness.

The lesson said,
"God is the Love in which I forgive." (L 46)
Your goal, as you come to understand love and forgiveness,
Is to know that when you love as God loves,
You are not sending energy,
You are not sending good thoughts,
You are not sending best wishes.
You are, in fact, giving your Self.
And when you love, that which you ARE,
The essence of your being, that which is a part of God,
Penetrates into and BECOMES that which you are loving.

Ultimately you will know, without effort or struggle,
That EVERYTHING is the recipient of that love,
And, therefore, the recipient of your Self.
And that you shall recognize as ONENESS.

Imagine some person, some being,
Whom you feel you love immensely.
Try to imagine what it would be
To give of yourself in such a manner
That you BECOME that other being.
This is not SENDING something TO another,
For that only imagines separation.
As you BECOME another being, in your loving,
You shall experience what it is to be ONE.

As an aside, you will eventually come to realize
That within this Oneness, there does exist individuality.
All of you (us) are ONE.
But within the infinity of Creation there is that which is YOU,
Which is but your Self, and yet is in no way separate
From any other aspect of Creation.

As you love another, and BECOME that being,
You are merely opening to what has always been true,
And to that which you are.

In the giving, in the becoming, you do not diminish.
And it is not possible for you to lose anything.
Rather, when you give of your Self
You expand and magnify that which you are.
Such is the nature of God.
Such is the nature of your Self.
Such is the purpose of Creation.

Try, if you can, to allow the truth of these words
To penetrate your being.
If you can get a glimpse, an inkling, of that truth,
You will have saved yourself years.
But if you do not,
Do not be discouraged.
For there is nothing you can do
To separate yourself from the Love of God,
Except, for a moment,
To imagine that you are separate from Him.
But that is, indeed, harmless.
So do not be afraid.

One of your lessons said, ''There is nothing to fear.'' (L 48)
And one said, ''God is the strength in which I trust.'' (L 47)

God loves you.
God has become you.
In His love, God is within you.
God's Love is not a thought He sends you,
But HIMSELF that He has given you.
That shall always be so.
And you are absolutely safe.

If you were the parent of a child who had a nightmare,
Believing (as you believe)
That he was separate and alone, and afraid,
You would know as the parent,
That your child was safe,
That the nightmare had no power to remove your presence,
Your protection, and your love for your child.
Such it is with God.

Try to imagine that Creation is, indeed, just like that.
You may then realize that God IS the strength within you,
That you CAN, indeed, trust,
That you ARE totally safe,
And totally free.

So take the lesson that says, "There is nothing to fear," (L 48)
And insofar as you are still locked within
Your thoughts and your imaginings,
Say to yourself,
"God is within me. God Himself is within my being.
God's strength, God's Love,
And the Light with which I will see,
Are deep within me.
They will never leave.
And I, in all the power of my imaginings,
Cannot make it go away.
Truly, there is nothing to fear."

Another of your lessons said,
"God's Voice speaks to me all through the day." (L 49)
This, if you understood it today,
Would be the completion of your *Course in Miracles*.
God is, in fact, deep within your being,
Separated from your awareness only by your imaginings
And the games you play with your thoughts.

The presence of God is within you always—
As a sense, as an urging, as an awareness,
Sometimes as an unrest, sometimes as a fullness,
Sometimes as a thought,
Sometimes as a Voice that speaks words.
BUT IT IS THERE, ALWAYS.
And you cannot separate your Self from it.

You can imagine this Voice to be but your own thoughts,
And try to isolate yourself from it.
But "trying" is all it will be.
For separation between you and the Voice of God cannot be.

I have spoken of this Voice as the Holy Spirit.
It is, in truth, the presence of God within you.
And you will learn to feel its presence,
To know that It is the Voice of God,
To understand the difference between that Voice
And the voice of your ego.
All of this you will come to know.

On that day you will become, even in your imaginings,
Perfectly safe and perfectly calm.
You will perceive truly
That you are sustained by the Love of God,
That there is nothing to fear,
That the strength of God knows every detail of every situation.
You will realize that when you live and think and act
According to the presence of God within you,
Then the expression of your individuality, as a Son of God,
Will be complete, will be safe,
And will be totally harmonious with All That Is.
Just as God Himself is in perfect harmony with All That Is.

For this moment, do not worry about how you will
Know the difference between that Voice and your ego.
Simply try to feel within that "There is nothing to fear."
Feel within that the Voice of God is there,
And will not, and cannot, leave.
Feel, if you can, with great confidence,
That you are sustained by the Love of God,
Protected by the strength of God,
And that you WILL see with the Light that is God.

Feel, if you can, that you will know in every circumstance,
With total certainty and calmness,
Exactly what to experience,
What to feel, what to say, and what to do.

I promise you, your life shall be completely free of doubt.
A certainty will accompany you
Every moment of your living on this earth.
And then you will need this earth no more.
For you will be free.

So allow yourself to imagine that this IS the way it will be.
I tell you, truly,
You have the power to make it that way this instant.
But to the extent that you still believe in time,
It is OK for you to say,
"It WILL become that way for me."
Allow yourself to believe that it WILL be,
While at the same time trying to believe
That it could be so this instant if you chose.

And imagine as best you can the scenario
In which God is, indeed, within you.
That strength, that love, that power,
That knowledge IS there, reaching to you,
Reaching through your thoughts and vain imaginings
To a calmness and a peace and a joy
You cannot yet imagine.

As you begin to imagine
That your life CAN be just as I have described,
It shall begin to become just that.
In fact, I promise you,
It already is exactly that way.
You simply don't know it.
As you begin to realize that these words of mine are true,
Then the other imaginings,
The separation, the fear, the grief,
The sickness, and the deformity
Shall already begin to pass away.

When the change arrives,
It may seem instantaneous to you.

So do not be dismayed if, right now,
You do not feel your fears passing away.
Simply allow yourself to imagine the presence of God,
And all I have said it will be.
Then know that in imagining it thusly
You are taking a giant step forward
To love and freedom.

Blessings upon you all. That is all.

LOVE I

Greetings again. I am Jeshua. I have come this day
To further, with you, my discussion of
A Course in Miracles.

Today I would speak with you more about love.
Love is something you have spoken of so often in your life,
And probably have never really understood.
Today I will help you begin to move
Toward the reality of what love is.

We spoke previously about the Love of God,
And how, when God loves you,
He, in essence, becomes you.
When I use the word "essence,"
I mean beyond your bodies, beyond your thoughts,
Beyond your imaginings.
For beyond those is reality.

So when God loves you,
In reality, God becomes you,
And God IS you.
But in reality, there is no "you."
Hear me well.
In reality, there is not even God.
You do, in fact, seem to have a measure of individuality.
And that measure you might always call your "Self."
But, in fact, it can never be alone.
It can never be unique.
It can never be separate.
Even God Itself is the same.

Creation was, in no sense,
The development, or the beginning, of different souls.
Creation was nothing more than an expansion,
An expansion of God Itself.
And out of that expansion came what seems to be,
In some measure, individuality.
That seeming individuality allows for measures of creation

Which seem to come from different sources.
However, that is not so.
For all is One.

The words "All is One" can be difficult for you.
But I have no choice but to keep saying them—
All is One.
You are One.
God has become you.
You have become your brother.
Over this you have no choice.
Such is the Will of God.
Such is also the will of your Self,
Whether you imagine it to be so, or not.

It is necessary for me to keep saying these words.
They are the vehicle through which we work
While you yet remain on earth,
In this sojourn of your imaginings.
Eventually the meaning, the understanding,
The feeling, and the knowing
Will go beyond the words.
Then you will BE One.
And then you will be free.

Hear the words again.
God loves you.
God does not SEND you something.
He does not send you energy, or good thoughts, or good will.
For even to say "send you something" implies a separateness,
A gap which must be bridged between sender and receiver.
I tell you that does not, and cannot, happen.
In God's loving you, God has become you.

Now I would speak of you, and your loving.
When you love another (Hear the word, "another"),
When you say you love another,
You are imagining separation.
And remember, separation cannot exist.

One of the first things you do when you love another
Is to imagine good for that person,
To imagine him well, to imagine him joy,
To imagine him free.

This is a valid step for where you are.
Do not make yourself wrong.
Do not decry the nature of this life you have chosen.
But soon, all of you will be able to move past the notion
That when you love another
You send a someTHING to someONE different from yourself.

Within your Self is everything.
Within your Self is God.
Within your Self is all beings.
Within your Self is all of Creation.
Especially, within your Self is all of
What you refer to as your physical universe.
All of it, every iota, is contained,
Completely and fully, within you,
Just as in the hologram.
You ARE the entire universe.
But you are far more than that which you call the heavens,
And the cosmos, and the physical universe.
That is but one drop in the ocean of creation,
One drop in the infinite ocean of experience
That is God.

The entire universe as you see it,
The magnitude of the heavens,
The bodies of the earth, the planets, the Sun, the stars,
Is an infinitesimally small aspect of what you are.
Do not be awed by this.
Only open your being to the wonder of what you are,
And rejoice.

So when you love another,
You cannot send to the other "someTHING."
For that you have already done.
When you love another, you become the other.
And in loving another, you become your Self.

Everything you see comes from a place
Deep, deep, within your being,
Wherein lies the God within you.
In your invulnerability, all that you see is truly your creation.
It cannot be otherwise. It can only be as you see it.
And the need you have for vision
Is your need to see TRULY.

When you see separation,
When you see differences, when you see individuals,
When you see wills which can be in conflict,
Or ideas that can be in conflict,
You are not seeing.
Do not delude yourself.

Begin now with the words,
Knowing that the experience will follow,
The experience preceding certainty,
And the awareness of what you are.
Begin with the words, the ideas, the thoughts
Which tell you that your world IS YOU.
Every aspect of what you label OTHER,
Whether it be another being, another animal,
Another plant, another chair, a distant star—
Everything which you call "other"
Is, indeed, your Self.
For you have become your friend.
You have become your enemy.
And neither of those sentences makes any sense.
For you have merely become your Self.

When you fully understand the truth of those words,
You will understand love.
If you do not understand it now,
Do not be frightened.
These words can seem difficult for you.
Simply rejoice that this world is a place
Where you can come to see things differently.

One of the lessons said,
You can look upon this world
As a place where you become free. (12)
And all you need do is shift your thinking upside down.
Instead of seeing the separateness which you have imagined,
See it as the Oneness of your own soul.
See it as your Self, and know it to BE your Self.

It is your thinking, your imagining,
That has created this world as you know it.
So now, for a moment, try to imagine
That you ARE the tree,
That you ARE the cat, that you ARE the star,

That you ARE your friend.
Do not say words to yourself,
Like "What does that mean?"
Rather try to be still, and allow the experience,
The understanding of that,
To seep into your being.

That understanding already lies within
The deepest part of your being.
It needs only surface, and you will be free.
Realize that all of Creation, every aspect,
Whether it be what you call physical,
Or what you call spiritual, is the same,
And is a dance.
It is a dance of Oneness.
It is a dance of all aspects of Creation,
The part of your Self you are calling you,
The part of your Self you are calling the animals,
The part of your Self you are calling the stars,
And the part of your Self you are calling the other humans.

And for them, the others
Whom you imagine to be separate from yourself,
It is the same.
For they are your Self.
And all of it is a magnificent dance,
A magnificent symphony of cooperation,
And sharing, and Oneness.
For without the full cooperation
(Note even the word "cooperation" implies separation)
Of all other aspects of the universe,
You could not experience it as you do.

Insofar as you believe that any of it
Does something different from that which you have desired,
What you experience cannot be real love.
That belief is the primary source of all this illusion.
That belief is the only source of your tears,
Your pain, your sickness, your grief,
Your worry, your anger, and your doubt.

Then, for you, love shall become the knowing
That you have long since BECOME,
That you long since ARE,
Everything that you see.

Imagine something which you do not like.
Then realize it is only an aspect of your Self.
Realize also that there is no goodness, nor badness, in you.
That aspect which you perceive to be something you do not like
Is but an aspect of your Self needing an experience,
Within the realm of your freedom and your joy.

As you accept that aspect of your Self you do not like,
Allowing it its freedom and joy,
And likewise accept, in its freedom and joy,
That aspect of your Self which you call yourself,
You shall realize that the two are one and the same.

Then how can you hate? How can you be angry?
How can you not forgive?
Recall, forgiveness is the purpose of this Course.
And your forgiveness is the realization
That YOU ARE YOUR WORLD,
That you cannot label anything as bad, or as good,
That you simply cannot judge at all.

For if you label one thing as bad, and another as good,
Then what you have done is split your Self.
And how can you live,
If you have been split asunder by your own imaginings?
When you talk about anger, or fear, or hatred,
That is, indeed, what you are doing.
You are trying to imagine that somehow
You have been able to rend asunder
That which is One, that which is you.

Then how can there be peace?
How can there be freedom?
Do you see now why I call this world insane?
Imagine trying to tear your Self in half, which is an impossibility,
Yet feeling the pain, in the belief that it could happen—
Imagine believing that such could be real—
And then somehow imagine that you like it.
Or try to imagine that upon so doing
You might not be in conflict.
Insanity, yes.

So realize that God, in loving you, has become you.
You are nothing more than the expansion of God.
And then your love and your forgiveness

Shall become the same.
For they are your awareness that
Your entire world is but the expansion of your Self,
Which is really the expansion of God.

Know this, and know it well.
Everything you see is your Self.
It is entirely possible to pick any aspect of this entire world,
And in your silence, in the absence of your imaginings,
In the absence of your thinking,
To see the entirety of your Self.
For that, truly, is what it is.

Try for a moment to imagine that this is so.
Take your world and turn it upside down.
Nothing is separate. All is One.
All is a splendid march in harmony and cooperation,
All of it orchestrated by you,
All of it orchestrated by every aspect of Being,
Which is also you.

As you begin to imagine thusly,
What you will most likely feel is an expansion within yourself.
You will feel as if your heart is growing,
Almost to a point where it would burst.
That feeling you may realize
Is the first stirrings within you of Real Love.
For Real Love comes when you know within your being
That everything is your Self,
That everything has become you,
By your own choice and your own creation,
Because you are God.

You are your Self. You are the universe. You are free.
Everything you see is but an aspect of your Self,
From the smallest blade of grass to that which you call God.
And as the experience takes you past these words,
You shall find your Oneness,
And your freedom.
And your forgiveness.
And your shall realize that all of it is love.

Blessings upon you all. That is all.

FORGIVENESS I

Greetings again. I am Jeshua. I have come this day
To further, with you, my discussion of
A Course in Miracles.

Today I wish to discuss with you
Some of the beginning notions of forgiveness.
You have already read
That forgiveness is what this Course is all about,
That forgiveness is your salvation,
That forgiveness is your happiness,
That forgiveness is the light in which you shall see.
The lessons also said, "God is the light in which I see." (L 44)
So forgiveness is of major importance.

In all likelihood, you do not understand forgiveness.
One of your previous lessons said that
You do not understand what anything is for. (7)
This is one time for you to open your being
And acknowledge your lack of understanding.
For as I speak to you of forgiveness, and what it really means,
Your experience will begin to move beyond this world,
Beyond your thinking, beyond your ideas,
Beyond all that which separates you
From the reality of what you are,
Which is the Son of God.

There is one thing about forgiveness
Which we need to mention very early on.
You will hear it again and again.
For those of you in this world, on this earth,
This is of extreme importance.
What I shall discuss right now
Is what forgiveness IS NOT.

Forgiveness is NOT, ever, for any reason, in any way,
Forgiving someone else for what he has done to you.

The traditional thought about forgiveness
Is based on the belief that SOMEONE ELSE

Has unjustifiably, inappropriately, done something to you,
That an action on the behalf of someone else—
Be it by an individual or by a group,
Be it by loved ones or by enemies—
That an action by someone, or someones,
Has done something which has made you unhappy,
Which has hurt you.
You are very familiar with this notion, I am sure.
And when you forgive,
The notion has always been that you would somehow
Look beyond, look past the wrong they have done.
And so you would say,
"I forgive you for committing this wrong against me."

That, in a sense, is your definition of sin.
But you have read in this Course,
And will doubtless hear again and again—
There is no sin. (13) There is no guilt. (14)
There is no wrong that any being can inflict upon another. (15)

Hear me well.
Whenever you take it upon yourself to even imagine
That you are willing to forgive another
For what he has done to you,
What you are really doing is attacking that person,
And attacking yourself.
For you are saying, are you not, that it is possible
That he could have done something (anything) wrong.
And if it is possible that one of your brothers
Could ever do anything wrong,
Then it is possible that you as well
Could do the same.

If it is possible that your brother could sin,
Then it is possible that you could sin.
Thus does sin become a reality in your mind.
When you take it upon yourself to consider saying,
"I will forgive you for what you have done to me,"
You are viciously attacking your own invulnerability.
And the lesson said,
"My attack thoughts are an attack
Upon my own invulnerability." (L 26)

Now again, hear me well.
You are the Son of God.

You are an expansion of the Mind of God Itself.
In that sense you are God.
And as God, whether you like it or not,
You are invulnerable.
What does that mean, again?
It means that absolutely nothing can happen in your life,
In this or any other form of your life,
Except that it be by your own will,
Your own design, and your own choice.
It is impossible for any being to do anything TO YOU.

We will say often, never look outside yourself.
For there is nothing there.
There is only your Self; and you ARE all of Creation.
That truth will become natural, second nature, to you.
But for now, if the notion is difficult, do not be upset.
Simply hear me again.
Nothing can be done TO YOU, by anyone, ever.

As you open more and more to that thought,
To that realization, and to the experience behind it,
You will come to know that everything you experience
Is, indeed, your own choice,
Even that which you call pain, and misery, and hurt.
And all of your vain imaginings
That you can be unhappy
Are but your own choice.

Hear me well.
If any other being seems to participate
In acting out your choice to be unhappy,
It is only out of love,
And because you wanted him to be there.
So how can you, when you should be saying, "Thank you,"
Turn it around, and say,
"I forgive you for the wrong you have done to me"?

It should be clear by now.
Forgiveness is never forgiving someone else
For what he has done to you.
It is impossible that anyone can ever DO anything to you.
If you are angry, never delude yourself into thinking
You are angry at someone else.
You are angry at yourself.

If you are hurt, never delude yourself into thinking
That another has hurt you.
For you have only hurt yourself.
So never feel it is loving, or appropriate,
Or kind, or gentle, to forgive another.
For he could not, can not, and will not
Do anything TO you.

What you will come to realize
At the innermost depths of your being,
When you contemplate forgiving another,
Is that forgiveness is just the realization within yourself
That there never is, and can never be,
Anything to forgive.
The issue doesn't even come up.

How about forgiving yourself?
Should you forgive yourself when you make yourself wrong?
Should you forgive yourself for not being fully enlightened?
What are you doing, if you feel you are wrong,
That you have CHOSEN pain, sickness, or injury?
You are believing in your thinking
That if you were more advanced,
Fully enlightened, as it were,
You wouldn't be feeling the pain.
And so you conclude, you must be wrong.

Do you see it is the same?
If you can sit in a moment of frustration,
And label yourself as wrong,
Or not perfect, as you see it,
Then your brother, likewise, becomes capable of error.
Thus you generate anger at him and at yourself
In exactly the same form, although perhaps more subtle,
As when you elect to forgive him,
Or blame him for doing something to you.

It there any difference between
Blaming your brother for doing something to you,
And blaming yourself for something YOU have done to you?

You are the Son of God.
You are the expansion of the Mind of God.
You are an all-powerful being, a being of Light,

A being of absolute truth, and of absolute Love.
There is nothing you can want for, or need.

And your sole purpose in being on this earth
Is to release everything that would keep you
From realizing that what I have just said is true.
Ultimately, since your forgiveness is your salvation,
And since your forgiveness is the salvation of the world,
Your forgiveness is only about
Forgiving all the things that would seem, in any way,
To keep you from the knowledge that
You are the invulnerable Son of God,
A being of Light and of Love.

Take that idea right now, and try to feel its reality.
True forgiveness is merely the dismissal of all the blocks
That would seem to separate you from your inheritance,
From your true nature as the Son of God.

Let us return for a moment to the notion of blaming yourself,
And then needing to forgive yourself for doing so.
If you think for a moment,
You will realize that whenever you blame yourself,
All you are talking about is time.

When you hear, within your being,
The truth that you are the Son of God,
That you are invulnerable,
You already know that you are perfect,
That perfect love and happiness ARE yours.
But what you feel, as you live on this earth,
Is that perfect love and perfect happiness
WILL be yours.
Do you hear the difference?

What you are doing when you would blame yourself
For not being perfect right now
Is worshipping time.
To the extent that you ever feel frustrated
Over not being fully enlightened,
Over not being completely peaceful,
Over not being healed of all pain, all sickness, and all sorrow—
What you are doing is substantiating what you call time.
And you are choosing time above the Voice of God.

Now, it is not wrong for you to do that.
For your choosing to come and live in human form
Is a choice to EXPERIENCE your body, and space, and time.
And your forgiveness will take you beyond all those blocks,
The major ones being your body, and space, and time itself.

In your forgiveness you will be freed
From the prison of space and time, and your body.
For they are but products of the thoughts you have.
And we have said often before that
Your thoughts do not mean anything.

Your forgiveness will lead you to a point
Where you will know, beyond your ideas and thoughts,
That your body and space and time itself
Are but your thoughts, which do not mean anything,
And ultimately are not real.
Therefore, you are free.

So in your forgiveness you will be free.
Hear me well.
I have said, you WILL be free.
For I honor, with love, your belief in time.
I do not make you wrong
For the choice you have made to be human,
To live on this earth.
Neither make yourself wrong.
When you feel frustration, when you feel sick,
When you feel deformed, when you feel pain in your life,
When you feel life is complex and you do not have the answer,
Realize that all you are doing is
Believing in time, and believing in space,
Mostly in time.

Now begin to feel within your being
That time shall pass away.
Then everything you label as frustration,
And fear, and doubt, and pain,
Will pass away—
Because in the absence of time, it cannot exist.

For a moment, play with that thought.
Imagine that there were no past;
Imagine that there were no future;

Then see what is left to fear.
You will realize at once, NOTHING.
Recall that the lesson said, "There is nothing to fear." (L 48)
When I wrote that lesson down,
I knew that space and time,
And all the blocks they present
To the truth of what you are as the Son of God—
They all are but your thoughts,
And do not mean anything.
For you are free.

For now, it is enough for you to be in the place
Where you realize that space and time SHALL pass away.
And as you grow into the beauty,
The peace, and the joy of forgiveness,
This is what you will be forgiving—
Space and time and your bodies.
For without those it will take you
No time at all to realize
That someone else cannot possibly do anything to you.
For you, along with God, are the creator of the universe.
And in that moment you will know your freedom.

For now, when you find yourself tempted to blame yourself,
Realize that what you are doing
Is trying to honor space and time,
And to honor thoughts which, ultimately,
Do not mean anything.

Then go back to the lesson where you said,
"I do not understand what anything is for." (7)
Go back to the lesson that says,
"God's Voice speaks to me all through the day." (L 49)
And always go back to the lesson that says,
"There is nothing to fear." (L 48)

As you release your fears,
Which are your belief in space and time,
You will begin to realize that God's Voice does, indeed,
Speak to you all through the day.
And you will begin to hear that Voice.
In those moments,
You will find the complexity of your life disappearing;
You will find yourself knowing what to do,

What to say, and what to be.
There will be a certainty within you.
The certainty will lead to peace.
From the peace will come joy.
In your joy you will know there is nothing to fear.
And in your release from fear,
You will be growing in forgiveness.

Never make yourself wrong.
Only go back and say,
"I do not understand what anything is for." (7)
Then do your best to open to the Voice of God,
Which does speak to you all through the day.
As you open, you will hear the Voice.
And the only thing that keeps you from following the Voice
Is your belief in space and time.

As you hear the Voice of God,
Do your best to say, "There is nothing to fear." (L 48)
For then you shall be moving
Toward your freedom,
And your peace,
And your joy,
And love.

Above all, do not make yourself wrong.
You cannot be wrong, for you are the Son of God.
You are the expansion of the Mind of God Itself.
You are the happiness, the joy, the light,
And the beauty of the entire universe.

Blessings upon you all. That is all.

GRIEVANCES

Greetings again. I am Jeshua. I have come this day
To further, with you, my discussion of
A Course in Miracles.

During the past week, you have been reading about grievances.
"Love holds no grievances." (L 68)
"Holding grievances is an attack
Upon God's plan for salvation." (L 72)
We will speak today of grievances.

Love holds no grievances.
The key word is love.
For Love, as the lesson said, created you like Itself. (L 67)
Indeed, God IS Love.
And YOU are Love.
All aspects of your world are Love.
For Love is all there is.
Truly, there is hardly a better way to define Love than that—
Love is All That Is.
Some people even define God as ALL THAT IS.
That is really nothing more than saying that God is Love.
Therefore, you, too, are Love.

Love is the completeness, Love is the wholeness,
Love is the Oneness that IS the universe.
But the universe is beyond
What you conceive of as your physical universe.

With regard to your physical universe,
Love is the energy, Love is the glue,
Love is the strength that holds it together.
It is that which gives it form, and of which it is made.
Love is each atom itself.
Also Love is the energy, in whatever form you imagine it,
That binds and holds the imaginary atoms one to another.
Love is all that which you deem to be
The physical particles that create your body.
But beyond that, Love is that living, breathing,

Vibrant force that seems to hold
The molecules of your body together
In that pattern you call your self.
All of that is Love.
And the only difference between
The love you call your body, and your world—
Between that and the love
You call another's body, and his world—
The only difference is the changes and variations
In frequency, or vibration.

When things blend perfectly, you imagine them to be one.
And when they don't blend
Into a perfect harmonic resonance, as you call it,
Then you imagine them to be different.
However, the imagined resonance, or lack thereof,
Is a product of your thoughts.
For it is your thoughts that have created
This image of your physical body,
And the image of your entire physical universe.

All of it is thoughts—
Your bodies, the differences you see in bodies,
The differences you see in resonance and vibration.
All of it is thoughts which do not mean anything,
And cannot be real.

All That Is is God. All That Is is Love.
Now imagine for a moment, that YOU ARE All That Is.
We have said this before when we said you are invulnerable.
Being invulnerable, you create every aspect of your world.
And everything that seems to happen to you
Is by your own design, by your own choice.

The truth of that goes beyond the notion itself.
For when I suggest to you in words
That what seems to happen to you is of your own creation,
I am still allowing for a thought pattern
Which suggests that what seems to happen to you
Is somehow different from yourself.
But indeed, that is not so,
And cannot be so.

YOU ARE All That Is.
Your entire world, all of it,

As you perceive it, as you experience it,
As you will come to know it when you move
Beyond your thoughts, beyond the illusions—
All of it IS your Self.
This is literally true.
Not in some sense of the imagination,
Not within some mental construct, but literally—
The world you experience IS your Self.

It is not sufficient for me to say,
Or for you to think, or feel,
That what happens in your world
Is a product of your own creation.
That is not sufficient.
It is only sufficient to say,
"What is there in my world IS, IN FACT, MYSELF."

Hear me well.
You are the raindrops. You are the Sun.
You are the energy that seems to hold
The Sun and its molecules together.
This is true even though it SEEMS to you
That the resonance holding the Sun together
Is different from the one holding your body together.
This makes it SEEM that you are different from your Sun.
But you are not.

Indeed, you could be at the very center of your own Sun,
Not change your consciousness,
And not suffer one iota of what you call harm.
Because you are the same.
You world would, indeed, call it a miracle.
But I tell you it would not be a miracle.
It would just be a statement that you ARE your world.

Imagine now, for a moment. Let your imagination play.
Suppose that what I have said is true.
You ARE your world. You ARE All That Is.
Just as God is All That Is.
And now try to imagine what a grievance is.

There are two succinct ways to express what a grievance is.
First, a grievance is literally an attack
Upon your own invulnerability.
Secondly, a grievance is anything

Which you perceive to be outside yourself,
Separate from yourself,
And which you would like to be different from what it is.

You ARE your own world.
And for you to imagine that you would like
Something in your world to be different
Is literally to desire that a part of your Self be different.
I tell you, you are whole; you are complete;
You are unified within your being.
There is no conflict within your Real Self.
The unity of what you are does not allow conflict.

In fact, conflict is an experience unknown to God.
Within God there is only completeness,
Wholeness, and Oneness.
And for you to imagine that any aspect of your Self
Should, or could, be different from what it is,
Is for you to imagine that the unification that is you
Should somehow be split,
And that a part of you should be different from what YOU are.

Imagine the conflict as you try to BE your Self,
Believing that part of you has been split off from your Self,
All the while needing to remain whole.
For whole is what you are.

This is truly the source of all the conflict in your world.
You imagine that you have been split asunder,
And that what you call ''other'' is different from your Self.
And in your belief that it IS different,
You want it to be a certain way.
You want it to change from what it is.
All of that is your grievances.

Love is All That Is. Love is your Self.
Your world is, in fact, you.
The aspects of your world are not merely your creations,
They are your Self—
Because you are totally invulnerable,
Because you are the Son of God, creator of the universe.

A grievance is for you to wish it to be otherwise.
A grievance is for you to wish
That there is an aspect of your Self

Which has been split apart from your Self,
AND OVER WHICH YOU HAVE NO CONTROL.
Every time you look at another being in your life,
Be it a stone, a tree, a plant, a raindrop,
Or what you call another person,
And wish that somehow it be different,
You are wishing for your Self to be split apart,
To be torn asunder.
Then in your insane imaginings,
You believe that splitting your Self thusly
Will bring you happiness and peace.
"Insane" is the correct word, is it not?

Hear this well.
Love is All That Is. God is All That Is.
You are God, and you are All That Is.
Your entire universe, in every detail,
Is just an expression of love,
Put into the dense form of energy you call your physical world.
It is put there by you out of your desire
To experience it at that level.
The world itself, and the glue that holds it together,
Is Love, and is your Self.

To do this Course, you must be willing to love your Self.
You must be willing to open,
First your thinking, and then your being,
To the truth of what you are.
I tell you, as you begin to open to that truth,
It will accelerate, and blossom, and grow
Until it touches your knowing within.
And then it will be as if the sunlight is burning within you.
Rather than feeling that you could be inside your Sun
And not be harmed,
You will feel as if your Sun is inside of you.
And that kind of light, that kind of energy,
That kind of warmth,
Shall pour out of you to your universe, to all your brothers,
To all that you see, and to all that you experience.
And even that, as you try to imagine it,
Is only a fraction of the joy, the light, and the beauty
That you will feel within yourself.

Begin now, if you can,
To allow those thoughts to flow within you.

Your universe IS you.
It is God, and it is All That Is.
And as you come to love your Self,
As you open to loving your Self,
You will realize that you are always
Looking at naught but your Self,
Always at your own wholeness.

Initially you may find yourself looking at your vain imaginings,
That which you have imagined to be fear,
That which you have imagined to be sorrow,
And misery, and separateness.
You may imagine that initially.
But then a shift will occur.
And when you truly see that your world IS your Self,
You will open to it, and see it as a light,
A beauty, and a shining,
Which is, indeed, your Self,
Which is, indeed, your freedom,
Which is, indeed,
Nothing more than an expression of what you are,
And what you can be.
So try, right now, to imagine that what I have said is true.
For I assure you, it is.
Your entire world is your creation,
And more so; it is, in fact, your Self.

Imagine it were true that
You have within your Self the glory, the love, and the power
To literally create this world.
Without you, without your will, without what you are,
It would dissolve into nothingness in an instant.

Then you would see Creation as a product of what you are.
You would see its beauty.
You would see that it is but a reflection
Of the creative power, and the wholeness,
That God gave to you when he expanded Himself into you,
In order to become you.

When you know that within your being,
It will bring you great freedom.
It will totally change the way you see your world,
And yourself, and your brothers.

Love holds no grievances.
Realize, moment to moment,
That you are always looking upon that which you have created.
All it would take for it to be different
Is for you to imagine it so.
And therein will be the expression of your love.

So as you look at the raindrops,
And the flowers, the trees, and your brothers,
Realize that none of them can ever do, or be, anything,
Except that it be your Self.

You may explore this any way you wish.
But never look outside as if to see
A brother, or being, who is different from you.
For it cannot be so.
And your belief that it can
Will only cause you the conflict
Of which this world is made.

Before we close for today,
I will make some comments about salvation.
For I have just now told you exactly what salvation is.
In this Course, we speak often of salvation.
Well, salvation is nothing more
Than your realization that you ARE All That Is.
It is your knowing that you are your world,
That there is nothing outside of you,
That there can not, ever, BE anything outside of you,
Just as there can never BE anything outside of God.

When you experience that,
Your entire world will become a unified whole.
There will be no conflict.
There can be no competition.
There can be no self which you deem
To be different from another self.
There will only be perfect harmony.
You may call it a resonance, if you will.
But it will only be perfect harmony, and perfect sharing.

Your salvation is your freedom from all the thoughts and ideas
Which allow you to believe
That separation and isolation can exist,

That you can be different from your world,
Or from another.

As you EXPERIENCE what we have said this day,
You will be saved from all the misery,
The pain, fear, grief, and sorrow
Which comes from your believing that you can be different.

In this Course, you come to realize that
What is the same is the same.
All is the same. And the same cannot be different.
That is what we have been saying.
Everything is the same. Everything is One.
And within this great Oneness, nothing can be different.

And when you know that
Nothing can be different from your Self,
Then salvation will be yours.
Salvation is not to be saved FROM anything.
Salvation is merely to move, at the level of your being,
Beyond all of the thoughts which would tell you
That the aspects of your world are separate, one from another.
For indeed, they are not.

As I said at the beginning,
God is Love, and God is All That Is.
You are the Son of God.
You, likewise, are All That Is.
Realize with freedom, with joy, with great peace,
And with that which you call love,
That as you look upon every aspect of your world,
You are always looking upon your Self.

Do this with joy.
Open to what you find there,
And your life will grow immensely.
For you will begin to perceive
The infiniteness of what you are as the Son of God.

Blessings upon you all. That is all.

SILENCE

Greetings again. I am Jeshua. I have come this day
To further, with you, my discussion of
A Course in Miracles.

Today I wish to speak to you, for the first time,
Of how to listen to, and how to hear,
The Voice for God.

You have been through a number of lessons
Which have suggested that you be very still,
That you move to a place deep within,
Where is to be found truth,
Where is your Real Self,
Where is the answer to all the illusions of the world,
All of its conflict, all of its fear,
And all of its guilt.
Such a place is truly to be found.
And like all else,
It is within you.

I realize that within your illusion, in this world,
It can seem difficult for you to find that place.
However, finding that place would take but an instant
If you could let go of all the illusions,
All of that which I have called grievances.

Insofar as you hold onto the grievance you call time,
It may take you a period of time for this to happen.
In this discussion, I will allow for both.
Truly, if you suddenly become free enough,
It can happen in an instant.
Try to constantly keep that idea in your thoughts.
For it is from there that it shall penetrate your awareness,
Which is beyond your thinking.
If you choose to have this take time,
Do not make yourself wrong.
Simply allow it to flow through

The minutes, the hours, the days,
Even the years, should you choose to have it take that long.

It is a promise I give you, that God gives you,
Indeed, that God has already given you,
And that can never change—
You are free,
And in your sense of time, WILL be free.
It cannot happen otherwise.
Have no fear. Have no doubt.
If you choose to take time in which to know that you ARE free,
It does not change the fact that you ARE,
Or in your terms, WILL become so.

How do we suggest that you listen,
That you be very still, that you find that place within?
How do you truly do it?
Today I will give you some guidelines.

First, God is Love. And you are Love.
Love is freedom. And freedom is forgiveness.
Forgiveness is your only function here in this sojourn on earth.
Your function and your happiness are one.
And your happiness is joy.

If you could experience within your being what I have just said,
You could cease this reading right now.
For you are God.
And God, in the expansion of Himself,
Created you and me, and all beings
In this vast Oneness of WHAT IS.
WHAT IS is the creation of life.
And creation is absolute freedom.

Your existence is as full and as rich
And as instantaneous as your imagination.
For whatever crosses your Mind, IS.
You have created it.
This happens without time.
And the only way you can conceive of it without time
Is to say *forever and ever.*

This is your existence:
Freedom of creation,

Freedom to imagine whatever it is you desire, forever and ever,
Ever changing, ever growing,
Instantaneously switching from one being to another,
From one form to another,
From one thought to another, from one sharing to another,
To the knowing that everything is complete and instantaneous
And full and rich, forever and ever.

You are the Son of God.
That is your happiness. That is your joy.
And the purpose of *A Course in Miracles*
Is to do nothing except to allow you
To remove all of the blocks
That keep you from knowing that is true.

So as you listen,
One of the first things you listen for,
And one of the easiest things for you to understand,
Is joy.
You simply listen for joy.
And with it comes peace.

As you are attempting to be still,
And try it now if you wish—
As you are still,
You move beyond all the busyness of your thoughts.
You move beyond all the restrictions
Formed by your thoughts and your concepts
(Which, remember, don't mean anything).
In your stillness,
You even move beyond the concept of what you are.
For even THAT concept, as we have said, has no meaning.

As you move to a point of stillness,
You are totally open to anything you can imagine.
As you try to hear that Voice,
Which is my voice, which is your own voice,
And which in this Course we call the Holy Spirit—
As you listen,
Listen for the feelings of joy.

When you feel joy, it will well up inside you.
It will seem, as we have said,
As if the Sun were shining within your being

With such radiance that it must burst free.
Indeed, it WILL burst free.
And that shall be your joy.
For joy cannot be contained.
In your joy, you shall become a Sun.
For as a Sun, you are truly a Son of God.

So as you listen,
As your imagination flows within you,
As you sense a lightness, a freedom, and a peace,
And an illumination within you,
Then realize that you are, indeed,
Hearing the Voice for God.

All that would keep you from hearing that Voice
Is your desire to bring with you
Your thoughts, your concepts, and your idle wishes,
Which only limit you,
And keep you from seeing what you really are.

If you think you are feeling joy,
And you can imagine something which could threaten it,
Then your joy is not full.
If it can be threatened, it still contains within it
A great measure of what we call the ego,
Which is comprised of your thoughts and your concepts.
So if it seems that you are truly joyful,
And you wonder if you are hearing the Voice for God,
Simply try to imagine whether anything, or anyone,
Or any circumstance could alter your joy.
And if it could, you are not completely, truly,
Hearing the Voice for God.

When you sense the joy and the peace that is of God,
Nothing can threaten it.
If you begin to sense the joy
And become aware that it could be altered,
Know that you are harboring within yourself
The grievances of which we have spoken.
For the grievances are the attacks
Upon your own invulnerability.
Your grievances are your idle wishes
That you not be the Son of God.
Your grievances are your idle wishes

That something could be outside yourself,
That something could happen to you.
Your grievances are your wishes
That you pull a shade in front of the miracles
To which you are entitled as the Son of God.
Your grievances are your desire to live in darkness.
And none of them can be there without that you love them.

So as you listen for joy,
As you begin to feel it welling up inside of you,
Check and see if anything outside you can threaten it.
If a person should act differently,
If someone should choose to die, as you call it,
Or if a circumstance should change,
Would your joy be altered?
If the answer is yes, then it is not real joy.
It is only another set of thoughts and concepts you have made.
It is but one more brick in the prison
You have created for yourself
By desiring that you be different from what you are.

So, in your stillness,
Listen for lightness and freedom welling up inside you.
Try to realize that in the lightness and freedom
You are perfectly safe,
And that nothing can change that same lightness,
That freedom, or that peace,
Except yourself.

If you can even imagine such a state,
Then you have heard the first real whisperings
Of the Voice of God.
You may apply this filter always.
If ever your joy can be altered,
Know that you are harboring grievances.
Know that, at some level, in your time,
You are not yet ready to be free.
Know that you are not ready, in your time,
To let go of the thoughts and concepts
Which hide from you the light within.

What do you do if you listen, if you try to be still,
And do not get a sense of joy?
For now, I suggest you do this—

Do your very best to imagine, within your thinking,
That it IS there.
Do your best to KNOW within your being that it is there.
See it as a goal.
See it as a mountaintop which you know you can reach.
Perhaps the goal seems too far in the distance for you to see.
Perhaps the mountaintop is covered with clouds.
Simply know that it IS there.
And in your imagining, in your knowing that it is there,
You begin to open your being to its presence.
And eventually it will come.
Do not doubt this.
The joy WILL come.
Over this you have no choice.

I promise you the joy is there.
There is nothing you can do to remove it.
You can pull the shades so you cannot see it or feel it.
But it is not possible to change its presence, or remove it.
Such is the nature of God.
Such is the nature of the Son of God, which you are.

So in your imagining, do your very best
To know that the joy is there.
And after a while, there will come whispers,
There will come little flashes,
Which might seem like little flashes of light,
And which will be your first steps toward vision,
Toward SEEING the joy that is, indeed, there.
You may have a moment when it wells up inside you,
Only to disappear in the next instant.
Do not despair. Rather rejoice.
For by that you will know
That for one brief moment you did, indeed,
Let go of the barriers to your joy.
And if you can do it for a moment,
Then, of course, you can do it forever.
For a moment is nothing less than forever.

It is very important that you not be discouraged
As you come again and again to this place of silence.
Do not despair when you realize that your experience
IS vulnerable to circumstances, and is not the full joy of God.

It is important that you not be discouraged in those moments.
It is important that you come again and again to that place.

For in that place,
You shall become more and more aware of your grievances.
And as the lesson said,
Every choice you make
Is between a grievance and a miracle. (16)
As you become aware of each and every grievance,
You are in a better position to let it go.
And as you release each grievance,
You come closer and closer to the miracle behind it.

Do not be dismayed today
If it seems that what I have said is too lofty,
It it seems to be too much of a struggle,
If it seems as if you've never been to the place of silence,
And can never get there.
Do not be dismayed.
Do not be discouraged.
Only know that you are absolutely safe,
And that you are absolutely loved.
For I am with you, and will never leave.
Over that, also, you have no choice.
There is nothing that can harm you,
In spite of all your vain imaginings.

So begin to realize, as best you can,
That the joy IS there.
When you find it for that first instant,
It will then begin to magnify, and grow.
And when you find the real joy of God,
Then this whole world of illusion,
Which but seems to bring you joy,
Will pass into nothingness,
As shadows before the morning Sun.
Rejoice.
For you are absolutely loved.
You are absolutely safe.
And truly, you ARE the Son of God.

Blessings upon you all. That is all.

ONE PROBLEM—ONE SOLUTION

Greetings again. I am Jeshua. I have come this day
To further, with you, my discussion of
A Course in Miracles.

Today I will discuss with you two particular lessons,
Number 79 and Number 80.
You may recall that the lessons said,
"Let me recognize the problem so it can be solved." (L 79)
And, "Let me recognize my problems have been solved." (L 80)

Based on all I have told you thus far,
Lesson Number 80 is the one which contains the real essence
Of what you need to experience—
"Let me recognize my problems HAVE BEEN solved."

In truth, you have no problems.
In truth, any problems you may think you have now,
Any problems you have had in what you call the past,
Or anticipate having in what you call the future,
Do not exist.
Over this you have no choice.

You are free to be whatever you would be,
And free to imagine whatever you would imagine.
Indeed, you can imagine that you have problems.
It is almost universal on this earth
For you to imagine that you do, indeed, have problems.
But, in truth, you don't.
Because you can't.
Hear me well.
Over this you have no choice.

Why can I say this?
Lesson 79 said that all problems are one. (17)
You have one problem,
And it IS the problem of separation.
In whatever form you imagine that you have a problem,
It is always, ultimately, a belief that you can be separate,
That what is the same can be different.

And because you think things can be separate,
You also believe that there can be conflict.

Try to imagine that you knew, even if only in your thinking,
That what is the same is the same.
Then where could there be conflict?
Try to imagine, and to FEEL as you do so,
That whatever you might perceive as separate,
As different from yourself,
Is, in fact, not separate or different at all,
But is actually your Self.
Where could there be conflict?
Indeed, there could not.

All of your grievances are based on a belief
That what is the same can be different.
They are based on the belief that you can be separate
From something else in your life.
Even the word "else" implies separation, does it not?
So when you have a grievance, you really, as we have said,
Are wishing that something else,
Something you perceive to be other than yourself,
Could somehow be different—
Be it a circumstance in your life,
Be it the behavior of someone you perceive
To be different from yourself,
A child, a family member, a spouse, a lover, an enemy—
Always you are wishing that someone "else,"
Something separate, be different.

For a moment, try to feel what I am saying—
That somehow you knew that "else"
Was not a word that even applied to your experience.
Imagine, and feel, for a moment,
That nothing could be different,
That NOTHING could be outside yourself.
Then how could you imagine that you would want
That which IS you
To somehow be different from that which is you?
That is why we say that
What is the same is the same, and
What is the same cannot be different.

So all of your problems are based on a belief in separation.
And the answer to all of your problems

Is something over which you have no choice.
For you are the Son of God.
And as the Son of God, you are part of God.
And God merely IS.
When we say IS, that means that all of existence IS God.
You are God.
All of those whom you perceive to be your brothers are God.
Likewise, all of that which you experience as nature is God.
For all of it is the creative energy of the universe.
And all of it is One.
There can seem to be variations in its expression,
In the form that the Oneness takes.
But, ultimately, it is all One.
And you cannot change that.

Do not be dismayed, but rejoice.
For there is nothing you can do that can EVER separate you
From the Oneness, the beauty, and the fullness that is God.
Even your vain imaginings cannot separate you
From your Oneness with God.
Ah, yes, you can imagine such.
But your imaginings don't change a thing.

Chapters in the Text talk about dreams,
And awakening from the dreams.
Think of it that way, if you wish.
In your dreaming, you can dream of problems;
You can dream of separation, and isolation, and differentness.
But then, in your realization that dreams are only imaginings,
When you wake, you will instantly know that it was not true,
That it was just a dream.

And truly, every time you perceive that you have a problem,
Be it what you call major, or extremely minor,
Every time you perceive any problem whatsoever
You are just imagining separation.
This applies to every problem you can imagine—
To enemies, even mortal enemies
Who would kill or destroy you,
To other countries who might destroy your country,
To persons you call friend, who might betray you,
To the subtle things in your life,
To the beliefs that you might not have enough money, or food,
To the minor things like a sigh of tiredness,

Or a wisp of discouragement,
To something as simple as stubbing your toe,
Or nicking your finger,
Or having a few hairs fall from your head
When you wash your hair—
All of these are but your dream.
All of these are your imaginings.
All of these are your attempt to pretend
That your problems have not been solved.
All of these are your attempts to pretend
That you can, somehow, be different, or separate,
From anything in your existence.

Again I say to you,
It cannot be so.
For there is only Oneness;
There is only completeness.
You are part of that Oneness,
And part of that completeness.
And though you imagine all manner of problems,
You cannot change the Oneness and the beauty that you are
As the Son of God.

Try, if you can, in your thinking,
To pretend, to imagine, to daydream, if you will,
That all of your experience, all of your world,
Is, indeed, not merely LIKE you,
Not just PART OF you,
But actually IS YOU, your Self.
Try to imagine, try to daydream, if you will,
What it might feel like to know
That your world IS, indeed, YOU.

Over yourself you have absolute dominion.
One of your lessons said, "My salvation comes from me." (L 70)
Truly that is so.
It cannot come from anywhere else.
Because there IS nowhere else.

Allow yourself, if you can, in your daydream,
To REALIZE what I am saying.
Your salvation, your peace, your joy,
Your freedom, are yours.
Over that you have no choice.

Because all that you experience IS you,
And IS your choice.

You can dream of problems and of separation, as we have said.
But in your waking, in your truth,
You have absolute dominion over your entire existence.
For you are the Son of God.
Even in your imaginings,
You have dominion over those selfsame imaginings.
So even in your illusions,
There is nothing that can seem to happen to you
Which you have not, in your dream,
Chosen and imagined of yourself.

There is never a time, in truth or illusion,
When you have a problem.
There is never a time, in truth or illusion,
When what is you can be different from you.
Truly, it cannot be.

So I urge you to daydream as often as you can
About freedom and dominion.
Even within your illusions,
Daydream that everything that happens to you
Is, in fact, yourself,
Is, in fact, your choice.
Nothing can happen to you except that you choose it,
Request it, and create it.

Daydream about that,
Even the things that you call problems.
Daydream that they are your own choice.
Even if it seems strange that you would choose them,
Realize that, indeed, they ARE your choice.

Then what may happen for you
Will be that which you might call a double negative.
For already this world you live in,
Which you think is reality,
Is a dream.
And if you can dream within that dream,
Your dreaming within your dream
May guide you back to reality.
If you can dream within your dream

Of what your reality actually is,
Then you may open the door through which
You can move back to that reality.

That is part of what we are trying to do in this Course
When we say it is a Course in mind training.
We are teaching you to use your thoughts,
WITHIN this world of thoughts,
To revert back to the world of reality
Where, indeed, there are no thoughts.
Because thoughts are always of separation,
And do not mean anything.

To clarify for a moment,
We said early on in the lessons
That your thoughts do not mean anything. (L 10)
The reason that they do not have meaning
Relates to our theme for today.
Your own thoughts are your own interpretations,
Based on your own concepts about what you are.
That, in its essence, defines separation.
So your thoughts, your own thoughts,
Must be a product of your belief that you are separate.

The thoughts that form your self-concept,
And thereby allow you to believe you ARE separate—
Those thoughts are all part of the same problem.
That is why we say you need to go
Beyond your thoughts to your experience.
You need to go beyond the notion that you are a separate being
To the EXPERIENCE of oneness.

In moving beyond those thoughts and concepts,
You will realize the problem has been solved,
That all of it was but a dream
Which shall pass away in a moment,
Your moment of awakening.

Truly, I tell you,
It is as possible for you to wake up this moment
And be totally free
As it is for anyone whom you imagine to be asleep in this world
To wake up and pop out of his dream
Into what you call his consciousness.

You can free yourself from this dream of illusions
Just as quickly, and with just as much certainty.
Hear me well.

You do get insights which come to you like that.
They are little pieces of your awakening from your dream.
Welcome them when they come. Do not fear them.
Allow them to be, and incorporate them into your life.

It may seem difficult, as a concept, for me to say to you,
All of your life IS YOU.
The approach we are taking in *A Course in Miracles*
Is to say that, to resay it, to respeak it, and reemphasize it,
So that beyond your thoughts, it will become experience.
When that happens, you will awaken from your dream.

Today's lessons can bring you closer to your awakening.
So don't treat them as analytical thoughts.
Don't treat them as something to be discussed.
Don't treat them as something to argue about.
For all that is of the ego.
Treat them as something you wish to experience,
That you wish to have BE, within yourself.

Try to feel what it means
To have your world BE yourself.
Try to feel what it means to know
That you have total dominion over your entire existence,
Be it illusion, or be it truth.

Try to feel it within the depth of your being.
For there, past your thoughts, past your analyzing,
Past your fears,
Is the truth of what you are.
And that truth is that what is the same is the same,
And what is One cannot be separate,
And what is the Son of God is, indeed, God,
And can never be separate from God,
Or any aspect of Creation.

Feel that within your being, daily,
Moment to moment, hour to hour.
Let it flow within what you are.

You are the Son of God,
And nothing can be separate from you,
Not one tiny aspect of your experience.
For you are the God of your own being.
Everything is One. Everything is Love.
Everything is peace, without conflict.
And everything is joy.

And all you can do to not experience all of that
Is to somehow vainly dream that it is not yours.
Take heart, and rejoice.
For I tell you this dream,
The dream of your illusion that you can be separate,
Will pass away,
And is passing away more rapidly than you can imagine.
And soon you will become free
To BE the Son of God.

Blessings upon you all. That is all.

LIGHT

Greetings again. I am Jeshua. I have come this day
To further, with you, my discussion of
A Course in Miracles.

Today I wish to discuss with you a concept.
The concept will be that of Light.

Bear in mind, as we have said, that concepts are of thought.
Thought is a reaction, an interpretation,
Based on the notion that you are a separate individual.
Your thoughts do not mean anything.
The purpose for your thoughts,
Including your thoughts about time,
Is for you to use them to become free of them.
That is all they are for.

As I speak to you about Light,
Be aware that this in not an idea for you to learn.
It is not something for you to study,
Not a thought pattern for you to master.
This is something for you to EXPERIENCE,
So that when your thoughts, when your interpretations,
When your imagined separateness goes away,
You will still have the reality of that which I share with you.
That reality lies beyond the thoughts and interpretations.

I will be talking to you about Light.
Light, as I refer to it in *A Course in Miracles*,
Is not the light with which you think you see.
The light you study in your physics and science courses
Is an electromagnetic radiation.
That light is one of the major forms of energy
Which you experience in your world.
But when I say Light in *A Course in Miracles*,
I am not referring to that light at all.

It is very important for you to realize that the Light,
The Light I refer to in *A Course in Miracles*,

The Light I referred to two thousand years ago as Jesus,
Is not the light of your electromagnetic spectrum.

The Light is beyond that.
You have access to the Light.
You are the Light.
You can experience the Light.
The Light will bring you vision.

That can happen, could happen, will happen,
Whether or not you have physical eyes in your head.
You could be a universe of beings with no eyes at all,
Or you could individually be blind,
And it would not change one iota
That which I will now tell you about Light.

Everything is One. God is One.
The Son of God is also One with God.
The Son of God is One with his own creations.
Indeed, your own creations ARE
Every aspect of this life you experience.
Your own creations are this entire universe which you perceive.
For truly, you have created it.
And you, in your own completeness, are One with all of that.

The Light is, in a sense,
The glue that creates that Oneness and holds it together.
The Light is not a physical thing you can measure
With any of your instruments.

The Light can be transformed down
To something which you call an energy,
Which you can then use, if you wish,
To alter the physical energies of your world.
As such, the Light, when it is active within your being,
Can seem to do what you would call miracles.
For the Light can alter any of that
Which you call your physical laws.

It is not essential that you learn to do this.
It is not even important that you do it.
In fact, it is probably as well
That you be oblivious to that possibility.

It is enough that you experience, within your being, the Light.
Hear me well.

Your being is not your body. You are not a body.
Your being is not your physical body.
Although that which you perceive of as your physical body,
And your physical world, is composed of Light,
It is the densest form this Light can take.
As such, it is nothing more than the true Light,
Almost imprisoned, if you will,
And yearning to break free the bonds
That have locked it in a world where it does not belong.

Again I tell you, everything is One.
And the Light is the glue that holds that Oneness together.
You can even call it Love if you wish.
God is Love, and you are Love.
God is Light, and you are Light.
For YOU are that which holds the Universe together.
The Light is, indeed, you.
And since everything is One, you ARE the Light.

How do you, in your thinking,
Deal with these lessons about Light,
When all I have offered so far
Is an abstract concept that says
You are the Light?

I have said to you, you are the Light of the world.
I have also said that the Light of the world
Brings peace to every mind through your forgiveness. (L 63)
And I have said, "The Light has come." (L 75)
Perhaps for your lesson today you have read,
"Miracles are seen in Light." (L 91)
And I will say to you,
Light and strength are of God, and are One.

I have said, as you recall,
Light is not that which you see with your eyes.
So if you do not see it, as you deem seeing to be,
How then do you perceive this Light?
Can you hear it? Can you touch it?
Nay.

The Light is beyond all your physical senses.
It is beyond that which you call the physical world,
Except insofar as your physical world is, indeed,
Comprised of that selfsame Light.

The Light, then, is something
You will EXPERIENCE at the depth of your being.
When I say to you, you are the Light of the world,
And when I say, you are that
Which holds the entire world together,
The Light to which I refer is a something
Which lies deep within your being,
Past your consciousness, past your concepts,
And past your thoughts.

There is a level within you
At which you EXPERIENCE, with FEELINGS.
Feelings, as yet, you do not fully understand.
Because most of your feelings you interpret with your thoughts,
And thus you distort what they are.

So beyond your interpretations, beyond your thoughts,
There is to be found that which we call FEELINGS,
Or EXPERIENCE.
And whenever you FEEL something, without defining it,
Without trying to interpret it
In terms of the parameters of your world,
Which are space, and time, and the past, and memory,
And all the thoughts you have about who you are,
And who other beings are—
When you experience something, anything,
Without the encumbrance of all those concepts,
Then you are experiencing Light.

In your eternity,
After you have passed through the barrier of time,
And out of this world,
What you are, and what you will experience,
Will be Light.

When you experience life in true freedom,
You are experiencing Light.
I tell you, you ARE the Light of the world.

In your freedom, in your joy,
In your joy that echoes through the universe
With unbridled childlike enthusiasm,
You become the Light of the world.

Indeed, you already are the Light of the world,
Whether you like it or not.
Over this, hear me well, you have no choice.
Even in this prison of thoughts you are imagining,
Even in this prison of physical illusion,
You are still the Light of the world.

None of this could exist
Without that you have FELT its presence into existence.
For there is that level at which you FEEL, and EXPERIENCE,
This world.
That level is beyond your concepts,
And beyond your interpretations.
That is the level of miracles.
That is the level of your reality.

I have told you,
The Light of the world brings peace to every mind. (L 63)
And when you become the Light of the world,
Living apart from this world,
When you become the Light of the world,
Living in this world,
Yet unfettered by its concepts, by its prison of thoughts,
Then your boundless freedom will affect every other mind.

In your unbridled freedom,
You will know that you are perfectly safe,
That there is nothing to fear.
Your brothers will sense your freedom and your joy.
And they will automatically receive
The blessings and the peace that you know.

Then, the Light to which we refer
Is the state of being that is your reality.
It is a state of being which is unfettered, totally free, unbound.
When you live in that state, which you CAN do on this earth,
You will extend freedom, and joy,
And peace, and absolute safety
To all beings.

All beings who come into your presence
Will know that in your presence, they are free.
They are free to be
Whatever it is they might be, or think, or feel,
Without judgment, without attack, and without disdainment.
They will know, in the absence of any attack from you,
That they can be at peace with whatever it is they would feel.
And they will then know they are safe.

In the Light you extend to them,
You must receive that selfsame Light in return.
You will, likewise, receive that same peace,
That same blessing, that same freedom,
And that same knowledge that you are absolutely safe.

Miracles are seen in Light.
And Light and strength are One.
Strength is that which leaves you completely safe.
Strength is that which leaves you with no reason to ever attack.
For with infinite strength,
How would you ever have fear of any attack
That might be directed toward you?
And how would you ever need to attack in return?
In the realization that you are the strength of God,
That you are invulnerable, beyond attack,
You will know that you are perfectly safe.

Your safety will allow you to be perfectly free.
Your freedom will allow you to be joyful.
Without freedom, you cannot be joyful.
Without safety, you cannot be free.
Without being invulnerable, you cannot be safe.
Without being the strength of God, you cannot be invulnerable.
One follows from the next, in either direction.
And all it says is that you are One,
That you are the Light of the world.

How then, do you experience the Light of the world?
We spoke before about how to listen for the Voice within.
I told you to listen for the joy,
And always to check to see if anything you can imagine
Could threaten your joy.
For if you can perceive it as threatened,
It is of the ego, and not of God.

So as you search for joy,
The path will lead you back through the chain I just mentioned,
Back to the Oneness.
And your joy, the joy that is unfettered,
That is safe, that is totally free,
That cannot be touched
By any of the imaginings of this physical world—
That joy will shine within you,
And shine out from you.
And all those whom you come near will sense it, and feel it,
Whether you speak of it or not.

So, in listening for your joy,
You are listening for that selfsame Light
Which is your true being.

I have spoken to you this day of a concept.
And if you just THINK about it,
The words will fall on deaf ears.
For in your thinking, you set up a block, and a barrier,
To your joy, to your freedom, and to your peace.

Search for the joy.
Search for the freedom.
Listen within to that which brings you joy, invulnerable joy.
You will then know that you are beginning
To experience the Light.

As I have told you, you are the Son of God.
Nothing can happen to you except by your own choice.
You have dominion over your entire existence.
You ARE the Son of God.
And as the Son of God,
You are the Light of the world.

In whatever way you may choose,
Feel that Light within you now.
Feel the Light.
For it will shine. It will blossom within you.
It will fill your being,
And with it will come the joy that cannot be harmed,
That cannot be altered.

If it does not come immediately,
Do not be dismayed.
It is there. And it WILL be there.
Never lose sight of the fact that it will be there,
That it cannot fail.

God's plan for salvation cannot fail.
There is nothing you can do to change the fact
That you are the Light of the world,
And that you are that which holds the entire world together
In its Oneness.

Rejoice.
For you are Light. You are Love.
You are strength. You are freedom.
And you are joy.

Blessings upon you all. That is all.

ONE SELF

Greetings again. I am Jeshua. I have come this day
To further, with you, my discussion of
A Course in Miracles.

Today, we will again talk about a concept.
The concept will be your One Self (capital S).

Be aware, as I speak of your One Self,
That I am speaking about the unity of what you are,
Your unity with all of Life,
Your Oneness with your brothers,
Your Oneness with God.
All of it is your Oneness with your One Self.

When I speak of your little self,
I am speaking of that which ultimately is not real.
Your little self is based on the thoughts you have made,
Thinking you had a problem, believing you were separate,
Believing that somehow you could BE separate,
Which you cannot, and could not, be.

Your One Self is of unity, and is of God.
Your little self is of your thoughts,
Is of that which you have tried to make,
As if to imagine that you could separate yourself from Life,
Or from anything.
Your little self is the source of all your problems.
For your little self is but a concept you have made.
As such, it shall eventually pass away.
Therefore, in reality, it does not exist.
For reality does not, and cannot, pass away.

Do not be alarmed.
Do not be disheartened by this.
This realization that your little self is not real
Is for you a source of great joy.
It is what this Course is all about.

So today, I will speak to you of your One Self.
Your lessons for this week discussed often your One Self.
Again, bear in mind as I speak of ideas and concepts,
That they are not things to be learned.
There will never be a test to determine
Whether you understand this within your thinking mind.
The goal of this Course is for you to understand your One Self
In your knowing, in your being, in your experience,
Beyond anything you think you think,
Or contemplate, or analyze.

So once again, I offer you an admonishment,
Which I will continue to offer you throughout this Course.
Do not think that your analyzing,
That your processing with your thoughts,
That your thinking diligently about all this
Will bring you salvation.
For it will not.

Know that your salvation lies at a level beyond your thinking,
At a level which you may call feeling, which I call experience,
But above all, which is a level of certainty,
Of peace, of light, and of joy.
So always, as you contemplate this Course,
Keep within your mind, keep within your heart
The realization that your One Self, and all of which I speak
Sings to you of light, and joy, and peace, and oneness.
It sings to you of a place where there is no conflict,
Of a place where conflict cannot even be fathomed,
Much less forgiven.

That is what I promise you.
For you are the Son of God.
That is your right, your gift, your inheritance,
Which shall never be taken away,
Which shall be yours throughout all eternity,
Beyond the end and passage of time.

I spoke to you before about how to listen for the Voice of God.
I told you the first step in your listening is to listen for joy,
A joy that simply wells up within your being.
I told you to listen for that joy.
And I told you how to know if you were experiencing real joy.

For if you can imagine anything,
Any circumstance within or without,
Which could threaten or alter your joy,
Then it is not real joy.
And it is not the Voice of God.

There is another tool which you can use
As you attempt to listen to the Voice of God.
It is this:
As you search within for the Voice of God,
For that which is your One Self,
Be aware that within the Kingdom of God,
Within your One Self,
THERE IS NO CONFLICT.
This is very important.
As you listen within for the Voice of God,
Which you may call the Holy Spirit,
Which you may call your One Self,
Know that within salvation
There is no room for conflict of any kind.

The word "certainty" showed up
A number of times in your lessons.
Certainty is absolute.
When you hear the Voice of God, it will be joy.
There will be nothing you can imagine
Which can threaten or change it.
Furthermore, when you hear the Voice of God,
It will be absolutely without conflict.

Try now to imagine, if you can,
Within your being, past your thoughts,
What it would be like to have NO CONFLICT,
To live a life of joy
Which could not be threatened by ANYTHING.
Try to imagine, try to feel within,
What it would be like to have no conflict OF ANY KIND.
If, even for a moment, you can get a feeling
Of what that might be like,
You are well on your way to salvation.

If you cannot get that feeling, do not dismay.
That state DOES exist within you, and it cannot be changed.
It cannot be taken away, no matter what you think you think.

So if you have that feeling of no conflict, rejoice.
And if you do not, rejoice anyway.
For it is within you, and cannot be changed.
It is your right and your inheritance as the Son of God.
And it SHALL be yours.

I have spoken to you of your One Self.
I have said that salvation comes from your One Self. (L 96)
I also told you that you are Spirit. (L 97)
That you are Spirit is just a reflection
Of what it is to be One Self.
I have also said,
You are just as God Created you, unchanged. (L 110)
That, also, is just a statement
Of what it means to be One Self.
When I used the words "One Self," I spoke of unity.
That is the reason for the word "One."
So when I speak of your One Self,
Realize I mean that your One Self is All That Is.

As I have said, you think of yourself as split.
You think of yourself as having facets,
Aspects, or parts of your being, of your personality,
Which are at war, which can be in conflict.
You are free, of course, to think anything you wish.
But in reality, there exists only your One Self.
That is the message of this Course.

When the understanding of what I have just said
Becomes part of your being,
You will no longer need this Course.
You will no longer need your body.
You will no longer need this earth.
For everything will be One.
And you will be free.

Do not take these words lightly.
They represent your freedom and your salvation.
I have said before, everything is One.
You ARE your experience.
I spoke at length about your only problem,
Which is the belief in separation.
I spoke of the fact that your only problem doesn't exist,
Because there is no separation.

And when I speak of your One Self,
I am only iterating
That there is no separation anywhere in all of Creation.

Always listen within for the joy,
The joy which cannot be threatened,
And which contains no conflict.

Then I said, salvation and forgiveness are the same.
So here is another aspect of forgiveness.
Salvation is your only function here.
Forgiveness is your only function here.
So what does forgiveness represent?
Forgiveness is simply your awareness,
At a level beyond your thoughts,
That there is, indeed, but One Self.
Forgiveness is your awareness
That duality and conflict and illusion cannot exist.
For they are not of God.

Try to feel within your being what it would mean to know that.
Try to feel within your being that you are One Self,
One with God,
One with all your brothers,
One with all of Life, including this earth.
Try to FEEL that you are invulnerable, unlimited,
Filled with light and peace and joy.
Try to imagine within your being
That you knew with absolute certainty
That Life could not be otherwise.
Try to imagine the freedom you would feel
If you knew the truth of those words.

Try to imagine all of that as often as you can.
For your imagining will lead you to experience,
Beyond your thinking.
And that will lead you to your reality,
And to your joy.

Blessings upon you all. That is all.

HAPPINESS

Greetings again. I am Jeshua. I have come this day
To further, with you, my discussion of
A Course in Miracles.

Your lessons for this past week have been about happiness.
Today we will talk about happiness.

A previous lesson had said,
"Salvation comes from my One Self." (L 96)
That is absolutely certain. That cannot be changed.
Over that you have no choice.
For there IS ONLY your One Self.

Just as salvation comes from your One Self,
So does your happiness come from your One Self.
So does your joy, so does your peace,
Come from your One Self.

I have spoken often about your experience.
I have tried to tell you in words
That you ARE your experience.
That is but a form of saying,
There exists ONLY your One Self.

We have talked about your invulnerability,
And the fact that everything in your existence
Arises NOT from somewhere outside of you,
But ALWAYS from within,
It being, literally, a creative expression of what you are.
Your world is the creative expression of what you are.
Your world, as you perceive it, is your Self.
For there is nothing but your Self,
Your One Self.

Let us return to our discussion of happiness.
The happiness of God is unshakable, unchangeable.
Nothing can take it away from you.
Nothing can alter it. Nothing can threaten it.

This I have already suggested
When I discussed hearing the Voice of God.
I said, as you listen for the Voice of God,
Listen for joy, which is your happiness.
And if nothing can threaten it in any way,
You are hearing the Voice of God.
Also I told you, if you are hearing the Voice of God
There can be no conflict.

Those ideas are much the same as saying
Your happiness comes from your One Self.
For within Oneness, there is only unity.
And unity means total harmony,
Without change, without conflict.
Indeed, as I told you,
When you are experiencing your One Self,
Conflict is beyond comprehension.
Only conflict, of course, can threaten anything.
So when you have no conflict,
You cannot imagine anything
Which could threaten your happiness.

So even the first two rules I gave you
For hearing the Voice of God
Are ultimately the same.
Hear me well.
This is the message of *A Course in Miracles*.
Everything is the same.
Everything is One.
When you know that,
When you feel it within your being,
With certainty, without conflict,
Then you will know salvation.

Let us try, now, to imagine what your happiness might be.
Remember, once again,
This is not a Course in learning about thoughts and ideas,
But rather in going beyond them to the truth of what you are.
So try now, as you read, to go beyond my words,
Beyond your thoughts, beyond your analyzing,
To your experience, to your feelings.

Let us try to find what happiness might be.
If you can, only for a moment,

Imagine that state of happiness,
And peace, and joy, and love,
(They are, of course, all the same)—
If you can imagine that state for even a moment,
You will save thousands of years of your time.
So try now, as you read, not to think, but to feel.
There is a place within you
Where your Spirit knows that you are One.
In your stillness, you can find that place.
You will find your home, that harbor within you,
Where your real One Self exists.
You will feel that all is One.
And as you feel that all is One,
You will be able to realize that, indeed,
Your experience IS One with you,
That your experience IS your One Self.

Now, as you read my words,
Allow yourself to experience what they represent.
As you read "Oneness," let the feeling be within you.
As you read "unity," let the feeling be within you.
As you read "peace," let that feeling be there, within.
Try to feel, to imagine,
That everything you have ever experienced,
Are experiencing now, or ever will experience,
Is a unified part of what you are,
In total harmony with your Self.

Try to imagine, if even for a moment,
That in your Oneness
It is not possible for anything to be "out there."
It is not possible for anything to be outside your Self.
And then, as you begin to feel
That Oneness, that unity, that harmony,
Allow yourself to become aware
Of just how safe you actually are.

Try to imagine within this perfect harmony
What there might be that could possibly
Bring you harm, or wish you ill.
Of course, you find nothing.
For all that you find is your Self.
And that is perfect harmony.

Now try to imagine, in this state where you are One,
Where you are in total harmony,
Where you are unified with everything,
Where you are totally safe—
Try to imagine being ABSOLUTELY FREE
To experience anything you can imagine.
Try to imagine dynamic, moving,
Flowing, changing, excitement.
Imagine yourself as a small child
Playing with your existence in a world
Where you can do no wrong,
Where there is nothing to even suggest anything other
Than that which brings you joy.
Imagine yourself free within a freedom
Which entails ANYTHING you might imagine.
And THAT shall BE your happiness.

This happiness of which I have been speaking
Is your right, and is your inheritance.
It is what you ARE as the Son of God.
Every being, every aspect of your existence
Is part of the One Self.
You ARE the One Self.
Just as I am the One Self.
Even God, the Creator, IS the One Self.

Try to remember a time in your life
When you absolutely knew that something would happen—
KNEW THAT SOMETHING WOULD HAPPEN—
AND IT DID.
All of you have had such times.
That is a statement of what your Spirit is, and how it functions.
Try to remember a time when for a moment, or longer,
You KNEW, without doubt, without conflict, with certainty,
That something was to be, and it was.

Imagine that feeling, that certainty—
Multiply it a thousand thousand times,
And you will have an idea of the certainty
With which God knows of your happiness,
Of your peace, and of your salvation.
Within God there is the perfect knowing
That you are only peace, only joy,
Only happiness, and only love.

And in spite of the wanderings that lead you upon
This sojourn through space and time and bodies
And illusion (and all of it is just that)—
In spite of your vain imaginings,
There is no doubt, there is no conflict,
There is only total certainty within the Mind of God
About what you are.
There is a certainty within the Mind of God
A thousand thousand times greater than any
You have ever known,
That you remain His Son.

You are part of God.
You are One with God.
And that same certainty MUST exist within you.
Try to imagine, now, if you can,
That such a certainty is driving you
Along the pathway to your own joy,
To your own peace and your own happiness.
There is NOTHING which can prevent
The goal of your freedom, and your joy.
Your imaginings that it is not so are truly as nothing.
Your imaginings that it is not so are as the most minor setback
Along a pathway such as you might have imagined above,
When you KNEW your goal WOULD BE realized.

Would that you might take
One millionth of God's certainty about you
And apply it to yourself as you experience this Course.
Would that you might, in every experience,
Know with that same certainty
That the experience could not be outside your Self,
Could not be other than your Self,
And that what you are seeing IS your One Self.
Would that you might know with that same certainty
That the body, be it yours or your brother's, is an illusion.

For there is only Spirit, your Spirit, your brother's Spirit—
And both are but expressions of the One Self.
Just as God knows of your happiness and your joy,
And knows of its inevitability,
Do your best to know of
That same happiness and joy for yourself,
And for all other beings.

As you do that, you will save yourself
The thousands of years we have mentioned.

To the extent that you can apply
That same knowing to your world,
Your grievances will quickly pass away.
You will find yourself safe
In the knowing that what seems to be outside you
Is nothing but an image formed by your Spirit.
And in that knowing,
All your physical trials, and aches,
And pains, and illnesses,
Will pass away.

You are unlimited. You are free.
You are free to forgive,
Which means to realize that
Illusion is but illusion, nothing more.
In your knowing that this world
Is but your brother's illusion as well,
You become free to save the world.

In the knowing of your One Self,
You shall become the saviour of the world.
Because your One Self is God, is me, is you,
And is all other beings whom you encounter.

Truly, salvation comes from your One Self.
Joy and peace come from your One Self.
Happiness comes from your One Self.
And Love, Love IS your One Self,
In its creative, growing, dynamic, flowing beauty.

Feel that deep within your being.
Feel its truth at the level where you are One.
And you shall be free.

Blessings upon you all. That is all.

ONENESS

Greetings again. I am Jeshua. I have come this day
To further, with you, my discussion of
A Course in Miracles.

One of the greatest struggles you have
In this world of illusion, in this world of the ego,
Is to try to understand what it means to BE One Self—
To truly understand Oneness.

What you have done, in this world of the ego,
Is made your own self (small s).
And as we have said,
That self which you have made
Is nothing more than the collection of thoughts
You have had about who you are.
And in this world of illusion, this world of falseness,
This world, literally, of insanity,
You have come to believe
That this self IS what you are.

So when I suggest to you, "Don't think, simply experience,"
Your self (ego) realizes that what I am suggesting is that it die.
In your world of concepts and thoughts,
This is, indeed, a very threatening thing.
In fact, this fear of the death of your "self"
Is most certainly the major block you all have
To the "willingness" of which I speak in *A Course in Miracles*.

For I have told you many times,
If you could but be WILLING to allow your Real Self to be free,
Then all would be peace, all would be harmony,
All would be joy.
And your salvation would have arrived.

What you ego does is equate that same willingness
With its own death.
And since you, your small self,

Believe that your ego is what you are,
You naturally feel extremely threatened by this notion.
I understand this. I understand it well.

The reason for this world, this universe of time and space,
Is for all of us, in playing with our creativity,
To imagine what it would be like
To try to be separate one from another.
Do not forget that this is an impossibility.
This is one of the things over which
You have no choice, and no control.

For there are those things which you cannot change.
You cannot change God, the Creator, Itself.
You cannot change the fact
That you ARE just as God created you,
His only Son, in perfect Oneness with all of Life,
Including all the others who, with you,
Are also trying to imagine themselves as separate.

What I want to do this day
Is help you to imagine and experience
Something of real Oneness,
So that you can then become more free and more willing
To let go of that pattern of thoughts
Which you equate with your own existence.
As you become able to let go, you will arrive at a point
Where you will feel happy about letting go of those thoughts.
You will even, eventually, move to the point where
You will give not one thought to your own death,
Which is what you imagine it would be
To let go of your self-concept.

Recall, this is a world of separation.
Your ONLY problem is that separation.
And once that separation is gone,
You will know your One Self,
And you will be truly free.

Even in this world based on a belief in separation,
It is not possible for you to separate yourself
From the knowing, deep within,
That you are always in perfect harmony

With All That is, that you are One.
Over this you have no choice.

In attempting to experience your Self as split,
Split within your own being,
Split off from the others
Who are also imagining themselves to be separate—
In imagining all that,
You are bound to experience disharmony, discontent,
And the lack of peace.

I wish to help you feel what it might be like to be One Self,
And to experience true joy.
What this requires is your realization that to BE One Self
Is to BE in that state of harmony, in that state of Oneness
Where all that exists is peace and joy, and CREATION,
Which is a dynamic of experience,
Ever new, constantly changing and flowing,
Much as clouds moving across the sky
Change, and flow, and ebb, and become,
And disappear, and re-form.

What it requires is your realization that all of this
DOES EXIST in the Kingdom of God—
And that all you need do to be there is to let go of the fear
That you will become as nothing if you give up your thinking.
And I assure you, there is no fear which can remove you further
From the truth of what you are.

To be One means to be in harmony.
Look at your own lives,
And you will see that you already know that.
Indeed, you cannot not know that.
For the Oneness is the Will of God;
And you cannot change the Will of God.

So much of your life here is an attempt to experience oneness.
In your intimate realtionships,
You are attempting to become One.
When you marry, you are attempting to become One.
With your best friends, from whom you keep no secrets,
You are attempting to experience the harmony of oneness.
When you appreciate a sunset, even then,

You are ultimately attempting to experience oneness.
Your popular songs, your stories, your plays, talk about love.
And all of it is an attempt to somehow experience
The harmony and the peace that comes from being One.

Bear in mind, however,
That the basis for this world of time and space
Is the belief that you are NOT One, but separate.
So realize that you are trying to become One
Within a world whose very design
Demands that you are NOT One, and cannot be so.
Seen this way, is it any wonder
That you find this a world of conflict?
And do you understand now,
Why I say this world is but an illusion,
And doesn't really exist?

For God cannot be split asunder.
Such cannot happen. It cannot be.
And you are God.

The world of Oneness is a world of harmony.
Harmony is peace. Harmony is joy.
Harmony means that you can live out your goal of Oneness
With total freedom.

I have stated in the Course, love is freedom. (18)
That is absolutely certain.
How often you find yourself,
As you search for your happiness and your oneness, saying
"I just want to be able to be myself."
What you mean with those words is that you desire freedom.
Look at your relationships in which you feel the most oneness.
They are the ones in which you are most free
To be, and to feel, exactly what you would be and feel.
They are the relationships in which
You are free to think whatever you choose,
Always finding that, no matter what you think,
You are accepted as whole, and complete, and beautiful.
And then you feel one.
And you, of course, find yourself wanting
To be in the presence of someone
Who allows you that freedom to be yourself.

Now try to be still and imagine within yourself
That you are One with every other being.
WHAT YOU ARE IMAGINING IS TRUE.
In your state of being One,
Anything that you can imagine,
Anything which you wish to experience,
Any thought which you wish to play with in your creativity,
Immediately, instantaneously, totally free of time and space,
Becomes a thought in total harmony with the entire universe,
With God, and with God's only Son.

What this means is that, whether you know it or not,
Every being in your existence automatically, instantaneously,
Supports anything you might imagine,
And loves you for what you have imagined.

This includes your thoughts here on earth
Of oneness, and peace, and harmony.
It also includes, here on earth, your thoughts of misery,
And pain, of murder, and robbery.
It includes your thoughts of enemies.

You are invulnerable.
If you imagine yourself as having an enemy,
If you try to imagine that there is a part of your Self
Which can harm you,
Then immediately, out of the harmony of All That Is,
You will experience another being who,
Out of love, and for purposes of his own self,
Will choose to be that which you have imagined.
If you imagine that you have an enemy who would harm you,
Then out of the Oneness there comes another being
Who will play, FOR YOU, the role of your enemy.

If you were to try to THINK of all this, it would be impossible.
If you were to try to sit and write a script,
Or to plan out, as it were, all the events of your world,
Assigning roles to the billions of you in such a way
That the result was perfect harmony
With everything blending into a unified whole,
You would realize that even your biggest computers
Could not do such a thing.

And so I say to you,
Don't think, just experience.
For at the level of your One Self, which only experiences,
That perfect harmony has already been accomplished.
In every instant, with every change,
In every dynamic aspect of your life,
It already exists.
Such is the power, such is the wonder
Of what you are as the Son of God.

You are invulnerable.
Whatever you might choose to imagine about your existence,
From within the harmony of the One Self,
It shall seem to be as you have imagined it.
Such is your freedom as the Son of God.
You can imagine absolutely anything,
And that which you imagine shall seem to be.

We shall now discuss your oneness further.
All your imaginings about separation cannot be real,
Because you cannot change God and what He has created.
As you imagine enemies, and struggles, and separate wills,
Even your own will separate from God's,
Rejoice that these things cannot be real.
Rejoice that they cannot exist.
For within God, within reality, there is only harmony,
And it cannot be otherwise.
And harmony is peace, and joy, and freedom.

Now for a few moments, try to allow yourself to feel
What it might be like to exist in a world of perfect harmony.
God, the Creator, expanded Himself,
Expanded His own consciousness.
In so doing He remained One Self, unified and whole.
But at the same time there arose, without limit,
Creativity and change.
Creativity involves awareness.
And awareness MUST BE at the level of experience.

You cannot be separate from the Oneness.
It is not possible to experience something
Which no one else could experience.
It is not possible that there be secrets.

There is only the One Self.
Everything you experience, everything you think,
Automatically becomes part of the awareness
Of every other being.
Such is the nature of your Oneness.

However, within the expansion that God created out of Himself,
There exists the beingness, the capability of exploration,
Of playfulness, of newness,
Of experiencing that which has not been experienced.
But always there remains the perfect harmony.

It is as if there were millions, billions,
Of sides to God Himself,
All of which were in perfect agreement,
And yet each of which was totally free
To imagine anything it wanted,
Was totally free to experience anything it could imagine.
Such is the beauty and the freedom of creation.

Try to feel, if you can,
What it might be like to be absolutely free
To imagine and to experience anything you wish.
Anything that can come to the level of experience can be yours.
And whatever it might be shall be immediately blessed
By every aspect of Creation,
With full harmony and with full support.
Such is the freedom of God.
And such is Love.

I tell you,
During times of your creating you will seem to be unique,
But you are always One.
Indeed, there will be times in which
You seem to be completely One,
Without needing the uniqueness.
It is not necessary that you maintain
A uniqueness about yourself.
For any time there is the desire and the playfulness to create,
Then that which you might call your uniqueness
Shall automatically seem to take form
And give rise to the creation of whatever is desired.

This that I have spoken is truly beyond your comprehension.
But perhaps you can imagine what it would be like
To have the creative uniqueness which is you
Ebb and flow, almost as if
When you are sleeping the uniqueness is quiet,
And when you are awake it is active and creating.
It only matters that you realize
You are free.

Love is absolute freedom to create and to be,
With the totality of Creation supporting you,
Loving you, and delighting in that which you create.
And nothing you create, nothing you can imagine,
Can be wrong, can be a sin, can be inappropriate.
For there is only freedom.

Now by way of introduction,
Guilt is the feeling you have when you attempt
To deny yourself the freedom God gave you.
If you could experience yourself as totally free, which you are,
Then there could be no guilt,
And you would never feel guilty again.
Indeed, guilt always comes from your imagining
That there is a Will, separate from your own,
Which knows better than you yourself
What you should do or be.
How absurd such a notion is.
For were it so, you would not be the Son of God.
And you would not be free.

For now, do what you can to realize
That every aspect of your creation,
Whether or not you seem to like it,
Is in perfect harmony with you.
For that is your invulnerability.

When you begin to know that your brother truly IS your Self,
And that to give and receive are the same,
Then what you will generate for your own life
Will be joy, and peace, and fullness.
And in your Oneness the entire world shall share that with you.
In their awareness of your peace,
They become free to make it their own.

Such is the manner in which you become
The saviour of the world.

You create your own world in all its beauty.
You are absolutely free.
You are One Self.
There can be no sin. There can be no guilt.
For there is only happiness and joy.

And as you explore your life with freedom and with love,
You shall touch the Mind of God,
And find your One Self.
And in your knowledge that that is all you can be,
So shall it be.

Blessings upon you all. That is all.

FORGIVENESS II

Greetings again. I am Jeshua. I have come this day
To further, with you, my discussion of
A Course in Miracles.

We have spoken before about forgiveness.
Today I will speak more about the same.
You will recall that I told you emphatically,
One thing forgiveness is NOT.
It is not ever forgiving someone, or something, or anything else,
For what they, or it, have done to you.

A great deal of your freedom comes
With the realization that such a thing cannot happen.
You are invulnerable.
You do, indeed, create your own existence,
Every minute aspect of it.
Nothing can happen to you without it being
Of your permission, and your choice.
So NEVER think of forgiveness
As forgiving another for what he, or she, has done to you.

Now to proceed further,
Forgiveness is your only function here.
Ultimately, forgiveness is the source
Of your happiness and your joy.

It is common, in this world of the ego, for someone,
When presented with ideas such as we are speaking of, to say
"How will this benefit me?"
For you still tend to think of yourself as separate,
As having special interests.
However, it is of no matter.
For just as forgiveness blesses your One Self,
It also brings great blessings upon your little self.
So as we speak about forgiveness,
Realize there is a difference between
The way your One Self will experience forgiveness,

And the way your little self will do so.
But only blessings come to both.

Again I remind you,
As you read these words, try not to think, try not to analyze,
As if this were some didactic teaching.
Rather, try to experience,
And to allow that which you feel
To become yourself.

Suppose it were true; just imagine, if you can,
That you ACTUALLY WERE invulnerable.
Try to imagine knowing at the deepest level of your being
That no one could ever do anything to you.
Then much of your forgiveness would already be there.
You would never blame another;
You would never blame another being,
You would never blame another circumstance,
For ANYTHING.
Hear me well.
You would never even blame God
For being the cause of whatever enters your life.

Now, as you imagine that NOTHING can HAPPEN TO YOU,
Where is your anger?
I have said in this Course,
Anger is never justified. (19) And that is true.
Every gift that you give, you give to yourself.
Every time you direct anger at your world,
Be it toward person or circumstance,
You but direct it at yourself.
And, in the knowledge that, as the Son of God,
You are truly invulnerable,
Your forgiveness frees you
From all the effects of your anger.

Try to feel, try to imagine,
What it would be like to never be angry.
Try to feel, to imagine what it would be like to never be angry,
Not by virtue of the fact that you are suppressing the anger,
But to never be angry by virtue of that fact
That anger is something your Spirit cannot comprehend.
Think for a moment of the times in your life

When you have been angry.
Think of how it makes you feel almost ill,
Of how you do not feel good inside,
Of how there is no peace,
Of how there is no love at that time.
Your forgiveness will free you from all such effects.

So, in the realization that you, as the Son of God,
Are the master of your life,
You become free of the deep unrest you feel
When it seems that someone has hurt you.
You become free of the deep unrest
Which must penetrate your being
When you are angry at another.
You become free of the fear
That someone else might do something to you.

Imagine, further, if you can, that aspect of your forgiveness.
In your relationships here on this earth,
How common it is to hold back,
To hold back your love,
To hold back your joy,
To hold back your spontaneity,
For fear that someone will,
UPON SEEING YOUR JOY AND YOUR LOVE,
DO SOMETHING TO YOU.
It might be as simple as a frown,
Or the words, "I don't approve."
It might be that they may literally
Strike out at you and take from you
Something which you value with your life.

Your forgiveness,
Which shall stem from the knowledge
That all the gifts you give are given to yourself,
And from the knowledge of your invulnerability,
Will free you from those fears.

So try again to imagine, if you will, that your fear IS GONE,
But not because you have pushed forward your chest
And decided to be brave,
And to face with courage what might come to you.
But try to imagine that your fear IS GONE,
Totally gone, as fog before the morning Sun.

Try to imagine that your fear is not there—
Because your being cannot comprehend it.
Imagine that it takes no effort to be free of your fear,
Simply because IT IS NOT THERE.

And whether you are living as your One Self,
Or seem to be living as your little self,
Forgiveness offers you just such freedom from your fear.
And who among you, given the choice,
Would not choose to be totally free of fear?

Remember, it begins with a calm, a peace, and a certainty.
It begins with the knowing that you, as the Son of God,
Are the creator of every aspect of your life.
Hear me well.

It does not matter at this point
Whether you are aware of the reasons for all of your choices.
In fact, you will move beyond
Ever needing to know the reasons.
So if, in your existence,
You seem to be choosing
Things which you believe you would not have chosen,
Things which you are actively NOT enjoying—
Then the key to your forgiveness, and your happiness,
Will be to hold to the realization,
Even when you seem frustrated,
That, at some level, you have, indeed,
Chosen that which you are experiencing.
Truly, you are invulnerable.
Truly, you ARE the Son of God.

So it is that the realization that you ARE as God created you
Is the key to your forgiveness,
And the key to your freedom.
Try to imagine, to feel these things
As often as you can.
For the more you feel it,
The closer you move to the day when it becomes you,
Beyond your thinking, beyond your analyzing,
Even beyond your concept of who you are.

I mention the concept of who you are.
I have spoken before, many times,

About the fact that your belief in yourself
As a separate individual
Is the cause of all your problems.
That belief is the basis of separation,
Which is the one problem of this world.
And so it is that your forgiveness will free you
From the pain, the fear, the doubt and the misery
Which your belief in separation brings.

Try again, for a moment, to imagine
That you ARE, as I have said, ONE SELF.
Try to imagine that there is no separation
Between you and any other being,
No separation between you and any other circumstance.
There is but ONE SELF,
Moving in a splendid harmony of existence,
All of which but reflects the fact that you are the Son of God.
There is, indeed, confusion in this world.
But the harmony of existence is always there.
You cannot destroy the fact that you are but One Self.
So try once again to imagine that there is but One Self,
And the entire world IS you.

This is the step which goes beyond the belief
That you, an INDIVIDUAL, are in harmony with your world.
This is the awareness that your world IS you.
Try, if you can, to imagine that.
Imagine that you KNEW that there was nothing in existence
Save for the completeness, the fullness,
And the Oneness of what YOU ARE.
For then your forgiveness brings you to a new freedom,
Wherein conflict and fear become incomprehensible.

In your true forgiveness, you will be able to release
The notion that there are separate aspects of your experience
Which need to be reconciled, or brought into harmony.
Your true forgiveness brings you to the point
Where you realize that all is One.
This is merely a different way of expressing the fact
That you ARE invulnerable.

So try to imagine KNOWING, in any circumstance,
That ALL OF IT, including beings in that circumstance,
IS, LITERALLY, your One Self, complete and whole.

For then, as you look upon an experience,
Which is really just your Self,
Your forgiveness will free you to experience,
With total openness and freedom,
Everything that is there.
Your forgiveness will allow you to BE,
Without thought of the past or the future,
Without concern for whatever a circumstance might bring you.
Try, within your being,
To EXPERIENCE your One Self.

If you have felt that, even minutely,
Then try to imagine feeling separate
From any part of your experience.
For the two beliefs are absolutely not compatible.
If you feel separate, then go back
And try again to experience your One Self.
First this shall be for you nothing but an idea.
Then it will move to what you may call a feeling of certainty.
And then it will become the reality of what you are.

Again, your forgiveness frees you from the belief
That any part of your existence is separate from you.
And if no part of your existence is separate from you,
Then you are absolutely safe.
So, whether it be at the level of your One Self,
Or at the level of your little self,
Your forgiveness will bring you safety, and peace,
And the freedom to experience without fear.

There is more, and we could go on.
But for now, it is enough if you can, for a moment,
Feel within your being the safety,
The freedom, the joy, and the peace
That your forgiveness will bring you.
Never forget that the goal is to go past the words,
Past the thoughts,
To your experience.

If, as you try to imagine it,
You do not experience that which I have told you,
Do not be dismayed.
Simply go back to the ideas.
Play with them like a small child.

Think of them as often as you can,
And allow them to grow into your being.
For in your world of time,
This is a very common way
For you to choose to become what you are.

Always remember, time is not necessary.
In an instant, you could be free.
Only insofar as you believe in the limitations of your time,
Will you choose to have it take time.

But in either event,
You are absolutely safe, and absolutely loved.
And I promise you,
You will come to know forgiveness
And the blessings it brings you.
For as you bestow forgiveness upon your own life,
You automatically receive it.
And all those blessings of which we have spoken
Shall be yours.

Blessings upon you all. That is all.

ILLUSION

Greetings again. I am Jeshua. I have come this day
To further, with you, my discussion of
A Course in Miracles.

Today I will begin to discuss with you
The topic of illusion, the topic of reality,
And the topic of what is not real.

"Nothing real can be threatened.
Nothing unreal exists.
Herein lies the peace of God." (20)
These words I have placed at the beginning of
A Course in Miracles.
These words represent, in essence, all that the Course is.

This world you think you see,
This world you think you experience,
This world you think about,
Truly, is not real.
It is extremely difficult for any human,
Steeped, lifetime after lifetime,
In the belief that this is not A reality, but THE Reality—
It is extremely difficult for such a person to be told,
"I tell you, this world is not real."
Today we shall discuss that in a manner
Which may make it easier for you to accept, and to understand.

You are as God created you. (21)
You are the Son of God. (6)
You are invulnerable. (22)
You are One Self. (23)
You are Spirit. (L 97)
All of those are true.
All of those I have extended to you
In *A Course in Miracles.*
All of those lessons you have read, thought about,
And hopefully tried to hear from the silence within.

For a moment, try to allow in your thinking
That all of those statements might be true.
Even if simply for the sake of argument, if you will,
Assume that all those lessons are true.
Then apply them to this world,
To this physical world you think you see.

You are Spirit.
Spirit does not have form. Spirit has essence.
Its reality IS its essence.
There is no form which can define, or contain, Spirit.
You would have to say that Spirit
Exists everywhere, and everywhen, simultaneously.
And in your world of illusion,
What can be everywhere?

You perceive that a body occupies
One point in space, and one point in time.
If I say to you, "What you are in reality
Is everywhere, and everywhen, simultaneously,"
Then either that statement is not true,
Or you are not a body.
And I tell you, the latter is true.
You are not a body.
You are Spirit.
Your being is an essence,
As free as the wind, unlimited, unconfined,
Part of the great creative force
Which makes up the Son of God.
And if you ARE Spirit, which you ARE,
It follows that you CANNOT BE a body.

What of your body, then?
Does it not follow that your body is an image,
An image such as you experience in your dreams,
An image such as you might see on a movie screen,
A mirage,
But NOT reality?

Nothing REAL can be threatened.
The essence of your Spirit remains invulnerable,
Untouched, forever and ever.
The image of your body is, truly, of no consequence at all.
In fact, it is just an image, or a mirage,

Made up of your thoughts.
Your body can, and shall, pass away
As easily as the thoughts themselves,
When once you become free.

You are invulnerable.
You create everything, every minute aspect
Of what you experience, of what you are.
This I have told you before.
And it is true.
So for a moment, suppose, without even knowing,
Even without certainty,
Suppose that what I have said IS true—
You are invulnerable,
You do create your own existence.

Remember that the essence of Life is comprised of Spirit.
When you create any aspect of your existence,
You are creating within the realm of Spirit.
Therefore, you are creating essence, not form.
This is initally difficult to comprehend.
It is perhaps even more difficult to accept.

But I tell you, you will grow to love and to feel free
Within the truth of what I have just told you.
What you create is essence.
What you create is experience,
Beyond words, independent of words, independent of thought.
What you create is a feeling
Which defies the description of words,
Which defies the limitation of form.

We can even say,
That what you create CANNOT BE of form.
For the form which you see as physical
Is just an illusion, simply a mirage,
And truly, does not exist.
Whereas the essence of what you experience,
And what you feel,
Is eternal, unlimited, and free.

What then, is this physical world you think you see,
Which you think you experience?
It is a representation,

An attempt on the part of the mind which thinks,
To represent upon this plane of illusion
That which you are experiencing.
Hear me well.
That representation can not take place
In a complete and perfect manner.
That which you EXPERIENCE cannot be perfectly described,
Or represented, in this world of thought,
In this imagined physical world.
So what you experience physically,
And what seems to BE your experience, and what you are,
Is really just a crude attempt
At expressing what you are experiencing,
Using tools too ill equipped to possibly represent, or describe,
What your real experience is.

Therefore it follows that what you experience physically,
That which is your PERCEPTION,
Is but a creation of your mind.
Always what you see in this world is what you perceive.
Hear this well.
I have stated that perception is absolutely consistent. (24)
What you see is what you perceive.

Do not be deluded.
What you see with your eyes, what you perceive,
Is an attempt to represent an essence lying deep within you.
And that cannot accurately be done.

The true perception of which I speak,
Which you SHALL come to,
Lies in experiencing the essence
Which dwells behind the world you see.
But that essence, the reality of what you are,
Cannot be described with the thoughts
Which you deem to be your sight.
It cannot be described with the thoughts
You deem to be your hearing,
Or your touch, or your senses.
It cannot be described with the thoughts your mind thinks.

The thoughts themselves are woefully inadequate
To describe your essence,

Even could they be based in the present.
But, as we have said,
Your thoughts are nothing more than reactions
To what you perceive you have experienced in the past.
As such, the thoughts are even more limited
Than you can realize.
So it is, this physical world you think you see
Is but a poor representation of the essence of your experience.
Then is it of any value to you?
Ultimately, the answer is
NONE WHATSOEVER.

One of the lessons suggests to you
Not to value what is valueless. (L 133)
And this physical world, which SHALL pass away,
Is truly of no value to you whatsoever.
Insofar as you choose to see yourself
As being in a physical world,
And wish to use the thinking and senses of that world
As tools to help you go beyond it,
Then it is of some benefit to you
To look upon your physical world
As a representation of your inner world.
Indeed, many of your guides have suggested this to you.
If you wish to function on that level, that is a valid approach.

But do not be deceived into thinking
That the internal world you discover
By looking into the mirror of your external world
Represents your reality.
For always, what you shall discover is thoughts.
And thoughts are always limited.
They cannot represent the essence of what you are.

When I say to you, "Nothing unreal exists," (20)
It is true.
What peace is contained in that statement.
For that which does not exist,
That which is of no value to you at all,
That which is not real,
Can never harm you,
Can never take away from you what you choose to experience,
Can never affect the true essence of what you are.

It can, indeed, SEEM otherwise.
But I promise you, it is not.
That which is real can never be threatened
By that which is an illusion, a representation, a mirage.
And herein lies the peace of God.
You are safe.
Within this world which you imagine to be physical,
Which you imagine to be real,
YOU ARE ABSOLUTELY SAFE.
None of it can touch the essence of what you are.

Bear in mind, none of the pain,
None of that which you call your misery and your fear
Can touch the essence of what you are.
None of the happiness that you find in,
And ascribe to this physical world,
None of the happiness your body seems to bring you—
None of that can touch, or affect,
The essence of what you are,
Which is the Son of God.

You have, indeed, chosen to imagine
This life in a physical world.
And I am not suggesting that you end that imagining
With your own death.
But you will be able to experience your essence
Much more freely and easily
If you realize that what your body seems to bring you,
Be it misery, or be it what you call joy,
Is, ultimately, not real.

Indeed, the things of the body are not your concern.
Your concern is with something which lies beyond it.
This I have told you before, and often.

Be very still,
And you will hear the Holy Spirit.
You will hear the Voice for God.
You will hear the One Self.
And the message you hear will be a message of freedom,
A message of peace, and a message of love.
It shall arise out of your awareness
That there exists but One Self,
And that everything you give is given to that One Self.

As you realize that there is no separation
Between these bodies you imagine,
Nor between any of the things in this world of illusion—
As you realize that,
You will find yourself free.

And when you realize that truth,
Because you ARE One,
Your realization, your knowing, will affect all of your brothers.
And when the time comes when all of your Spirits
Blend into the knowledge of the One Self,
Then shall your freedom be complete.
Then shall the Light come.
And you will no longer have any need
To imagine this illusion you have chosen.

Do not make yourself wrong for having chosen this illusion.
Do not make yourself wrong
Because of the fact that it is not real.
For in part, your need for salvation arose out of
The exploration of your total freedom to BE,
Which was given you by our Creator.

All of it came and went in an instant.
This is nothing but a dream, a dream of experience,
In order that we might better understand
The essence of the One Self,
Which is what you, and I, and we, are.

Do your best as you read these words,
Perhaps over and over again,
To go beyond the words and thoughts,
To the feelings and the experience,
Which shall tell you that indeed, you ARE Spirit,
You are NOT a body,
You ARE free,
You ARE unlimited,
You ARE invulnerable.
If you can, for one moment,
Come close to feeling the essence of what I have told you,
A thousand years will be saved.

I remind you that you are the saviour of the world.
Your function here is salvation.

And that shall be your joy.
And that shall be your freedom.

You shall grow to where forgiveness is what you wish to share.
You will realize that the forgiveness is of this illusion itself,
Is of the belief that any of this can be real, or can even exist.
Rejoice.
Truly, I tell you,
Rejoice that such is the case,
And is your truth.

In this moment, as you become silent within,
Attempt to feel yourself unlimited, free,
Unbound, totally safe, totally loved,
And One Self.
For that is indeed the essence of what you are.
And as I have said,
There is nothing you can do to change that.
As you begin to experience all of this
At the deepest levels of this mind you have,
Then such joy, and such peace, and such freedom
Will come to you,
That you truly cannot comprehend
How beautiful it will be.

Blessings upon you all. That is all.

VALUES

Greetings again. I am Jeshua. I have come this day
To further, with you, my discussion of
A Course in Miracles.

The lessons for this past week
May have been very difficult for you.
For they can seem to be extremely negative
In the way that they seem to be telling you
To negate your feelings about this world.
"The world I see holds nothing that I want." (L 128)
"I loose the world from all I thought it was." (L 132)
Others of the lessons maintain a similar pattern.
I will discuss those lessons with you today.

God's gift to you is Love.
God's gift to you is peace,
Which is the goal of this Course.
There is nothing in the design of the universe which shall ever
Bring you anything except that peace, and that love.
And there is nothing in *A Course in Miracles*
Which would ever take away from you
Anything of value, or anything which is real.

When you feel threatened,
When you feel as if the lessons of this Course
Would suggest that you give up something of value,
I assure you, it is your misperception.
It is your ego, your little self, coming into play,
Fearing for its own existence.

One of the lessons said,
"I will not value what is valueless." (L 133)
Then it suggested that
Anything which will not last forever is of no value whatsoever.
If that is true, and I assure you it is,
Then it immediately follows that this world of form,
This world of space and time, is of no value whatsoever.
For all of that which you perceive to be time and space,
Your world as you perceive it, shall pass away.
It will pass away into nothingness.

The things of God do not pass away.
The Love of God is unchanging.
The peace of God is unchanging.
The peace of God is with you always,
And even goes beyond your understanding,
As the Bible suggests.

The body, which so many of you have identified with yourself,
Will pass away, and be no more.
And when that happens,
Your Real Self, the essence of what you are,
Will exist in all its freedom and all its glory.

Truly, as this Course suggests over and over again,
The body is an encumbrance, a design of separation,
An illusion which serves to bring you
Misery, sadness, grief, and the belief in death.
And I ask you now,
Of something which brings you your fears,
Your dying, your separation, and your grief,
What value is it to you?

Its only value would be found in your dying.
For the body's death would mean
That you would no longer exist,
Therefore to be free of the pain and misery and grief.
But I tell you, that is not so.

Indeed, I doubt any of you would have come
This far in *A Course in Miracles*
Without some measure of belief
That your reality continues to exist after your body dies.
Indeed, throughout the ages of mankind,
There has been the quiet, incessant, knowing within
That there IS an existence beyond that of the body.
And you are right, of course.

So since this body brings you misery, and fear,
And aging, and ultimately death,
And since it passes away while YOU continue to live,
Of what value is it?
Its value is only, as I have stated in this Course,
That of a vehicle for communication, (25)
Which shall help you to realize, in this world of form,

The Oneness you share with your brothers,
And the bonds that make you the One Self.

The question then always arises,
"Are you telling me to hate the world?"
The answer is no.
Am I telling you not to VALUE the world?
The answer is yes.

Your values are synonymous with
That which you believe you NEED.
And what you need you will cherish.
And what you cherish,
You will protect, FROM . . .
From what?
From anything, it doesn't matter.
Anything that you value, you will try to protect,
In order that it will not go away.

Now, if you value anything of the body,
Or anything of this world of form,
All of which MUST pass away,
Then in your meager attempts to prevent just that,
You bring upon yourself pain, and fear,
And misery, and separation,
And all that which is not of God.

Again, when you value something,
You feel it necessary that IT be in order for YOU to be.
When you DEFINE yourself in terms OF something,
That something is always of FORM.
And when you define yourself in terms of some form,
Then the loss of that form means, at least in part,
Your own death.
And the loss of that form entirely
Means your own death entirely.

What a source of fear, and of pain!
And whether you know it or not,
That is what your body represents to you,
Insofar as you equate it with yourself.

When you become free,
You will realize that your body is, in no sense, you.

Then you will no longer value it.
You will no longer fear its loss,
The loss of any part of it, or the loss of any of its functions.
You will then be able to use your body
Only as a means of communication,
Which is its real purpose for you, on this earth.

Even then, do not VALUE it as a means of communication.
For your communication is always beyond your thinking,
Beyond the form, beyond that which the body represents.
So you may USE it as a means of communication.
But never cherish it, or fear its loss.
For the communication which arises from your One Self
Cannot be harmed by changes in your body,
Or even its entire absence.

So I have told you that
The world you see holds nothing that you want.
The word "want" is the key.
For that which you want, you cherish,
You want to keep, and you want to protect.
And you only "want" something
If it serves to create that which you call yourself,
Your self-concept.

But the world you see, I assure you,
Can do nothing to create, or alter, in any way,
That which you REALLY are.
For, as we have said, and will say again,
You are as God created you.
You are Spirit.
You are One Self.

The world you see cannot be part of your One Self.
For its problem is separation.
Thus it denies the One Self.
The world you see is not, in any sense, what you are.
For the world is not of Spirit.
This you already know, intuitively.
So this world, which I tell you offers nothing that you want,
Indeed, offers you nothing to make you your Self,
To help you become your Self,
Or to make you, in any way, more than you already are.

The only thing this world can do is,
As you believe it to be real,
As you cherish it, and value it,
Detract you from the truth of what you are.
So this world, at worst, totally separates you
From any awareness of what you are as the Son of God.
And this world, at its best, is a thing which you can forgive
As you see through and beyond it to your true One Self,
Which is only Spirit, and only of God.

You have chosen to come here to explore, to search,
Ultimately to find what it is to BE the Son of God.
You will, indeed, find that.
But you will not find it, I tell you, in this world.
The knowledge that you are the Son of God
Is your peace, and your happiness, and your joy.
And this world will not bring that knowledge to you.

When you feel that this world, with its form,
Is bringing you joy,
Realize that the joy will not last, that it will pass away.
The laughter ringing in your joy
Will one day be the tears that echo through your being.
Such is the world, in its frailness, in its fickleness.
For it SHALL pass away.

The peace of God, I tell you, does not change.
It lasts, shines, and shines, and grows, and becomes, forever.
You are free.
You have come here in your freedom
To explore your creativeness, as the Son of God.
And all the beings here are exploring it with you,
Within your One Self.

Indeed, as you look upon this world
You can see that creativeness.
You can see that which is the offspring of the Son of God.
You can see, in the comings and goings of your lives,
The intricate design which you, in your Oneness,
Have created here.
You can see that creativeness in yourself, and in others,
In plants, and animals, and the heavens.
And truly, as you look upon that WITHOUT VALUE,
You can see God.

Hear me well once again.
If, and when, you confuse any of this world with what you are,
You only wish for your own death.
And you WILL find it, in the form of fear,
Be it even a sigh of tiredness,
Or the panic that can come as you approach with fear
Your own death, or illness, or pain.
But it IS a wish for your death,
And you WILL find it.

But if you cease to value this world, then you will be free.
In your freedom, you can create whatever you wish
Of this sojourn in space and time.
So I do not say to you, hate the world.
For there is no hate.
There is only love.
And I do not say to you, reject the world.
For there is only the Oneness that is God.
And nothing of God can be rejected.
And I do not say to you, spurn the world.
Rather I say to you,
Love, and be joyful,
And be free.

If you choose, in your creativity, to be free,
Then you shall find joy here on this earth.
But I promise you that everything you value
Shall bring you pain.
And everything you value is a wish for your own death.
And I promise you,
If you can see that this world offers nothing that you want,
Because it has nothing to do with what you truly are,
And if you can see that the reality of what you are
Lies beyond this world,
Then you shall be free.

In your freedom, you can play on this earth
Just as the little child I once said
Should inherit the Kingdom of Heaven.
Your freedom to be as that child,
Your freedom to be as God created you,
Your freedom to live here as a true Son of God
Lies in your freedom from valuing anything here.

Truly, this world offers nothing that you want.
For you are Spirit. You are as God created you.
And nothing here can change that.
You are absolutely safe,
And absolutely free.

I tell you there is nothing here worth valuing.
For in your valuing, you only try to change,
Within your own belief,
That which you are as the Son of God.
So as you look beyond the world,
And as you free it from your valuing,
Then you yourself shall be free.
That freedom shall bring you joy.
And this earth shall become for you a place of joy,
For as long as you choose to walk it,
Be it in this lifetime, or in others to come.

Your freedom and your salvation lie in knowing
That you, truly, are Spirit,
That you truly are as God created you,
And that nothing can change that.
Your safety and peace, here on this earth,
Lie in that same knowing.
And as you let go of your value of this world,
You shall be free to love it,
And to find within it the joy you have sought.

Blessings upon you all. That is all.

ILLNESS

Greetings again. I am Jeshua. I have come this day
To further, with you, my discussion of
A Course in Miracles.

Last time we talked about valuing,
And how it is that when you value something
You see it as a needed part of your existence.
Therefore, you ultimately see it as a part of what you are.
And therefore, you see its absence as, in part, your own death.
So your valuing of ANYTHING of this earth,
Of anything at all in any universe,
Is a desire that you die.
For all of space and time shall pass away.
And you must see its passage as your own death.

One of the primary examples of valuing
To be found in this world of illusion
Is your own illness.
The lesson said,
"Sickness is a defense against the truth." (L 136)
Indeed, that is exactly so.

As I have told you, time and again,
You are Spirit,
You are free,
You are exactly as God created you,
Which is unencumbered, unconfined,
Totally free to be whatever you can imagine.

It always seems, does it not,
That sickness is a thing which happens TO you.
But I have told you that nothing happens to you
Without it being your choice,
Without it being an expression of that which you wish,
And what you desire.
It can seem frustrating, indeed,
To have someone tell you, almost glibly,
That your illness, your pain, your struggle,

Is something which you have chosen,
And which you desire.
It especially seems frustrating when, within your thoughts,
Your illness is something which you despise and do not want,
Above all when it brings you pain and limitation.

So how is it that illness arises?
First, when you think thoughts
Other than the truth about what you are,
You generate conflict.
Also, you cannot see illusion
Without that you value what it is you think you see.
When you see your body, and deem it real,
It MUST BE that you have valued it.
For the lesson said, perception is absolutely consistent.
Perception reflects your thinking;
And your thinking reflects only what you value.
You cannot see a world you have not accorded value. (24)
And that is true.

Be aware that it is entirely possible to walk this earth,
Seeming to have the form of a body,
But without valuing it in any way whatsoever.
In that state, you are free.
In that state you will not experience sickness.

For you, in the absence of your valuing,
Will not defend yourself.
And in not defending, there can be no attack.
Not defending involves many things,
Including, as I said in the lesson,
Not even planning what you will do one hour,
Or one minute from now. (26)
This seems somewhat absolute
To those of you steeped in this illusion.
Indeed, it seems very difficult.
But truly, it is not so difficult as you think,
When once you adjust your perception,
And head in the direction of truth itself.

So ultimately your illness MUST BE
A statement from within that you have valued your body.
When you perceive that your body is,
Totally, or in some measure,

WHAT YOU ARE,
Then you have identified the body as yourself.
To have done that, you MUST have valued it,
And MUST BE creating conflict.

The conflict arises because you ARE One Self.
Your One Self knows you are NOT a body.
This puts your thinking mind at odds
With the truth of what you are.
And this produces the conflict,
Stemming from your one problem,
Which, you recall, is separation.
When you perceive that your body is in any sense real,
Then you are valuing it,
And you will fear its absence, or its change.

When you fear,
You create all manner of havoc in your universe.
For as you fear that your body might leave you,
Or that it might change,
That IT might do something different from what YOU desire,
You begin to sense that you are a victim of that body.
And in that valuing, in that fear,
YOU CREATE YOUR OWN DEATH.
For death is always the result, in one form or another,
Of your separation, and your fear.

So you have, out of your own creative power,
Structured a world in which
There SEEM to be bodies walking around,
But which are merely shadows of separation.
You seem to have structured a world
In which these bodies are born, live a while, age, and then die.
And you think that the cycle through which the body goes
Is the cycle through which YOU go.

That is not true.
For you are the Son of God.
You are Spirit.
And you, like God, are unchanging, are forever,
And are invulnerable.

Perhaps it seems to you like so many hollow words.
I am sure it can seem like preaching

When I seem glibly to say,
All of your illness is but your choosing.
All of your illness is but your fear.
Give up your fear, and you will be fine.
I know how frustrating that can be,
When it seems that you want to give up your fear,
And somehow it does not go away.

So I have come, in love, to speak with you this day.
I have come to share with you
How you might more peacefully approach your own illness,
Your own body, and even its death,
If you choose that to happen.
And most likely you will.
Very few of you choose not to die physically.

Remember, the world you see is a reflection, only a reflection,
Of that which is within.
The external and internal worlds are not in complete correlation.
Furthermore, the correlation does not function
In both directions.
It is true that what you see in your external world,
Including your body,
Is a reflection of your world within.
But it is only a reflection.
Because the physical world cannot possibly represent
That which you are in Spirit, which is the Son of God.

Any time you seem to experience grief, or pain,
Or loss, or tiredness, or illness, or death,
It but reflects that which is within,
And that which is really just your thinking.

However, it does not follow
That when you seem to have no illness,
Your mind is free of conflict.
Some of you have chosen to come here
And not experience illness,
Simply to live a life free of physical pain, until you die.
And even your dying can be without pain.
And that is simply your choice.

Some of you have come here and chosen a life of illness,
And struggle with seemingly persistent pain.

That too, is nothing more than your choice.
Neither is good. Neither is bad.
Nor is one better or worse than the other.
So if you are ill, do not think yourself wrong.
Just realize that it is what you have chosen.

Your illness commonly does reflect a poison within.
But your health does not reflect a goodness.
And your health does not reflect
An absence of that same poison within.

Hear me well.
When you, in your desire not to be ill,
Value your body and its absence of symptoms
As something good, as a desirable goal,
You are not focusing on what you actually ARE.
For your focus is still on the body.
And the body remains the source of your conflict.
Your separation, and your pain.

So I said in the lesson,
"Only salvation can be said to cure." (L 140)
If you have chosen some symptom, however minor,
And if you choose to use the power of your thinking
(And powerful it is indeed)
To make that SYMPTOM go away,
You are still living within, and valuing, this world of illusion.
And you are not yet free of your conflict.
You only seem to be free if you equate, incorrectly no less,
The absence of illness with the presence of truth within.
So be careful, as you deal with your illness,
Not to attempt only to free yourself of your SYMPTOMS.
For that but keeps you in this world of illusion.

The only real cure for your illness,
The only real cure for the problems of this world,
Is your forgiveness.
And your forgiveness ultimately means realizing
That none of this world is of any value whatsoever.
In that realization you become free.

It should be clear by now.
If you value something, then what you value you will see;
And what you value you automatically equate with yourself.

For that is simply what valuing means.
And the fear that it will disappear,
Which is the fear that YOU will disappear,
Is the belief in your own death,
And the wish for the same.
All of this shall pass away.
Even you, in your thinking, know that.
When you value any of it,
All the while knowing it shall pass away,
You are creating your own death,
And the fear of the same.

Once again, your forgiveness is nothing more than
The realization that there is nothing here to value.
So when you perceive yourself to be ill,
When you perceive yourself to be in pain,
Know within that your illness is nothing more than a reflection,
A validation that you are valuing something here,
Within this world.

When you go beyond the valuing of this world,
Truly there will no longer be illness.
You will no longer need the experience of pain.
For pain is just a reflection of your fear.

So for those of you who have chosen illness in whatever form,
From severe chronic pain, to occasional discomfort,
To the slightest allergy or sniffle,
You have chosen an easy way.
Because, in your wisdom, you are presenting yourself
With evidence that you are valuing this world.
And your symptoms are merely the reminder of your valuing.

As you come to know that this is so,
Try, as best you can, over and over,
To come back to the realization that you are Spirit,
That you are free,
That you are not a body.
Try to realize that your mind, in its reality,
Holds only the thoughts you think with God.

As you become still within, and attempt to let go of your fear,
Which you do by focusing on the thoughts you think with God,
Then the fear will pass away.

It will not pass away because you have fought it,
Or struggled against it.
It will pass away because you have simply LET IT GO.
You will not have let go of your fear through struggle.
But you will have let it go
Because you have chosen something more precious,
Indeed, something that IS worth valuing.

What you will have chosen
Is the thoughts you think with God.
And your forgiveness frees you from the belief
That any of the thoughts you think with God
Are centered here upon earth.
For indeed, nothing here is to be valued.

Lest your mind wander into conflict,
Be aware that you can walk this earth in peace,
In love, and in joy,
Without valuing anything here.
In the absence of your valuing
You shall BE without fear,
In total safety, without illness,
And without your own death,
Until such time as you might choose to move on,
And to change form.
To walk this earth thusly shall be your goal.
And that shall be a form of your salvation.

There is much more, beyond, of which I cannot even speak,
For you could not understand.
Be content to know that you are blessed,
And you are free, as the Son of God.

There are those of you who have not chosen
A great deal of illness,
Who have not chosen a great deal of pain.
Do not mistake that for the absence of your valuing.
Rather, your job is, perhaps, more difficult.
If you have what you call a "good" body,
Which behaves well for you,
And lets you do the things you want to do,
It becomes far easier to value those things,
And to want to keep them.
But as we have said,

In your valuing you create fear,
And the belief in your own death.

So you have chosen a variation on the path to salvation.
What you can do, then, since you seldom choose pain,
Is be diligent and look carefully at that which brings you joy.
And if that which seems to bring you joy
Is dependent upon something of this earth,
So that your joy would pass away
If the earth should pass away,
Then let that be your illness.
Realize that when you find joy in what this earth offers you,
Then to the point that you value it,
That shall be your illness.
For it WILL lead you, eventually, to pain.
Because it too shall pass away.

You can learn this by being aware of your thinking.
If you find joy in something of the earth,
And you find yourself able, within that joy,
To experience it IN THAT MOMENT, in that instant,
Then you are free.
But if there is the slightest fear, the slightest worry,
Of whether you will be all right
When the source of that joy passes away,
Then know that you are valuing,
And are bringing about,
Just as in the case of illness,
Your own death.
Above all, do not be deceived into thinking that
Because you are not ill, you are free of the valuing.

This issue is very important for you to be aware of.
It IS an issue of thinking.
And even the thinking shall pass away.
In the time when you no longer think,
Your valuing will not even be an issue,
And you will BE totally free.

You do not even have to struggle against your valuing.
For it WILL go away, in the same way
That everything of this earth will pass away.
Be aware that I have merely given you concepts
For you to apply your thinking to.

Such application of your thinking
Shall help you to move beyond it.
Be whether you choose to follow these suggestions or not,
You are absolutely safe, and absolutely loved.

So the issue is not your illness.
The issue is not the absence of your illness.
The issue is that your freedom comes
From not valuing that which is valueless.
Your freedom comes from realizing
That there is nothing in this world
Which you can want enough to value,
Or to desire that it BE yourself.

In the absence of your valuing,
You will become truly free to walk this earth
For as long as you wish,
In joy, and in love.
And all your brothers will see that joy shining in your face,
And in your eyes.
They will perhaps seem to be confused by some of it.
But at the deepest level of what you are,
There is only Oneness,
There is only the One Self.
And they will know of your experience.

As you truly cease to value anything of this earth,
As you come to the joy that lies in knowing
That you are totally free of anything here,
Because you ARE Spirit,
Because you ARE the Son of God,
Because you ARE co-creator with God,
Then you are truly free.
Your brothers will sense in you that freedom.
And you will truly be one of the saviours of the world.

Blessings upon you all. That is all.

TIME

Greetings again. I am Jeshua. I have come this day
To further, with you, my discussion of
A Course in Miracles.

Recall the initial reminder I gave you.
A Course in Miracles is not a Course to learn.
It is a Course to LIVE.
It is not a Course of ideas to be mastered, or understood.
The ideas only function to help you go beyond them.

In going beyond the ideas,
You move to the level of experience.
Always keep that in mind.
Never value the ideas I seem to be giving you.
Never value the reactions you seem to get
As you read these words I offer you.

Of late, I have been speaking with you of valuing.
We spoke of valuing, what it was, what it meant,
And how it is that valuing is a construct of your ego.
It is the form you use to define your self-concept,
Your beliefs about who you are.

Whenever you value anything of form,
Of this world, or your body,
You are valuing something that will pass away.
Therefore you are demanding that you shall pass away,
And that you shall die.
So, as I have said before,
To value anything here is to believe in your own death.

And I tell you, again and again,
In the Kingdom of God, there is no death.
There is no conflict; there is no pain.
There is only peace and joy,
Forever and ever.
And it is the "forever and ever" part
That I wish to discuss with you today.

For without that you always know it,
One of the major values that you ascribe
To your life upon this earth
Is the value of time.
I said in the lesson,
"If you choose a thing that will not last forever,
What you choose is valueless." (27)
And I tell you, time shall not last forever.

That can seem a difficult concept.
For time seems to be a thing independent of your world,
Which simply flows, which merely IS,
And would seem to BE,
Whether or not your world physically exists.
I tell you, that is not so.

That which you perceive as time,
That which you value as time,
Is truly just another form of form itself.
As you have created the physical world, which is an illusion,
As you have created your body, which is an illusion,
As you have created your own thoughts,
Which, yet too, are illusions,
So have you likewise created time,
Which also is an illusion.

Think for a moment about your pain, and about your fear.
Essentially all of your pain, and all of your fear,
Is because you value time.

Ultimately what you are doing, is saying
I do not choose to value what I am experiencing in this moment;
I rather will value that which I call a memory of the past,
Or more usually, that which I anticipate will be the future.
Essentially, all of the time when you bind, or constrict, yourself,
It is because of some imagined fear
Of what your future will bring.

In the one lesson, which you may even be reviewing today,
"If I defend myself, I am attacked," (L 135)
I tried to make it clear that time, and the belief in time,
Is one of the major defenses you create,
And with which you attack yourself.
And, of course, an attack upon yourself

Brings you pain, or conflict, or discontent.
They are all the same.

And trying to plan for the future,
Even to the point of organizing this day,
Is a defense, ultimately is an attack upon your Self,
And will bring you distress,
And the absence of peace.
How is that so? you might ask.
When you plan for the future,
Think of what it is that you really do.
You are saying, within your thoughts,
"What is it that I, ego, want to experience,
Not now, but at some point in the future?"

Then you attempt to structure the moments to follow,
All of which are also in the future,
In such a way that moments in the more distant future
Will contain that which seems to make you happy.
In this context, being happy seems to mean
Experiencing what you WANTED to experience.

And is it not true,
That even while you are experiencing that which you desired,
There is the knowing within that this too shall pass away.
So ultimately, there must be a frustration,
And a sadness, associated with it.

And what has happened?
What you have done is valued a thing in the future.
And YOU, the Son of God,
Free of conflict, free of pain, free of disease,
Free of all restrictions, free of your body,
Free of your thoughts,
And free of time,
DO NOT EXIST IN THE FUTURE.

I have told you, one of the major barriers you have
Is the concept of yourself,
The ideas you have formed about what you are.
And those ideas of what you are
Are based upon what you call the past.
In your plans for the future,
What you are really doing is trying to structure

That same self-concept
So that at some point, which has not yet come,
You will have a particular, seemingly desired,
Feeling about who you are.

But within your being, within your knowing,
Within the awareness of your One Self,
You always know that all of it,
Including the concept of who you are,
Shall pass away.

Remember, in your valuing
You are worshipping and creating your own death.
And in your valuing of the future,
Which is not your Self,
And is not of God,
And is not of the Son of God—
In your valuing of the future,
You are looking TOWARD a concept of yourself,
Which may not come at all,
And if it does, shall pass away.

Never can you be content within such a framework.
And what creates all of that for you?
Your valuing of time.

Time is, for many of you,
Even a grander illusion than that of sickness.
For sickness is generally not subtle.
If you have a headache, if you are coughing, if your foot hurts,
You are directly aware of it at that moment.
And to the extent that you realize
That all should be peace in your life,
When you are sick, you know right then
That something has gone awry.

Ah, but time.
Time is a much more subtle master.
So subtle, indeed,
That when I say to you
"Time itself does not exist,"
It is even hard for you to believe my words are true.

If I say, it is possible that you be healed,
Because illness is an illusion,

And all illness, from a slight sniffle to the worst cancer,
CAN pass away in the twinkling of an eye,
There is something inside of you that, generally, will say,
Well, yes, I think that may be true.
Even if you do not feel, or believe,
That you can effect such a happening in your own life.

But when I say to you, as ultimately I am saying,
Time is the grand illusion, even more than your own illness,
I am saying that to be free you must free yourself of time,
And even the belief that it exists.

When I say to you, in earnest,
Take no thought of tomorrow,
Take no thought of the next hour,
Take no thought of the next minute,
Truly, most of you feel a clutching within your heart.
And what that clutching is
Is your belief within yourself,
That, truly, if you took no thought for tomorrow,
If you took no thought beyond this moment,
You would surely die.

That, indeed, is the proof of your valuing.
Do you understand?
When you believe that you could not exist
If you did not plan your future,
You are being the victim, by your own choice,
Of your own thoughts.

I tell you,
God did not create time.
God does not know of time.
For what God wills IS.
And what God imagines IS.
And your existence as the Son of God IS.
And your freedom IS.
And your health IS.
And your power over your own existence IS.

And when I say IS, obviously I mean
RIGHT NOW.
To think that there is anything of God
Which somehow God could not create until tomorrow

Is such a limitation on God
That surely you would laugh as I said it.

And I tell you now,
You are no less limited than God Itself.
For what you deign to be, IS.
In your imaginings, what you imagine, IS.
And what you HAVE imagined is a world of form,
And of time.

So you have taken your Spirit,
Free as the wind, free to dance throughout all of existence,
Unlimited by space and time,
Unlimited by anything you can imagine—
You have taken that freedom, and in your playing with it,
Have imagined that it doesn't exist.

And what this Course is about
Is your coming realization
That you are free.
And, truly, it would be this instant
If you could open to the knowing
Of what I have just said.

So in your thinking, think often about time,
And the value you place on it,
And how it is that when you fear for the next moment,
You are wishing to die.

Further in this Course we will speak at length
Of the Holy Instant.
All the Holy Instant is
Is the state you come to live in
When your forgiveness encompasses time.
And your forgiveness, as I have said,
Is your realization that nothing of this world
Is worth your valuing,
None of its form,
And especially time itself.

It is very important in this Course
That you EXPERIENCE, at whatever level,
What I have spoken of today.
The IDEA that time does not exist,
Whether you believe it or not in your thinking,

Will do you no good at all.
But if you can FEEL within your being, for one instant,
That your belief in time does, indeed,
Create your own death, and your desire to die—
If you can, for one instant,
Say, "But that is not my nature as the Son of God,"
Then you shall move thousands of years closer to your freedom.

If you could have within your being
One great moment of total freedom from all of time,
Then you could leave this earth,
And would never need to return for any of its lessons.
For the lesson of valuing time and the illusions that it brings
Is one of the greatest that you have to learn
In your sojourn on this earth.

All of this form,
All of that which you call your body,
All of that which you do to protect your body,
Whether it be for its comfort,
Or to keep it from being ill,
Is illusion,
And is of no value whatsoever.

The belief that you are not complete as the Son of God,
RIGHT NOW,
That you cannot be full of joy, RIGHT NOW,
That there is some limitation which you cannot overcome,
RIGHT NOW—
All of that is the grand illusion of time.
And time itself shall pass away.
Time itself is of no value whatsoever
To you, as the Son of God.

Hear me well.
You are free. You are unlimited, unrestricted.
All that you are is peace, and joy, and love.
None of what you ARE understands space, or form, or time.
And as you cease to value space,
And especially time,
As you forgive, within yourself and in others,
Your belief in space and time,
You shall become truly free.

Blessings upon you all. That is all.

VALUING

Greetings again. I am Jeshua. I have come this day
To further, with you, my discussion of
A Course in Miracles.

I have been speaking to you of late of valuing, and your values,
And trying to give you some sense of how it is
That your valuing is ultimately
What traps you in this world.

I said in one of the lessons,
Perception is absolutely consistent. (24)
It is impossible to see two different worlds. (L 130)
And you MUST SEE the world you have accorded value. (24)

So the seeing, the experiencing of a given world,
Is for you a demonstration of what your values are.
And remember that valuing is the internal statement
Of what it is that you feel is necessary
For your self to be.
If you value your body, then you are automatically
Making a statement, within, and without,
That your body is, partly or completely, what you ARE.
If you value anything of this world,
You are making a statement, within and without,
That what you value represents, in essence, YOU.

The words of a previous lesson were
"The world I see holds nothing that I want." (L 128)
That statement becomes clear
When seen within the scope of what we are discussing now.
There is nothing in this world
That is, or can ever be, what you are.
So none of it is worth valuing.
Because if you value it,
You merely confuse, within, what you are.

And what are you?
Over and over again I have said,

And this is the whole truth—
You are the Son of God.
You, like God Itself, are Spirit.
You are not a body.
You, like God Itself, are free.
You, with God, are co-creator of the universe,
Ordained thusly and created thusly,
By God Itself.

Remember, *A Course in Miracles* is not to be learned,
But to be lived.
So in your meanderings with your mind,
Take what I have just said to you,
And try to feel within your being
Its reality.

Be not content to hear it as ideas, and to say within your mind,
"Ah, yes, I understand."
Rather, attempt to allow that experience,
At the level of feeling and awareness, beyond your thoughts,
To become part of you.
As you do that,
You move thousands of years closer to your freedom.

I also told you in one of the lessons that
The power of decision is your own. (L 152)
Indeed, that is so.
Ultimately, that lesson is also about your valuing.
As I have said,
There is nothing you can experience
Anywhere in your universe
Without that it be your own choice.
For you are the Son of God.

And so you ask,
How is it that this world I see
Doesn't behave according to my every whim?
And the answer, which I have come to discuss with you today,
Lies in your valuing.

There is one problem; there is one solution.
The problem, as you recall, is that of separation.
For there is, indeed, One Self,
A Self that is you, and which you are in its entirety,

A Self that is the entire universe, and of which you are a part.
Both are true.

There exists, within the universe of reality,
Within the universe that has meaning—
There is within the world of truth,
But One Self.
Hear me well.
This world you see is not your Self.
This world that you see has nothing to do with what you are.
But as you value this world, which is but your perception,
Which is your choice within your mind,
Then you will see it as real.

It is true that its existence reflects a great sharing
Of the thoughts you all hold in your minds.
But, the thoughts that have created this world
Are NOT the thoughts you think with God.
So this world, by its nature, and by your own choice,
Is a reflection of your fear,
Of your desire to be separate one from another.
And in your experience of this world,
To the extent that you see it and think it real,
You are valuing that separation.

There are those aspects of your life
Which might seem to be strictly individual,
Belonging only to you.
And there are those aspects of this life
Which seem to be collective, for lack of a better word.
And it would SEEM reasonable
That some aspects of your life you could control,
While others might be more difficult to control.
Ah, remember the words,
There is no order of difficulty in miracles. (28)

So as you see this world at all
In your desire to experience it FOR YOURSELF,
In whatever aspect,
You are worshipping and cherishing separation.
You are, therefore,
Worshipping and cherishing your desire
To be separate from God,
And to be separate from your One Self.

It may seem, as you think about it,
That some things in this world
WILL happen according to your wishes.
But ultimately your thinking will demonstrate
That not EVERYTHING happens as you wish.
That is because in your desire to be separate,
You are desiring that things be allowed to happen TO YOU.

In your Oneness,
If one of you wanted it to rain,
Then all of you, as One, would choose the rain,
And it would BE.
In your dream of separation that cannot be.
It does not happen in your world
That every single, separate being
Wants it to rain at exactly the same time.

Then wherein lies the problem?
I have told you that nothing happens to you
Without that it be your own choice.
And what if it rains when you do not choose to have it rain?
Hear me well.
You cannot become what does not exist.
You cannot, as co-creator with God, create what does not exist.
You cannot, as a Son of God, BE what you are not.
Over that you have no choice.

You can imagine your separation.
You can imagine the pain, the tears, and the grief
That the separation brings.
But you cannot change, with your imaginings,
Your Self.

The Voice for God speaks to you always.
And in this Course,
When you come to the point where you value only truth,
Only that which has meaning,
Only the One Self which is your reality—
When you value only that, there will be no separation.
And all your problems will disappear.
I tell you, you CAN walk this earth in such a state.

So start by realizing, in your thinking,
That the world you see holds nothing that you want.

There is nothing in this world that reflects, or represents,
In truth, that which you are.
And any time that you would try to alter, to change,
To manipulate that which you see as your physical world,
You cannot even make that attempt
Without that you have valued the world you see,
And believed it to be yourself.
And insofar as you believe it is yourself,
You are apart from truth.

Rather, as you wish to live on this earth in peace and harmony,
And in the joy of your One Self,
Do it thusly—
There is WITHIN YOU all that you are.
There is within you your Creator, God.
There is within you, even as you walk this world of illusion,
The Voice of God, which is ultimately your One Self.
And as you loose the world from all you thought it was,
You will hear the Voice for God speaking,
No, singing, within you.
That Voice is your own voice singing within you.
Then, truly, I tell you, miracles will enter your life.

I have spoken to you about how to listen to the Voice for God.
I have said that the Voice for God always leads you to joy.
It cannot lead you to fear, or doubt, or guilt.
Now I tell you further,
The Voice for God will not cause you, ever,
To value anything of this world.

You are the Son of God.
You have created this world.
It is your right that you should experience your creation.
This world is your child,
Just as you are the Child of God.
And as you see it for what it is,
A creation of your thoughts, an illusion, a sleight of mind
That shall pass away with a change in your thinking,
Then you will be free to experience it as you wish,
Without fear,
With whatever joy you choose,
And to let it go at any moment you desire.
For THEN you shall be free.

As you become free of any valuing of that which is here,
As you move, in your thinking,
To the realization that none of this is, or can be,
What you are as the Son of God,
Then you will be free within
To HEAR the Voice for God.

It will speak of joy. It will speak of laughter.
It will never speak of fear. It will never speak of guilt.
And it will teach you, hear me well,
That you are One Self.

As I have told you in the lessons,
Everything you give, you give to yourself. (L 126)
All of your thoughts are directed at your Self.
For you are All That Is, One Self, united with your Creator.
The Voice for God will never suggest
That you are separate from another.
The Voice for God will never suggest that there is a difference
Between what you wish and what another being wishes.
The Voice of God will only speak of love,
And peace, and harmony.
So as you sense that there are any differences,
Or conflicts, or clashes
In your life,
Know well that you are valuing something here,
That you are choosing to say,
"This is what I am."
And I promise you, when you say that,
You are choosing the world of pain.
Ah, yes, it is nothing but your imagination.
But imagined pain still feels like pain.
This you know well.
For you walk this earth.

Your freedom lies in your valuing.
Your real freedom lies in not valuing anything of this earth.
For it is not, and cannot be, what you are.
As you do not value anything here,
From any possession, to any circumstance,
To that which you sense is your self,
To any relationship—
As you value none of that,

Your mind will become unfettered.
You will find within you a song.
And it shall be the song of your One Self.

Truly, I tell you,
Beyond the words, beyond the thinking,
The promise I have made to you is true.
As you cease to value this world,
There will be a song within you.
That song will guide you every moment,
Moment to moment.
It will not speak of the past.
It will not speak of the future.
It will only speak of NOW,
Wherein you are totally free,
Wherein you are One Self.

And in that song
There will not be an arrogance that says
You need to create the circumstances of this unreal world.
Because you will know, within your being,
Where to go, when to go,
What to say, what to do,
To the last detail.
And your joy, and your peace,
And the Voice for God, which is your One Self,
Shall be your guide
For as long as you choose to walk this earth.

Imagine being able to walk this earth like a small child,
To enjoy every moment,
To play with your creation
With the abandon of a very small child,
With a twinkle in your eye and lightness in your step,
No fear for the morrow, or for yesterday.
And that is what I meant when I said
You must become like a little child
To enter the Kingdom of Heaven.

What is it that will make you like that child?
It is the freedom from your valuing.
I tell you with so much love,
Do not value anything of this earth.
For it is not your Self.

And as you let go of all the values of this earth,
You will find yourself as a little child.
Then you shall walk this earth in joy,
For as long as you choose to do so.
And then you shall move beyond it to another form of joy.
And that shall be whatever you shall choose it to be.
For you are the Son of God,
And co-creator of All That Is.

Blessings upon you all. That is all.

SPECIALNESS

Greetings again. I am Jeshua. I have come this day
To further, with you, my discussion of
A Course in Miracles.

Of late, I have been discussing with you
Your values, and your valuing.
Indeed, your valuing is a very, very significant part
Of all this Course is.
It might even be said that in significant measure
The essence of this Course
Is for you to understand your valuing,
What it does, what it creates,
And how releasing yourself from all your values
Brings you freedom.

We have spoken about valuing as it has to do with your illness.
We have spoken about your valuing as it brings you freedom.
We have talked about your value of time,
And how time is one of the major values you use
To create that which you think you are.

Today I wish to discuss with you relationships.
In *A Course in Miracles*, I speak often of special relationships.
Always I say that special relationships
Are a hindrance, are a block
Which separate you from your peace, your freedom,
And your ability to experience this Course.

In a word, your special relationships are the ones you value.
So when I say "special" relationship,
I just mean one of those to which
You have applied some value in your life.

In the Text, I have said, quite directly,
"You do not want anything you value to come of a relationship.
You choose neither to hurt it
Nor to heal it in you own way." (29)
The essence of those words is that love is only freedom.

Remember, now, of your valuing—
When you value something,
You ultimately feel that its presence is necessary
In order for you to be what you are.
So your valuing is looking outside yourself at a thing,
Be it a body, be it time, be it a circumstance,
And saying that you require that thing
In order to be what you are.
And anything you see outside of yourself
Is of this world, and shall pass away.
So in your valuing
You create your own death.

So it is also with relationships.
The search for love,
The search to be loved,
Is what so much of your world seems to be about.
Your books, your songs, your poetry, your themes,
Are all about love.
And they are, indeed, almost to the piece,
About special relationships.

For they are about valuing a relationship.
And the words ''I need you''
Are presumed to be a statement of caring.
In fact, that is not so at all.
For, as I have said before,
When you need anything,
You have made it a part of your self.
And when you need a relationship, likewise,
You have structured a self, which is really a self-concept,
And based part of that self-concept on the relationship.
Thus is becomes to you, special.

Then if that relationship alters,
You must alter your self-concept,
Which is to alter your self.
Then enters fear, resistance, pain, and grieving,
And all of that which you associate with the loss of love.
And I tell you,
All of that which is associated with the loss of love
Is nothing more than the measure to which
You have believed that specialness is love.

In this world,
You have chosen the illusion of separation,
And have chosen the illusion of bodies.
I guarantee you, when you try to discover who you are
In terms of that separation and those bodies,
You will fail.
In this world, where the loss of love
Is based on what another body does,
When changes in the behavior of another body
Threaten your self-concept, and what you are,
You but see the world of specialness,
And of pain,
NOT the world of love.

I have said in the Text,
The pursuit of specialness shall always bring you pain. (30)
And that is true.
What I am saying is this:
To the extent that you value a relationship,
To the extent that you value
What another being does, or says, or thinks,
You are making that other person's actions, words, or thoughts
A necessary part of what YOU are.
To the extent that you value a relationship,
You will always find pain.
For all of it will pass away—
The body, the actions, the words, the thoughts.
And when it passes away,
As with anything else you value,
You will believe that part of you has died.

So valuing, even in relationships,
Is nothing more than the creation of your own death.
Hear me well.
The pursuit of specialness is the desire to die,
And to be in pain.

It would seem,
To those of you so steeped in the belief in specialness,
And the belief that specialness is love,
That I am telling you to deny love.
Truly, that is not so.
What I am trying to teach you, rather,
Is the love that brings you freedom,

Which brings you peace,
And brings you joy.

To love another so much
That you allow that being total freedom,
Total freedom to run and dance,
To flow through this life, or any life,
With the joy of a small child—
To love someone in that way is,
Indeed, to truly love.

As soon as you even BEGIN to define who you are
In terms of a relationship,
You immediately have chosen for that being
NOT TO BE FREE.
You have chosen for that being
To run and dance and play and laugh
Only insofar as it substantiates your concept
Of what you think you are.

Your One Self is of God, is of freedom, and is of Love.
Your One Self, in its reality, has no fear of being alone.
For it knows there is no such thing as aloneness.
There is only Oneness.

In your specialness,
As you desire another person to substantiate
That which you think you are,
It is a form, not of love,
But of hatred.
I said, thousands of years ago,
Those of your own household shall become your enemies.
And what I meant was this—
In your relationships that define who you are,
Be they brother, sister, parent, lover, friend—
It is in those relationships
That you feel resistance to another's freedom,
In which you feel pain when another
Chooses to be free.

So I tell you,
To love is to allow total freedom.
And to desire anything else for another

Is but a form of valuing, within yourself.
And that is the desire for specialness.

In order to become like a small child,
To dance your life with joy, with freedom, and with true love,
Then what you need do is not value any relationship.

This is not an aversion.
It is not the absence of love.
Rather it is the giving of love itself,
In the form of freedom, and joy.
When, within yourself, you need nothing from outside yourself,
Then you are free to love.
This applies especially to your relationships,
Of which I have been speaking this day.

It shall become more clear as we progress
Towards your freedom and your joy.
But for now, hear me well,
When I speak of your values,
And when I urge you not to value what is valueless.
Hear me well when I tell you that you are not a body,
That you are not of this earth,
That you are not of space and time,
That you are free.

The relationships of which I have spoken this day
Are the ones which you perceive
To be based upon bodies, upon space and time,
And actions that bodies seem to perform.
As you do not value those,
As you become free,
Free to love, and to give freedom without judgment,
Regardless of what any other being does—
As you give that freedom,
Then that is what you shall receive in return.

All that you give is given to yourself.
And as you give freedom,
Which you can only give when you do not value,
When you do not NEED,
Then that is when you shall receive that selfsame freedom.
And that freedom shall be your joy.
Hear me well.

These lessons can seem difficult.
These lessons can seem to be negative.
But indeed, they are filled with love.
And they are filled with a truth which,
When you hear and understand,
Will bring you your joy, your peace, and your freedom.
You shall then give to others their joy,
Their peace, and their freedom.
And you shall become among the saviours of the world.

The step which shall take you there is not to value,
And not to need—
Rather to allow, and therefore to receive,
Your freedom.

Blessings upon you all. That is all.

FREEDOM FROM VALUES

Greetings again. I am Jeshua. I have come this day
To further, with you, my discussion of
A Course in Miracles.

I have spoken often and consistently, of late, of your valuing.
Indeed, your realization of valuing—no,
Your experiencing the absence of valuing—
Is the biggest step you have on this earth
On your path to freedom.

For your values truly are the blocks
To your peace, to your freedom, and your joy.

I have discussed with you how it is
That your values create your own illness.
Indeed, your values create everything of which you are afraid.
Your values even create that which you believe to be yourself.
And it is the threat to that which you believe yourself to be
That creates your fear.

As you move to your awareness
Of who you are as the Son of God,
Then the valuing of that which you thought you were
Will pass away.
And with it shall disappear all your fears.
And without your fears,
Life shall be love,
And joy,
And light,
And freedom.

I will repeat for you one more time,
Nay, not one more,
For there will be many times I will repeat this for you.
Your forgiveness is nothing more
Than the release of your self
From your values.

Forgiveness merely means that you have realized,
Experienced within your being,
That nothing here is to value,
That nothing here has anything to do
With what you are in truth.

You are as God created you.
You are Spirit.
You are Mind,
Created only by Mind,
Living only in Mind.
It is that awareness which you wish to receive,
Which you wish to know and experience,
And which, in your forgiveness, and your love,
You shall give.

Today I wish to move past the DISCUSSION of valuing,
To try to help you experience,
Or to get an inkling of what the experience will be,
When you give up your valuing.
So try to imagine with me, for a little while,
What it would be like to leave this world.
I do not mean to leave it physically,
But to leave it in the sense of your valuing.

Try not to think, try not to analyze,
But to let my words flow into your being,
And to attempt, as you read,
To experience something beyond this world.

I have said in the Text,
You cannot imagine how beautiful
Will be the world you see
When once you have forgiven. (31)
Of that I shall speak now.
Try to imagine, to feel, what it would be like,
To KNOW that your brothers and sisters are not bodies—
Truly, ARE NOT BODIES, but are Spirits.
Try to imagine what it would be like
To know within your being
That whatever any one of them seemed to do,
In the form of a body, or using this illusion of the body—
Try to imagine what it would be like to KNOW

That anything they did was truly
Of no consequence whatsoever.

By that I mean,
See if you can feel within your being
What it would be like to realize that nothing whatsoever,
However small or however great it may seem—
That nothing at all could have any effect
On WHO YOU ARE.

To digress for a moment,
Remember that your fear comes from the belief
That the action which another seems to perform with his body
Can somehow change who you are.
Hear me well.
Nothing is further from the truth.

Try to feel for a moment the freedom you will know
When you realize there is nothing any other being can do
Which can affect your reality in any way.
Imagine a knowing deep within
So secure and so strong that
Any words another might say,
Any feelings another might have,
Can have no effect on you—
Because you are free.
Try to imagine how free you will be
When you realize that no action at all
Can change who you are.

In the extreme, try to imagine that another
Could take the step you call murder,
And seem to kill you.
I tell you, that would not change in any way what you are.
Attempt now, if you can, to feel that.
Feel the safety that will be within you
When you realize that nothing, no one,
Can harm you in any way.

Then, where is your anger?
When you know that you are safe, and you are free,
Then I do not need to admonish you not to be angry.
For there would be no anger within you.
Try for a moment to feel the ABSENCE of anger,

Not something suppressed,
But something truly unborn.
And see how free you feel.

At a level less than the destruction of your body,
So often you fear the actions of another
Because they seem to disrupt the plan you have for your life.
And remember, when you want to maintain that plan,
You feel the desire to defend . . .
Of that we have spoken previously.

Now imagine that truly
Everything is an echo of the Voice for God,
That the plan you have created
Out of YOUR OWN thinking
Is of no value whatsoever.
As you read on,
Try to feel deep within that which you read.

I do not imply that you should not live this life
With joy, with freedom, and with love.
NOT TO VALUE DOES NOT MEAN NOT TO LOVE.
To value means to insist that your own plan be preserved.
The release of that insistence shall bring you your freedom.
Try to imagine for a moment
That you did not fear for,
Or concern yourself with,
The past, or above all, the future.
Try to imagine that you truly
Flowed through your life like a small child.
And as circumstances seemed to change,
You merely adapted and allowed the experience
To flow over you,
Without recourse, and without resistance.

And as you did this,
Imagine that there was a knowing within
That YOUR plan for the future was truly of no consequence.
Imagine that your real joy was in the change,
And the freedom of allowing things to flow,
And to be.

Do this kind of imagining often.
And as oft as you shall do it,

You shall strengthen your awareness of your Self,
Your One Self.

Whenever you catch yourself valuing,
Feeling the need to defend what you think you are,
Or feeling the need to preserve the plan
You have made for the future—
Whenever you feel that struggle within,
Pause for a moment,
And imagine what it would be like
If you did not have that fear,
And did not have that need to preserve your future.
As you do that, you will, bit by bit,
Feel freedom seeping into your soul.

It is true that time is an illusion, a trick, a sleight of hand.
You could, indeed, release all of those fears now, this instant.
But to the extent that one of your greatest values
Is the belief in time,
Then you may choose to have this take time.
And that is quite all right,
For you are free.
When I suggest that you WILL
Slowly feel freedom seeping into your Spirit,
That is my acknowledgment
That you may choose to value your time.
Always realize, however,
That it is not necessary to do so.
For you are free, and could,
At any time,
Release time itself.

So try, whenever you can,
To imagine not valuing.
As you do that,
Try to let the experience flow,
Almost as a daydream about
The freedom that shall come to you.

As I have said,
To give and to receive are one in truth. (L 108)
Also I have said,
You shall give the miracles you have received. (L 159)

For that is naught but Oneness.
And all of that is so.

So as you imagine the freedom
That shall be yours when your values are gone,
Above all imagine giving that freedom to another.
For that is when it shall become your own.
As you seek out your own values in this world,
Try in your imaginings
To sense that you have released the world,
And the others in your world,
From the values which you impose upon them.
See them in their freedom, and in their joy.
As you do that, you shall see yourself as free.

I use the word, "see."
As you "see" your brothers free,
You shall not be seeing them as bodies.
For you shall know that their bodies are not what they are.
That is the step to the Vision of Christ.
As you see them beyond their bodies,
In the Light which is the Son of God,
Then you, likewise,
Shall see your Self in Light,
Not as a body,
But as a wisp of freedom,
Free of the past, and of the future,
Free of all time, and likewise of space.

Hear me well.
It is entirely possible that you walk this world
For as long as you choose,
Without your values.
That which I suggest to you this day
Is not an impossible, nor even unreasonable, goal.
For as I suggested in one of the lessons,
There is a way to walk this world
In which you are not part of it. (32)
And that path involves only the release of your values.

Imagine that you should be FREE,
Here on this earth,
To experience anything your heart could imagine.

Then what would you be imagining?
You would be imagining that no one, no thing,
Would ever castigate you for what you were choosing,
Would ever call you wrong,
Would ever suggest sin,
Would ever suggest that they might deprive you of something
Lest you change your behavior.
Imagine that you were totally free,
Always accepted exactly as you were,
For whatever you imagined,
And in whatever you chose to experience.
For THAT is the Love of God.

As you allow that same freedom to others,
You receive it yourself.
Hear me well, this day.
As you practice, as you play with what I have suggested,
As you do so openly, without resistance,
With courage to seek out the subtle, hidden values
You most need to release—
As you do just that,
You shall save yourself years and years
And lifetimes of your time.

Every value you release shall put a light around your being.
You shall shine, and glow, and radiate
Love and freedom.
And every value you release
Shall put that same light around your world,
Around your circumstance, and all other beings in your world.
And you shall see them as free, and beautiful,
Just as you are.

Indeed, you are the Son of God.
And each brother and each sister is the Son of God,
Each one totally free,
Each one deserving nothing less than total freedom,
Just as you are deserving of the same.
And all that would ever take away
Any of that freedom,
Any of that joy,
Is the values of which we have spoken.

Try diligently to imagine
The absence of the values in your life.
For as you experience that,
You will truly feel that freedom,
That love, and that joy
Coming to you,
And to your entire world.

Blessings upon you all. That is all.

LOVE II

Greetings again. I am Jeshua. I have come this day
To further, with you, my discussion of
A Course in Miracles.

Over the past few weeks,
I have spoken much of your values, and your valuing.
It is so important you realize that
Your values are what create the entire world you see.
You cannot see anything, ever,
Which you have not accorded value. (24)
If you see your body, and believe it to be real,
You have valued it.
If you see the world, and believe it to be real,
That is simply a reflection of your values.
To the extent that you know within that you are but Spirit,
The Holy Son of God,
Unfettered and free,
Unconstrained by what you perceive to be space and time,
Then that is what you value.

As I have spoken of your values,
I have told you
Do not value thus and thus.
Do not value this world, and the things you see in it.
Do not value time.
Do not value circumstance.
Do not value relationships.
Do not value anything in this world.

I know those words can all seem very negative.
But to the extent that they DO seem negative to you,
Know that they are informing you of where your values lie.
If I suggest to you that
You not value a particular thing or circumstance,
And you feel a resistance, or a tightness within,
Know that therein lies a value
To be explored and released.

Freedom from your values brings lightness.
Freedom from your values brings joy.
Freedom from your values brings, above all,
The awareness of freedom.
Since I have spoken so much of values,
Be admonished to diligently pursue,
At the level of your thinking,
That which you seem to value.
Do this that you may discover what it is you value,
In order that you may find your release and your salvation
By allowing the values to dissolve,
And pass out of your life.

Today I wish to move beyond.
I will move to something which you might feel is more positive.
However, I admonish you, with great love,
Do not cease to be aware of your valuing.
Do not cease to be diligent in your goal
To not value what is valueless.
If I do not speak of it, week after week,
I am aware there is a tendency for the diligence to subside.
I admonish you, do not be caught in that trap.
Do not forget the importance of your values.

Today, I would speak with you again, about love.
I shall speak about love
In the context of the absence of your values,
As applied to this world.
Love, as I have said, is freedom.
Love, as I have said, is joy.
Love, as I have said, is peace.
I have also said that Love is the substance of the universe.

What does that mean,
For Love to be the substance of the universe?
The words may sound a bit lofty.
And so, what IS the substance of the universe?
YOU.
And what IS the substance of the universe?
GOD.
And what IS the substance of the universe?
ME,
And all of those whom you call brother.

And what is also the substance of the universe?
EVERY OTHER BEING.
There may be those whom you would not wish to call brother,
Albeit in your misunderstanding.
Those whom you call friend,
Whom you would be glad to call brother,
Those whom you do not call friend,
Whom you might resist calling brother—
All of them are the substance of the universe.
All forms in which the universe appears
Are reflections of its substance.
And that is you.
For you ARE, in your magnitude, Love.

As an aside, for a moment,
I have spoken in the Text of littleness and magnitude. (33)
Littleness is that which you try to give yourself.
Littleness is that which you feel you need and want,
Based on the self you have made.
And indeed, as I have said,
Even that which you believe to be yourself
Is made by you, is a product of your thinking.
And as such, it shall pass away.

The greatest form of littleness
Is your belief that any aspect of what you are
Is different from, or separate from,
The substance of the universe,
Any aspect of it whatsoever.

As you value, what you do is DEFINE.
But your real nature, as the Son of God,
As the substance of the universe,
Hear me well,
Has no need to, and does not, DEFINE anything.
For what you define is a product of your thinking.
Of this we have spoken before.
Your thinking, ultimately, is not real.
So anything to which you give definition,
Anything which you specifically give substance,
(The word "specific" is important here)
Out of your thoughts,
Out of your wishes,
Out of your desires,

Be it positive or negative—
Ultimately is not real.

I have said to you
The natural state of the mind is complete abstraction. (34)
And I was referring to DEFINITION.
The natural state of what you are
As the substance of the universe, as Love itself—
The natural state does not DEFINE anything.
That can seem difficult,
Especially within this world of illusion.
For the illusion itself, all of it,
Is definition.
All illusion here,
The illusion of this earth,
Of this universe,
Of your bodies,
Of the separateness,
Could not exist without that
You had specified, and defined,
Within your being and your thinking,
What it should be.

How is it that you could even exist
Without a definition of what you are?
Of this I have spoken before,
I am sure you have heard the words about your thinking,
And how it ultimately does not mean anything.
How is it that you can exist without definition?
Hear me well. This is most important.
Definition, especially the definition of what you are,
As a body, as a separate being, as an entity—
That is what keeps you from the natural state of your mind.

Therefore, that is also what keeps you from love.
For right now, accept what I will say here
As a lofty goal to be pursued, insofar as it brings you joy.
As long as your mind needs to DEFINE what you are,
You cannot know the meaning of love.
Until such time as you are willing to release yourself
To complete, perfect communication,
Wherein there shall be no separation,
And no secrets of any kind,
You will not be fully able to know your Self as the Son of God.

This is not a condemnation.
For you ARE,
Independent of whatever you might think or define,
The most Holy Son of God,
The most free, the most undefined,
The most loved being you could imagine.
If you choose, for a while yet,
To need to define what you are, and therefore to do so,
Do not feel that I am calling you wrong.
For indeed, all I call you is my brother,
And worthy of all the Love of the universe.
Indeed, not only are you worthy of that Love,
You ARE that Love.

This is what shall happen to you as we proceed.
First, I have said, do not value.
Ultimately I mean do not define.
Do not constrict those whom you would call brother.
Do not confine, do not constrict
That which you would call yourself.
Do not feel there is definition or constriction
In what you call this world.
For it is nothing more than your thought itself,
Projected upon your mind.
And this we call illusion.

As you learn about real Love,
You will go beyond the definitions and constrictions
Which your thinking naturally places upon this illusion.
And as you grow in your understanding,
And your knowledge of love,
You shall also grow in your knowledge and understanding
Of that which you are.
For they are the same.

Do not be confused.
When you reach the point where you know what you are,
You will have no need to DEFINE what you are.
For you shall be free of that limitation.

I have also said
There are but two emotions, love and fear. (2)
Do you know what fear is, in a word?
DEFINITION.

And I have said,
All of this world is a product of nothing but your fear.
How is that so?
It is so thusly.
As you, in your thinking,
Define this world, as you define your brother,
Then deep within you
You have created something which shall pass away.
You call that death, for lack of a better word.
And really, what is death but the belief in nothingness?
And in your illusion of time
You believe that the things you have defined will pass away.

Your freedom from death shall come with your awareness
That this world is NOT something which will pass away,
But rather is something which has never been.
So as you attempt to DEFINE anything,
In that selfsame instant you create within your thinking
The awareness that what you have defined shall pass away.
And therein lies your fear.
To the extent that you free yourself from all definition,
From all specification of what you are,
Of what your brother is,
Of what life is,
Then to that extent shall you be free.

The natural state of the mind is complete abstraction.
In the state of abstraction there is what I call awareness,
And experience, and freedom.
In that state there is knowledge.
And there is Oneness.

There are, indeed, that which appear to be different minds,
Without definition.
But there is, in fact, only One Mind, without definition.
Both are true.
And only in the state of complete abstraction
Can you know that.

One of your lessons recently mentioned
Going "beyond words." (35)
The place beyond words is the state of abstraction.
That of which I speak when I mention going beyond words
Is the absence of definition.

So in your silence, when you use your words,
Use them only as a beginning.
Then allow yourself to BE.
Try not to think,
For then you define.
Try to go beyond the words without,
And this is important,
Without needing to define that which you will experience.

As you can open yourself to that which you will experience,
You are opening yourself to the substance of the universe.
You are opening yourself to your real One Self.
You are opening yourself to your brothers,
Who are One with you.
You are opening yourself to God.
But you are opening yourself,
Most of all,
To Love.
For that is what you are.

Blessings upon you all. That is all.

LEAP OF FAITH I

Greetings again. I am Jeshua. I have come this day
To further, with you, my discussion of
A Course in Miracles.

You have come a great distance in your learning.
But learning, as I have said,
Is not what *A Course in Miracles* is about.
So now it is time to begin to realize
That it is beyond learning you must go.

I have spoken to you the words.
It is not your thinking.
Do not think. Only experience.
There is, indeed, a way in which
You can live your life in that manner.
And the answer lies, as always, in your valuing.
This I cannot overemphasize.

It is not the purpose of this writing, henceforth,
To discuss nothing but valuing,
And to merely continue saying to you,
Thou shalt not value anything in this world.
But, hear me well,
If that is all I did,
And it caused you to eventually
Give up all value you place in this world,
It would be enough.
For you would then be free.
And if that were the approach which you, personally,
Wished to take, it would, indeed,
Reap for you great rewards.

You just read the words,
"Give up all value you place in this world."
That is, for most of you, what your perception entails.
Because of the fact that you do place value in this world,
You feel that it is a matter of "giving up" something

Should you let those values go.
When just the opposite is the truth.

Ceasing to value is not at all a "giving up."
Ceasing to value is a victory, a coming home,
An arriving at the truth of what you are.
Ceasing to value is not a matter of disdaining the world,
Or of developing an aversion to the world.
Rather, ceasing to value is the process of opening your arms
To the freedom that is within you.

If you could only imagine that, in its truth,
For one instant, that would be enough.
For in that instant of feeling the absence of all your values,
You would sense the truth of what you are
So powerfully and so fully
That you would open, without effort,
To the awareness of your true nature.
And you would never be the same.

For most of you,
To truly learn this Course,
To truly experience this Course,
There must come a moment in which you take
What you might call a leap of faith.
This leap of faith is a choice to go, a choice to move,
A choice to become something which you, as yet,
Do not know.
The oddity is that this leap of faith,
Which I shall discuss today,
Shall take you home.

Once again, the problem with this world,
The problem with the valuing that creates this world,
Is that it keeps you from your home.
It keeps you from the awareness of what you are.

As I begin now to guide you on your journey home,
Which is what I am doing,
From now on, try as best you can not to fear.
Try as best you can, in your thinking,
To imagine that the words I have spoken are true.
The measure that will come to you as you do that,
You cannot fathom.

So what is this leap of faith that I say will do nothing except
Move you back to the place where you already are,
That will take you home?
The leap of faith is a thing you do with your mind.
Now, faith does not exist in the Kingdom of God.
Faith is not something to value.
Faith is a tool of your thinking
Which you can use to become free.

What is this faith?
Faith is what you do, whatever you do,
That allows you, in your thinking,
To first, believe,
Second, imagine,
Third, feel,
And fourth, know
That you are the Son of God.

The last step, the knowing, is not something you can do here.
However, do not fear.
For God Himself comes to wrap you in His arms
And carry you, safe and secure,
Into the knowledge of what you are.

Again, I have spoken to you, over and over,
These past few weeks,
Of your valuing.
I have said,
Do not value anything of this world.
Again, all I have meant is for you to realize that
Nothing of this world,
Nothing you see with your eyes,
Nothing you hear with your ears, perceive with your senses—
Nothing of that has anything to do
With what you are in truth.
So when I advise you to let go of your valuing,
I am merely saying this—
In your thinking, realize that your senses,
Which you have created for the purpose of
Functioning within this illusion—
Realize that your senses
Do not speak to you of what you ARE.

If you but realized that,
Then, of course,

You would at once cease to believe
Any of the things your senses seem to tell you.
And that will be the leap of faith of which I speak.

How is it that such a leap of faith
Will eventually bring you home?
Imagine with me, for a moment, as you read.
Imagine that you were actually aware
That your senses do not speak to you of what you are.
Imagine that you knew, in your thinking,
That each person's physical eyes see a different image;
That one million of you could look at
What you would call the same object,
And what would be perceived
Would be one million different images.

Ah yes, you all speak of the image.
And there is similarity enough,
Stemming from your Oneness,
To allow you to speak of the image,
And to believe that you are seeing with your eyes,
The same thing.
But indeed, you are not.
What each of you is doing
Is perceiving the expression of that which is within.
Always, in your perception, that is what happens.

Likewise, imagine, with your hearing,
That a thousand of you heard a sound,
Or more clearly, listened to words spoken by another.
Truly, one thousand of you would hear a different thing.
That, I am certain, is easy for you to realize.
You can attend a lecture,
Or watch something on your televisions;
And I am sure you have, many times,
Shared the hearing with another,
And then attempted later to speak of it,
Only to find that what you heard
Was dramatically different from what the others heard.

It is simply that your senses
Do not report to you anything of truth.
Your senses only cause you to become aware,
At some level, of that which is within you.

Imagine, likewise, that a thousand of you
Touched the same surface, to feel what it was like.
The result would be a thousand different responses.
If you find this not easy to believe,
Spend some time thinking of this.
Watch, in your own experiences, for its evidence.
Quite soon, you will come to realize the disparity that exists
When you compare what you think you have seen,
Or heard, or felt,
With what another has seen, or heard, or felt.

There is nothing reliable,
There is nothing of truth,
There is nothing of meaning,
There is nothing of the Kingdom of God
In what your senses report to you.
But, indeed, you have valued your senses.
For it is those senses
Which have caused you to respond with thinking,
And to form the concepts of what you are.
And that concept of who you are, as I have said,
Is just one more value.

So the leap of faith of which I am speaking
Will bring you to a point
Where you can say
"I DO NOT KNOW."
And from there you will jump safely and securely
Into eternity, and into your freedom.

This day I have spoken to you of faith,
And the leap of faith that will take you beyond this world.
I have suggested that you begin
By coming to believe, in your thinking,
That your senses do not bring you truth.
Images, yes. Truth, no.

If your thinking, if your senses, do not bring you truth,
Then wherein lies the truth?
The answer is simple.
And I have been saying it all along.
The truth lies beyond your thinking.
And again, how do you get there?
By saying, "I DO NOT KNOW."

The purpose, ultimately, of *A Course in Miracles* is
To bring you to a point where you can say,
"I do not know,"
And still be unafraid.
When you arrive there,
You will find yourself at the doorstep of eternity.
The door is unlatched, and opens at your touch.
If takes no effort to swing open the door to your true Self,
The door to eternity.

Remember, your valuing is nothing more than that
Which separates you, which binds you to this world,
Which causes you to believe that this world
Has something to do with what you are.
None of that is true.

In your thinking, as you work within it,
Over and over again, say to yourself,
And feel the response as you say,
"The world I see holds nothing that I want." (L 128)
The world you see cannot tell you of what you are.
If you do that, over and over again,
You will come to a point
Where the words will yield to a feeling
Which comes as you say, "I do not know."
And that feeling will be a giant step toward the realization
That you are the Son of God.

You exist.
That you do not seem to doubt.
And that is enough.
When you come to believe that this world
Does NOT tell you of what you are,
So that you do NOT know,
And yet realize that you DO exist,
Then what will happen?
You will open.
And what will be opening is your real Self.
What will be opening is the door to eternity.

What shall then enter your mind
Is a different awareness from anything
You have felt before on this earth.

There shall come an awareness
Of that which you truly are.
That awareness shall erase all of your fear,
All of your doubts,
All of your pain,
All of your grief,
All of your sorrow.
That awareness shall erase your past.
That awareness shall erase your future.
That awareness shall erase all thought of sin.
And all that shall be left is light, and joy, and freedom.
For that is what you are.

Blessings upon you all. That is all.

LEAP OF FAITH II

Greetings again. I am Jeshua. I have come this day
To further, with you, my discussion of
A Course in Miracles.

Last time I spoke with you about the leap of faith,
And how it was that your valuing,
Rather your release from valuing anything in this world,
Would set you free—
And how it is that your valuing is nothing more
Than the delineation of that which you believe yourself to be.
Then I said that the leap of faith which you may take,
Indeed, which you MUST take to free yourself from this world,
Is to come to the point where you can freely and joyfully say,
"I do not know."

Now, for you to say, "I do not know,"
Is an extremely positive statement.
It is a statement of such great freedom,
And of such great release,
That if you knew what joy it will bring you,
You would move to, and beyond, that point,
In the twinkling of an eye.

For when you say, "I do not know,"
You are not, in fact, referring to your One Self.
You are referring to your thinking,
To that which binds you to this world,
To that which has created this world you think you see.

So when you move to the point where you say,
"I do not know,"
What you are really saying is,
And you can say it with celebration,
I DO KNOW that this world is not myself.
You are really saying,
I DO KNOW I have an identity as the Son of God,
Which is beyond this world.

You are really saying,
I DO KNOW that, to the extent that God is joy
And peace and freedom,
Then so am I.

So I want to emphasize for you that to say
''I do not know''
Can, and should, be a thing of great joy unto you.
For when you say, ''I do not know,'' and realize as you say it,
That this world has nothing whatsoever to do
With what you truly are,
Then you may be assured as you say those words,
That you, in reality, are standing tall,
Spreading your wings, and saying aloud,
I AM FREE.

Now, it seems, for those of you who still believe
That this world, in some measure,
Does have something to do with what you are,
That to say, ''I do not know,''
Can be quite fearful.
For as we have said, to say, ''I do not know,''
Means that you must let go of
That which you believe yourself to be.
And if you do, it seems, you will surely die.

But I tell you, to say, ''I do not know,''
To say that this world cannot bring you
To the knowledge of your Self,
Is, indeed, your freedom.
For what happens in the instant
When you realize within your being that you do not know—
In that instant there comes the awareness of God.

And all that keeps you, any of you,
From the certainty of what you are as the Son of God
Is the valuing of this earth.
Indeed, ultimately, your values are your statements
That say, ''I do know.''
And in your valuing, what you are saying is,
I believe that MY thoughts are the creator of All That Is.
I believe that my thoughts and my perceptions
Have displaced those of God.

I am sure when you see it that way,
You can surely smile,
As a parent would at a small child
As he plays his silly games.
You can, indeed, chuckle as you see yourself
Imagining that your thinking,
With all its bonds, with all its fear,
With all its misery,
Somehow supersedes, and becomes instead,
The Voice of God.

Is it as if a whisper could overcome the power of a hurricane.
But as you whisper, "I do know,"
Because you ARE the Son of God,
It is given that your whisper can, indeed,
Seem to you to overcome the mightiness of God.
Your imagining that you do know
Can have such power for you
Because that IS the power you have
As the Son of God.

Rejoice in the awareness that your illusions
Can have such strength, and such magnitude.
For they are a reflection, albeit a tiny reflection,
Of the strength and magnitude
Of the reality of your One Self.

So your goal, then, is merely this—
To cease the whispering,
To cease the tiny voices that urge you to say,
"I do know"—
To let go of the value you place on the self
You have defined in terms of this world—
And thereby to open to the mighty Voice of God,
Which shall fill you with the awareness
Of what you truly are.

So I have come to tell you this—
If you can come to the point where,
Even in your thinking, even academically,
You can say, "I do not know,
For I AM the Son of God"—
That speaking of the words, that academic understanding,
Which is NOT the reality of what you are,

Shall slowly seep into your being,
Until one day the awareness, the certainty,
And the experience beyond the words
Shall be yours.

When you say, ''I do not know,''
You do not leave a vacuum which can remain empty.
When you arrive at the point
Where you can take this leap of faith,
You will find there is nothing to fear.
For your tendency is to think
That in not knowing you shall cease to exist.
But I have come to tell you,
With the entire love of the universe,
There is no vacuum there.
There is no ceasing to exist.
There is only the immediate blossoming and awareness
Of your reality as the Son of God.

That experience shall come, perhaps in an instant.
That shall be the moment
In which your thinking passes into oblivion,
And your experience becomes what you are.
You, in your power, can choose to have this take time.
If you do choose thusly,
Do not make yourself wrong.
Simply realize that it is your power as the Son of God
That allows you to experience whatever you will,
To take as much time as you wish.
And even that realization shall bring you closer
To the point where you can let go,
And in that instant be free.

So what am I really saying to you this day?
I am saying to you,
The prison of this earth, and prison it is,
Is the product, the representation,
Of that which you value.
Even if it be that which you consider beautiful,
Still it creates your prison.
For it shall pass away, and you shall grieve.
And you must live in the fear of the time
When it shall, indeed, pass away.

Because God, and Real Love, cannot change,
The things of this Earth are not,
And cannot be, of God.
So as you let go of your valuing,
Knowing that it cannot be of God,
You simply let go of that which binds you to this earth.

And as you say,
"I do not know," you are, in reality,
When you can MEAN those words,
Smiling and laughing and spreading your wings of freedom.
All it demands you do is spread your wings.
And then the wind,
Which is your real nature as the Son of God,
Shall become a presence flowing beneath those wings,
Lifting you and carrying you,
Without effort,
High and higher and beyond,
To a joy and a peace and a knowing
That you, as yet, cannot imagine.

Hear me well.
You SHALL be able to walk this earth
For the remainder of the days you choose,
With wings unfolded,
And the breath of God being the wind beneath those wings.
And a joy which shall lift you to the heavens of your mind
Will be yours, moment to moment.

The key that shall bring you that joy
Is your forgiveness.
Forgiveness is your only function here. (36)
And remember that forgiveness is just
Your awareness that there is no value in this world,
That there is nothing in this world
Which can speak to you of what you are.
As you realize that what you are is beyond this world,
You shall rejoice as you say,
"I do not know."

And before you finish the words,
There shall come the breath of God beneath your wings.
My brothers, let go of your values.

Do not approach this with fear.
Do not see the statement,
''I do not know,''
As negative.
Rather see it as your step to joy,
And a flight that shall take you
To heavens beyond what you can even imagine.

Blessings upon you all. That is all.

SPIRIT

Greetings again. I am Jeshua. I have come this day
To further, with you, my discussion of
A Course in Miracles.

Throughout the Course, thus far,
I have ultimately been speaking to you of values.
As I stated at the outset,
The first section of the Workbook is designed
To help you let go of, to break down,
The false beliefs which cause your illusions.
And the second section is to help you replace them
With the true beauty of what you are,
Which is the Son of God. (37)

To the extent that you have chosen time,
And choose to have this take time,
Then there is much for you to learn.
We will proceed as if that is your choice.
Because for most of you it is.
Never forget, however, that you are always free
To complete this Course in an instant,
And to be, in that same instant, totally free.
And when you are totally free,
You shall walk this earth with joy,
With freedom, and with the total absence of fear,
For as long as you like,
And then dismiss it all in an instant,
At such time as you choose to do so.

So it is that I have spoken to you of your values,
And the fact that your values are nothing more than
The beliefs you hold about what you are.
Your values create, within this world of thoughts,
What you are.
Those same values are therefore that which separates you
From your real nature as the Son of God,
And as Spirit.

It is that of which I would speak today.
You are Spirit.
You are not a body.
You are not confined.
You are not constrained.

All of that which you have chosen to believe about yourself,
And therefore to value, is not true.
Insofar as you still see yourself as a body,
Constrained to walk this earth
With small steps upon its surface—
Insofar as you see yourself constrained
To communicate with naught but words,
Be they spoken or written,
You limit yourself.
And indeed, limited is not what you are.
You are Spirit.

Some people say, "free as the wind."
But I say to you, compared to the wind,
Your freedom is infinitely greater.
For the wind is the movement of that
Which you imagine to be air, and molecules.
It is confined to a place, this earth.
It is confined to speed, for it can only move so fast.
It is even confined to where it can go;
For there are barriers which cut out the wind.

But you, that which you truly are,
Are Spirit.
You are everywhere.
You, the Son of God, Spirit,
Are not of space and time.
That which you believe to be yourself (this body)
Is limited by your space and time,
Confined to little finite points of both.
Ultimately, space and time are the same,
Being but slightly different perceptions.
And you are not of space, nor time.

When I say to you,
"Be still . . . Forget this world, forget this Course,
And come with wholly empty hands unto your God." (63)

I am saying to you,
Do as you can to release all belief
That you are limited by space and time.

It is one thing to say you are everywhere.
But, hear me well,
To say that you are everywhere
Is predicated on a belief that a "where" exists.
But for you, as Spirit,
There is no "where."
There only IS.
As a Spirit, you are so free that
Whenever you experience anything,
Whenever the FEELING permeates your being
(That indeed, is what your experience is, your FEELINGS),
That experience, that feeling,
Simply IS.
And there is no aspect of all of Creation
That does not become aware of
Exactly the same feelings you have created.

There is no limitation based on "where," or even on "when,"
To the sharedness of that experience.
For Spirit simply IS.

Whenever you choose to FEEL something,
You are using the power of your creative ability,
Given you by God.
And God Itself,
And all other aspects of the One Self, the One Spirit,
Are co-creators with you.

If you wish, think of it this way—
I have told you, there are no private thoughts. (5)
That is so true that those of you
Who still believe in bodies and space and time
Must find it frightening.
Everything you experience
Is instantly and completely known
By all of Creation.
Everything that ANY aspect of Creation experiences
Is known fully, in that instant,
By all other aspects of Creation,
Including you.

Note that I am still using the word "you."
But do not forget what I have told you.
"You" are the collection of thoughts and beliefs and values
By which "you" are defined within your thinking mind.
And "you" does not exist.
For those thoughts are not of reality.

Because you are Spirit,
Insofar as you can FEEL at that level,
You shall realize the truth which I have just spoken.
Your leap of faith is to come to the point
Where you say, "I do not know."
And that leap shall take you to your freedom.
For when you say, "I do not know,"
Even to not knowing what "you" are,
You automatically open to the experience of the One Self,
Which IS what you are.
In that moment,
You shall joyfully release all the limited thoughts
Which would constrain, or confine you
To this world of illusion.

Ah, yes. Hear me well.
You are not a body.
You are free. (L 199)
There is no "where" you cannot go,
Indeed, where you are not already.
So nothing of this world of limitation
Can have anything to do with what you are.
It is as if you took the wind in its freedom,
Made it solid by condensing all its molecules
Into one little block, dense and heavy,
Set it upon the earth,
And then tried to imagine that it was still free.

The freedom you give up when you imagine yourself
To be a body, instead of the Spirit you are,
Takes you, in contrast, farther away from your real nature
Than is the wind from being one frozen block of molecules
Upon the earth.

You are not a body.
Rejoice in that.
Rejoice in the fact that whatever you experience

Is an expression of the creative power of God,
Which you cannot lose.
You ARE the Son of God,
And that cannot change.
Indeed, as you think now about this earth,
About what you perceive to be your body and its surroundings,
About your air, and the wind—
As you think about all of this
In light of the truth that you are Spirit,
Realize that all of that which you experience
Is a reflection of the creative power
Given you by God.

Rejoice in the fact that your pain can seem so real.
Rejoice in the fact that your fear can terrify you
To the last fiber of your being.
Rejoice in the fact that your imagined illnesses
Can violate every seeming aspect
Of that which you look upon as your body.

Why do I say rejoice?
I say rejoice because when you,
With new vision, can say, "I am Spirit,"
And can say, "Yes, all that I experience IS
A reflection of my creative power as the Son of God"—
Then you become free to rejoice in that power.
If you looked upon your body,
And it seemed to be ethereal, and of no moment,
Then how weak would be your power as the Son of God.
But as you all know,
Your body can seem so real
It is difficult for you, initially,
To imagine the truth of what
I have been saying these many weeks.

The power with which you can create, and choose, illusion
Is but a fraction of the power you have as the Son of God.
So as you see your illusions, use them.
Use your pain, use your misery, use your fear,
All as things which demonstate to you,
Lovingly,
How great is the power within you
That creates whatever it is you would experience.

Now, hear me well.
When you come to realize that
Only your values and thinking create this illusion,
And when you come to realize that
You, Son of God, ARE Spirit,
Then you shall see the world anew,
With the eyes of vision.
You will truly see the world
As a reflection of your power to create
And to experience anything you wish.
I tell you,
When that truth first goes beyond your thinking to experience,
When you have that first instant of awareness that
That power IS within you,
That everything in your existence
Is the result of that power in action—
In that same instant will you know yourself to be free.

In that instant you will invariably decide
That your fear, your misery, and your illness
Are a source and a matter of laughter,
And not of great import.
With a laugh, and a chuckle,
You will let them go.
Truly, I tell you now, 'tis that easy.
A moment of laughter, a twinkle in your eye,
And it is done.

And what it requires is that you EXPERIENCE,
Beyond your thinking,
The reality of what you are.
So I say to you again, this day,
You are not a body.
You are free.
You are One Self.
And all that you imagine IS,
Unencumbered by space and time.
Rejoice in that awareness.

This is a Course in mind training.
What we are doing is helping you to think differently,
All the while telling you not to think.
For your thinking truly is of no consequence.

So for you, as long as you choose
To believe in this illusion of space and time and bodies,
Your goal shall be to discipline your thinking
So that you can let it go,
And move beyond it.

So my advice to you this day is this:
Never lose sight of what I have told you about your freedom.
Every time you think of this Course,
Think to yourself,
"I am not a body. I am free.
For I am exactly as God created me." (L 201)
Always begin and end your thinking about this Course
With that idea.

And insofar as disciplining your mind and your thinking
Can cause your thinking to change,
That will be a significant step towards your freedom.
For as you say to yourself the words,
Which are thoughts, and have no meaning,
Slowly, in your time,
You will begin to FEEL the truth of those words.
And each time you do,
You will be thousands of steps closer to your freedom.

And then the day will come when,
Beyond the words, beyond the thinking, within your being,
Shall come the awareness and the knowing,
"'Tis true, I am NOT a body. I AM free."
And in that instant, FREE is what you shall be.

Blessings upon you all. That is all.

GRATITUDE

Greetings again. I am Jeshua. I have come this day
To further, with you, my discussion of
A Course in Miracles.

Today I would speak with you of gratitude.
Your recent lessons may have spoken of gratitude.
It is true that gratitude, as gratitude really is,
Is difficult to understand.
For as you, in your world, think of gratitude,
The tendency is nearly always to feel that
Gratitude is something you extend in response to
A gift or blessing you have received from someone else.
You likewise view gratitude as something
Which is returned to you by someone
To whom you have given a blessing or gift.

There is a tendency within the world
To feel that gratitude is, somehow, an obligation.
If someone gives you a gift,
Be it material, or a gift of the spirit,
You feel it inappropriate not to say, at the least, ''Thank you,''
Which is to honor the giver of the gift.
The counterpart is that if you extend
A gift of love to another being,
You have a tendency to feel that the receiver
Should (hear the word ''should'') acknowledge, somehow,
The gift you have given him,
Even if with nothing more than a simple
''Thank you.''
And you call the return,
After the receipt of a gift,
Gratitude.

I have come to tell you today,
That is a misperception of what gratitude really is.
Gratitude is a blessing so great you can hardly imagine.
Gratitude is a blessing that comes to you,
Without recourse, automatically,
When first, and when at once, you love.

Hear me well.
I have spoken to you these many weeks
Of love, and the Love of God.
Love, which is your reality,
Love, which is of God,
Love, which is the glue of the universe,
Is not possible so long as you value anything of this world.
And love and gratitude, real gratitude,
Go hand in hand.
Likewise, so long as you would value this world,
You cannot know the blessing of your own gratitude,
Or the seeming gratitude of others.

When you receive a gift from another,
And you feel, in some sense,
That you should, or want to, return a thank you,
That being a measure of gratitude,
Then you are valuing.
And what you have done, in that moment of perception
When you have felt gratitude toward another—
You have felt, and you have created
A SEPARATION between you and the other being
Whom you perceived to be the giver
Of the gift you felt you received.

For is it not true that,
In order for you to receive a gift FROM ANOTHER,
Even be it a gift of love,
You must first have defined within your thinking
A being SEPARATE from yourself
Who could extend to you that love,
Or that something, which you did not have.
And I tell you, that is an impossibility.

That notion is the source of your earthly gratitude.
Hear me well.
In this moment, in every moment,
Be it of the past, or of what you call the future,
There exists nothing, ever, which you do not already have.
Try if you can, for a moment,
To allow yourself, beyond your thinking,
Beyond the academics, beyond the imaginings,
To FEEL something of what I have just said.
Always, in every aspect of your existence,
In this world or apart from it,

There is nothing which you, your One Self,
Does not already have.
You have everything.

Now, hear me well, once again.
You ARE everything.
Try to feel, within the depths of your being,
Beyond your thinking,
The fullness, the richness, the peace,
The aliveness, the certainty,
That must be yours when once you realize there is nothing,
Nothing in the world of Spirit,
Nothing in the world of illusion,
Which is not already yours.

You are not a body.
You are free.
You are just as God created you. (L 201)
And God created you thusly—
That whatever you choose to create,
To imagine, to feel into your existence,
Is yours.
Hear me well, once again.
I have told you, seemingly over and over,
You have created every aspect of your own existence.
Now I say it but once again.
There is nothing outside your Self to give you anything.
There is nothing outside your Self
To receive the little gifts you might imagine you have given.

Remember, in your imaginings of this world,
You are actually wishing for, and creating, separation.
And ultimately, your true gratitude,
And therefore your love,
Will rest upon your awareness, within your being,
That you ARE the Holy Son of God,
Co-creator WITH All That Is,
And co-creator OF all that is.
And in that awareness,
You shall know that separation is not possible.

Now, I have said to you,
You cannot love, you cannot know gratitude,
If you still limit yourself by your values.
How is this so?

Remember, your values are the constructs you have formed,
Out of your thinking,
Which you have come to believe
Have something real to do with what you are.
In your valuing, which begins with your thinking,
You start with the belief that
You can have thoughts which are yours alone.
You start with the thought
That you can have a feeling, an awareness,
Which belongs only to you.
That is not so.
There are no private thoughts. (5)
For you are One.

However, in your valuing, based on your thoughts,
You come to see YOURSELF, just as with your thoughts,
As separate.
In your belief in separation
You perceive that which others have which you do not,
Or that which you have which others do not.
Sometimes you see this as misery which is yours alone
While the others seem to be blissfully happy.
Sometimes you see it as a blessing
Based on sufferings you do not have,
While others seem to suffer, for one reason or another.
It is your valuing that has created for you
This belief in separation.

You may now perhaps recall the previous time
When I spoke to you of your one problem, separation,
And the one solution, its elimination. (L 79–80)
Salvation IS your One Self.

Now let us reflect further about
Gratitude, and love, and your valuing.
You are One Self.
God is One Self.
I, who speak to you this day, am One Self.
Every brother whom you perceive,
Be it in love, or in hatred, or in anger,
Every brother is the One Self.
You, and I, and he, and she, and God are One.
And every aspect of every being whom we perceive
Is part of what we are.

Every aspect of every being whom you see, or perceive,
Helps to make you complete as the Son of God.

To turn the statement around a bit,
I cannot exist as One Self unless I realize, and feel,
That every aspect of all of Life, as I see it and know it,
Completes me in what I am.
This is not really different from saying that
I am Spirit, I am co-creator with God;
And all that I am, and see, and perceive,
Is a creation of my own, of my One Self.

So you see, on the one hand you say to yourself,
All that I perceive, all that I experience,
Is, indeed, my own creation.
And on the other hand,
You look out at your world, as you are still wont to do,
And you say, every being, every brother whom I see,
Completes me, and makes me full in my One Self.
Without him, or her, or God,
I cannot be complete.
And if I am not complete,
There will be within me a hollowness,
A lacking, a fear, an emptiness,
Which can but reflect, somehow,
A belief in death.

So when I look out at the world of OTHERS,
Which is the perspective associated with this earth,
And I realize, first, that I have cherished and chosen
Every aspect of that which I see;
And secondly, that every aspect of what I see
Is offering me the blessing of God,
And my completeness as the Son of God—
Then what I shall feel is love.

Again, hear me well.
To the extent that I look out upon the world of illusion,
The world of separation,
And see aspects of my One Self
Which I deem undesirable,
Or which I deem desirable,
I but look at my own values.
And those values shall cause me to desire

To bring to myself certain aspects that I see;
Just as they shall also cause me to want
To separate myself from certain aspects
Which I deem undesirable.
And always any desire to be separate
Is to disclaim that what I am seeing
Is part of my One Self.

Now I would speak to you again of love.
Love makes no judgments.
Love does not compare.
Love is not based on values.
Love merely IS.
Love does not editorialize experience into categories
Of good and bad, desirable and undesirable,
Free and not free.
Love merely IS.

As you free yourself of your values,
Of your editorials,
You shall be free to open
To all aspects of this life you have created for yourself.
And then you shall, at last,
See that all of it is beautiful.
For all of it is experience.
And all of it is lessons God would have you learn. (L 193)
In all of it, if you forgive, if you release it from your values,
You shall see it differently.

Your gratitude, then, is your awareness within your own being
That EVERYTHING IS YOUR GIFT TO YOUR SELF.
Your gratitude, then, is your awareness within your being
That you already have EVERYTHING.
Your gratitude, then, is your awareness
Within this world of illusion
That every being IS your One Self.
And since every being, including your Self,
Has everything,
Then there is nothing that you can, could, or would want to
Withhold from your brother.

In this world of illusion,
Gratitude goes out to your brother
For loving you enough to be,
Within the perceptions of your mind,

That which you need him to be—
Never forgetting that you are the same.

In love there are no values, and no judgments.
Love merely IS.
In your love,
You know that everything which you perceive
Is of your Self,
That nothing can ever be done to you,
Or given to you,
Or taken away.
In your gratitude,
You know that every gift you can seem to give
Is ultimately given to your Self.

It matters not, in this world of illusion,
Whether someone deems to say thank you.
For that is merely illusion.
And there is nothing in this world that has any effect
On the reality of your One Self.
So there is nothing in this world you could possibly want,
Including a thank-you.
For all of it, in truth,
You have already received within your Self.

Your love shall offer freedom to all your brothers.
And then you shall find yourself free.
Your gratitude shall extend
To every aspect of the world you see.
And your gratitude completes you as the Son of God.

And as you extend that gratitude,
Your forgiveness will but happen.
You will see all of life differently.
You shall see a light and a love shining within all that you see.
Then you shall realize, immediately,
That the same light is shining back
And illuminating your own soul.
Then you shall smile, and know this within—
I would give everything to everyone,
In gratitude.
For all of it is mine.

Blessings upon you all. That is all.

FORGIVENESS III

Greetings again. I am Jeshua. I have come this day
To further, with you, my discussion of
A Course in Miracles.

You have now moved into what I have labeled
Part II of the Workbook.
There is a very important shift
Which you almost certainly wish to accomplish
In your practicing, in your learning.
We have spoken of going beyond your thinking,
Of going beyond your words. (35)
Indeed, the more you can accomplish that,
The better will be your learning,
The faster will be your progress,
And the stronger will be your Spirit.

When I say,
Go beyond the thinking, beyond the words,
I mean different things.
As I have said so often,
Your thoughts are not the measure of your reality.
Rather, your thoughts are actually a distortion
Which would confuse you,
And move you away from what your reality is,
Which is the Son of God.
So it is that to go beyond your thinking,
To allow yourself not to think and not to analyze—
That is to free yourself from the barriers which separate you
From the reality of what you are.

Secondly, in your reality as Spirit,
In the reality that you are not a body,
In the truth that you are free,
You will find that the reality of what you are
Is to be found, not in your thinking,
But in your EXPERIENCE, in your FEELINGS.

These many weeks we have spoken of thoughts,
And of mind training.
So if you need a label, you might say
That now we will switch to FEELINGS training.
So henceforth, as you practice,
As you spend your time in silence,
With your One Self, with the Holy Spirit,
In the presence of God,
Be aware of, and constantly have as your goal,
Not your thoughts you have
But the feelings, the experiences.

Indeed, if you find yourself saying, within your head,
Words which represent thoughts,
While in your awareness you are feeling something different,
Be aware that the reality, the creation,
Lies in your feelings.
So make this shift as best you can.
Never lose sight of the fact
That the importance lies not in your thoughts,
But in your experience, in your feelings.

If, as you practice, you find yourself
Feeling something which is not joy, which is not peace,
Try to be still and allow the barriers, allow the blocks,
To dissolve.
For then reality will enter.
I tell you, this WILL happen.

Insofar as you have chosen, and believe in, time,
It may seem difficult at first.
But the power of your Spirit which chooses to believe in time
Also chooses to allow you to learn in time.
So, while an instant is all that you need,
Your belief in time blesses you with a belief in perseverance.
So as you choose time,
Also choose perseverance.
And you will be rewarded, indeed.

As you find that your feelings may not be commensurate with
The joy, the peace, and the certainty of God,
Simply try to be still and allow other feelings,
Which ARE of God,

To replace the ones you had.
Persevere, and it WILL happen.
But never lose sight of the fact that you have within you
The total capability of allowing all of it to happen in one instant,
If you choose.

I wish to speak to you again, this day, of forgiveness.
We have spoken of forgiveness as being many things.
I would speak to you again of forgiveness,
With intent to aid you in your shift
From your thinking to your feelings.
I have told you
Forgiveness is not ever forgiving someone else
For what he, or she, has done to you.
I have told you that forgiveness is
Nothing more than the realization that, indeed,
There is nothing to value here on this earth.
I have said to you, forgiveness is nothing more
Than your awareness that nothing whatsoever in this earth
Has anything, really, to do with
What you are as the Son of God.

I have told you that forgiveness is your freedom
From all valuing of anything here.
I have also said that your valuing is ultimately
That which creates your sense of identity,
Your beliefs in what you are.
So your forgiveness must also encompass
The realization that the constructs,
The thoughts you have designed about who you are,
Are not of God,
And ultimately do not exist.

Your forgiveness, then, will take you to a place
Where you are aware that you, and I, and your brothers,
Are but One Self.
I have spoken to you of the separation,
And how it is that your forgiveness
Is the release of all belief in separation itself—
Or rather, the awareness that separation does not,
And cannot, exist.

I speak to you again this day of forgiveness,
Because your goal now is to move beyond your thinking,

Beyond you mind training,
To your feelings.
If it is so, and indeed it is so,
That nothing from outside yourself can ever be done to you,
Or happen to you,
Then you are truly invulnerable,
And you MUST BE the creator of every aspect of your life.
When I say that forgiveness is your only function here, (36)
In large measure, it would be sufficient for you to totally own,
At the level of experience, the level of feelings,
The truth of those words.

Be aware of what that would mean.
Simply this—that always, automatically,
As second nature, without pause,
You would realize fully and openly, that every event,
Every circumstance, every relationship,
Every happening in your life,
Is simply and totally your own choice, and your own creation.
Now imagine how your life would be if you FELT that reality.
Imagine that with every minute circumstance in your life,
Your response was always,
"I KNOW that I have created this."
If you were confused, you might say,
"Why would I choose this?"
But never would you doubt that it was your own creation.
Imagine that you FELT the reality of that.

Certain things could not enter your mind.
The most important of these would be anger.
Insofar as your feelings are aware
That everything is YOUR OWN CHOICE,
Then anger at another, or a circumstance,
COULD NOT EXIST.
So the statement that forgiveness is not, ever,
Forgiving someone else for what he has done to you
Becomes a statement without meaning.
So you may see, that in the reality of what you are,
Forgiveness itself is an illusion,
And shall pass away.

So while you still use your minds and thoughts a while,
Always attempt, in your practicing and your learning,
To pause until you can, first, think,

And second, FEEL, within yourself
That you are the creator of your own life—
And that all gratitude is due unto yourself.
Try to FEEL deep within
That any brother, any circumstance in your life,
Is there simply at your request, to complete you,
And to complete that which you have chosen to experience.

So it is that your gratitude is due only unto yourself.
Therefore, the only response due any of your brothers
Is that of gratefulness for being in the circumstance
YOU have chosen, and requested of them.
Always do this, if you would learn forgiveness.
Always do your very best to interpret every single circumstance
As but your choice.
If you feel a threat of fear,
If you feel the presence of anger,
Pause, and be still.
And in your stillness, say to yourself, in words,
"I am the Holy Son of God.
There is nothing that can happen to me
But it be my own choice.
And I shall extend my gratitude
To that which I perceive as my world,
For helping me to be free to choose that which I will."

Insofar as you still choose to need mind training,
And most of you do,
Use that statement many times per day.
Pause, initially, many times per day.
For in the few seconds you take as you pause
To allow yourself to be free of this world
And the value you place upon it—
In those few seconds, repeated over and over,
You shall gain yourself weeks and months and years
In your progress toward peace,
And the awareness of your reality as the Son of God.

The second thing I would suggest
Relates once again to your valuing.
Whenever, in your moments of time,
You find yourself choosing upset, or uncertainty,
Always it is fear.
And always your fear is of your own death.

Always your fear is for the loss of something you have valued
Here, in this world.
Once again, forgiveness is your only function here.
When you feel upset, or pain,
Know that you are feeling fear.
And know, as I have previously told you,
That you have chosen, of yourself,
That same fear.
Know that you have chosen that fear through your valuing.
And in your forgiveness, pause, and do what you can to be still.
For in your stillness shall come your One Self,
Shall come the Voice of God.
And in your stillness you will become aware
Of what you have valued,
And which is causing you pain.
And then, with love in your heart,
You may release the value,
And move on to joy without fear.

I admonish you again,
From henceforth, let your goal be that which you FEEL,
Not what you think.
When you pause, in your moment of silence,
Always be aware of the feeling.
When the feeling of peace shall come, cherish it, reinforce it,
And return to it as many times as you can,
That it may become stronger and stronger within your mind.
And when you find a certainty
Creeping into your being that says,
Indeed, you have created your own existence,
Then do your best to return to that feeling again and again,
As oft as you can,
That it may grow and prosper within your Spirit.

And soon, you shall no longer need the words.
For the feeling shall be there in your silence.
And with it shall come the Voice for God.
And when you, in a moment,
Find yourself peaceful,
Realize you have understood
There is nothing in this world to value;
There is nothing in this world that can affect
What you are, as Spirit, as the Son of God.
And as that feeling comes,

Pause as often as you can,
To allow that feeling to grow
And prosper within your awareness.
And as you pause more and more often,
And FEEL the peace of God within you,
You shall grow into the full awareness of what you are—
And, indeed, much faster than you think.

You move now to a new phase of your learning.
As you do, be excited that you are working with your feelings,
Which are not new,
But which are to be emphasized more and more
Along the pathway to your peace
And the awareness of what you are,
Which is the Son of God.
At the level of your feelings,
Never stop pausing to say these words,
And to feel their reality growing within you—
I am not a body.
I am free.
For I am still as God created me. (L 201)

Blessings upon you all. That is all.

SALVATION

Greetings again. I am Jeshua. I have come this day
To further, with you, my discussion of
A Course in Miracles.

Remember, in this second part of your year of learning,
We have switched somewhat.
Earlier we spoke of a Course in mind training.
Last time I spoke with you, and told you
This can now be thought of as a Course in feelings training.
For the reality of what you experience, and of what you are,
Is not your thinking,
Indeed, is beyond your thinking,
And is that which you EXPERIENCE.

Actually, that which you are,
As co-creator with God, as the Son of God,
Is even beyond what you call feelings.
So if you get, somewhere deep within,
A sense that even the feelings
Are not quite what it's all about,
Be aware that, with that feeling,
You are sensing truth.

However, while you walk this earth,
You cannot go to the realm of knowledge.
So be it sufficient now to realize
That your thinking is not the answer,
Indeed, is the problem,
And the source of the problem.
Your feelings are much closer to your reality.

Today I would speak to you of salvation.
The question in your Workbook says,
"What is Salvation?" (38)
Once again, as you read these words,
Try not to hear them with your thinking.
Rather, let them become experience,
And feel their meaning.

Hear me well.
Salvation is not even necessary.
Salvation does not even exist in the Kingdom of God.
This is true in the same sense that forgiveness is not necessary;
And forgiveness does not even exist in the Kingdom of God.

You are NOW, this instant,
The perfect Son of God.
There is nothing you can do to change that.
Truly, you can imagine all form of complication,
Just as you have imagined this entire world.
And in your imagining, you can even believe it true.
But it has no effect whatsoever on what you are.

Try, if you can, to let the feelings flow through your being.
You are perfect.
You are absolutely loved.
You are totally free of sin and guilt,
Have always been free of them,
And will always be free of them,
No matter how long you choose to imagine that time exists.
You are complete.
You are whole.
And you cannot change that.

You have been given all power within the universe,
As co-creator with God.
But there is one power you do NOT have,
And that is the power to change what you truly are.
This world is a reflection of the power
Of what you can imagine.
Indeed, it oftentimes, usually,
Seems so real to you.
That is but a reflection of the power of your imagining.
But your imagining cannot change
The truth of what you are.

What is your salvation, then?
Your salvation is your freedom
From your vain imaginings that this world is real.
Your salvation is your freedom from your vain imaginings
That you can ever be separate from God,
That you can ever be split within your being,
And harbor conflict;

That you can ever sin or have any reason to know guilt.
Your freedom from such vain imaginings
Is, indeed, your salvation.

Do I speak to you of salvation?
Traditionally, you imagine that means
You need to be saved FROM something.
'Tis only your vain imaginings
From which you need to be saved.
And what does it take to be saved
From that which you have imagined,
But which is not real?
What it takes for you to be saved from your imaginings
Is merely this—
Hear me very well.
Your salvation requires but one instant
In which you wholly, totally, EXPERIENCE,
At the level of feelings, beyond your thoughts and words,
The truth that vain imaginings is all it is.

In that instant, when within your being
There comes a certainty, a knowing,
That indeed you ARE Spirit; you ARE free;
And truly this world IS but illusion,
That which you have imagined—
In that instant, you shall be free.
And never again shall you look upon this world
With the same eyes.

Salvation is very interesting, as you choose to THINK about it.
For salvation does not require that you DO anything.
Salvation is not something you can achieve.
Salvation does NOT require hard work,
And struggle, and tears, and toil.
Salvation requires ONLY that you let go of the imaginings.

Now, hear me very well.
Do not think that you will let go of the imaginings
As the result of your struggle, and your effort.
For in your struggle, and your effort,
You but further the imagined reality of your illusion.
In a sentence, then,
To achieve salvation merely do this:
Relax your mind; release your thoughts, and let them go.

And that is all.
TRULY, THAT IS ALL.
Relax your mind.
Release your thoughts.
And let them go.

I have spoken to you, many weeks,
Of your values, and your valuing.
Indeed, it is your valuing of the illusion,
Of the vain imaginings you call this world,
And your life, and your self—
It is the valuing of all of this that keeps you from
Relaxing your mind, releasing your thoughts,
And letting them go.

It is your valuing that tells you, in your thinking,
That if you let go, you will surely die.
I tell you today, as I said two thousand years ago,
He who would lose his life, shall find it.
And this is exactly what I meant.

To let go of your thoughts,
To release your mind,
To relax your total being,
Is simply to realize that none of it has any effect
On what you really are as the Son of God.

And when you HAVE relaxed your mind,
What then must you do to achieve your salvation?
The answer is this:
ABSOLUTELY NOTHING.
For your salvation is not to be achieved.
It is already yours.
And your only task is to let go
For the one instant it takes
For that certainty to well up within your being.
And then your awareness,
Beyond the level of your thinking,
Your awareness of what you are as the Son of God,
As co-creator of All That Is,
Shall well up within your being
With such power that you will never be the same.
For you will be free.

I have said often in the Text,
All it takes is the little willingness. (39)
Truly, you need DO nothing. (40)
And the reason is this—
Your true nature IS.
You cannot change it.
You cannot even toss it aside.
All you can do is use your power
To imagine that you are something different.

As you let go of the values which tell you
That your thinking and your imaginings are real,
As you let go of those values even for an instant,
Then automatically, without effort,
The memory of your true nature shall be there.
It is not that the memory will return.
For it is already there.
Only your imaginings hide it from you.

Indeed, the key to your salvation is to do nothing.
The key to your salvation is letting go.
The key to your salvation is to feel within your being,
"I am not a body. I am free.
For I am still as God created me." (L 201)
In your thinking, always come back to those words.
And as you do, always try to go beyond the words,
To the feeling, to the awareness of what they are,
And what they mean.

You cannot structure it.
You cannot make it happen.
The key, as strange as it may seem,
Is to allow yourself to focus your mind
So there are no distracting thoughts,
And say only this:
"I am not a body. I am free.
For I am still as God created me." (L 201)

And then, do as you can
To relax your mind and your thinking,
And to let go,
Even of the words themselves.
Let go of all thoughts you have of good and bad.

Let go of all thoughts you have of right or wrong.
Let go even of that which you have learned
In this *Course in Miracles*.
Let go, and be still within.
And in that stillness shall come rushing toward you,
Within you, and through you,
A mighty wind that shall be the breath of God,
But shall be nothing more than
Your own awareness of what you ARE as the Son of God,
Nothing more than your awareness in that instant,
That indeed, that is what you have always been,
And that is what you shall always be.

In that instant,
As you relax and still your mind—
That instant shall be your freedom, and your salvation.
And you will realize that it took no effort whatsoever;
Only the letting go of all that you value.

Blessings upon you all. That is all.

KINGDOM OF GOD

Greetings again. I am Jeshua. I have come this day
To further, with you, my discussion of
A Course in Miracles.

Today I would speak to you of the Kingdom of God.
Ultimately, that is all of which we speak.
For the Kingdom of God is the goal, the end result,
The state to which you go
As you proceed through your sojourn on this earth.

But more importantly, which we have said in different ways,
But cannot overemphasize,
The Kingdom of God merely IS.
The Kingdom of God is not a state
Which you are progressing toward.
The Kingdom of God is not something
Which you will one day achieve.
The Kingdom of God, rather, is your natural state.
For you were created part of that Kingdom.
And God's Will demands that you never leave it.
Over that you have no choice.

The Kingdom of God IS what you are.
And your existence, in reality,
Is an expression of that Kingdom.

What really is the Kingdom of God?
Ultimately, the Kingdom of God cannot be defined,
Cannot be known by you on this earth,
Cannot be fully experienced
While you yet dwell in human form.
However, do not be disheartened by that fact.
Merely realize that it is the limitations
Of this humanness you share
Which make it impossible for you
To fully experience the Kingdom of God here.
I will speak to you now, in words,
So that from these words you can experience
That which is close to God's Kingdom.

IN A WORD, THE KINGDOM OF GOD IS FREEDOM.
The Kingdom of God is freedom in a sense so free,
So unbound, and so unencumbered
That those of you walking this earth
Cannot fully comprehend it.
Again, do not be dismayed.
For freedom is a state you can find,
And come close to,
On this earth.
And your freedom shall be your peace and your joy
For as long as you choose to stay here.

The Kingdom of God is freedom. (41)
The Kingdom of God is love. (42)
And as I have said many times before,
Love is, indeed, freedom— (18)
And really, nothing more.

So what is this freedom of which I speak?
The freedom that is the essence,
The hallmark of the Kingdom of God,
Is your creative power given you by God.
That freedom is the creative power
Which allows you to be, and to experience,
Anything you can imagine.

In the Kingdom of God there is, of course, no time.
But you on this earth still think in terms of time.
So this freedom of which I speak is your freedom of creation,
To be and to experience whatsoever you wish,
Any time you wish to experience it,
For as long as you shall choose to do so in this world of time.

The Kingdom of God is freedom in the sense that it is absolute.
Were God to have created you with restrictions,
And yet like unto Himself,
Then God Himself would be restricted,
And would not be free.
I tell you that is not the case, and has not happened.
God created you like Himself, unfettered and unbound.
Such is your freedom, and in the sense of your time,
So shall it always be.
Over that you have no choice.

Indeed, I tell you, in the Kingdom of God
Everything you experience is always
The expression of your creative ability manifesting itself
As whatever it is you wish to imagine.
And that is exactly what you find represented
In your life here on this earth,
Or in as many lifetimes as you imagine
You have chosen to live on this earth.
Each of them, each moment you experience,
Is absolutely and completely
The expression, in a form chosen by you,
Of that creative power given you by God.
That is why I have said to you so many times before
That nothing can happen in your life
Which is not completely and totally
Your own choice.

For you ARE of the Kingdom of God.
Nothing can ever be part of your experience
Lest you, of your creative power,
First, imagine that it is so,
And second, choose to experience it.
Truly, this sojourn upon your earth,
With all its struggle and pain and grief and misery—
All of it is what you have imagined,
And chosen to experience.
And in part, for a very good reason.
God, in His own freedom,
Created you free.
You are Spirit, unbound, unfettered,
Freer than the wind,
Able to be and to experience anything you wish.
And all of Creation shares with you, in delight,
Whatever it is that you wish to imagine,
And to experience.

Then what is this earth about?
This earth and all its toils
Is the result of you, in your freedom,
Imagining what it would be like
To be separate from the rest of the universe,
From the rest of Creation.
So those of you who have come here
Are playing that out in your Oneness.

And your creativeness is so real, and so effective,
That those of you here, for the most part,
Actually believe this experience to be real.

Indeed, I tell you,
You will laugh with me the day you see
The truth of all this illusion.
A chuckle, a smile,
And you shall be free.

How is it that those of you here choose to stay
In this world of misery and toil and fear and death?
If you are, indeed, free,
Why would any of you do this?
The answer is to be found, once again, in your values.
Recall, when you value something,
You believe its presence in your life
Is necessary in order for you to be happy, or peaceful,
Or even for you to exist.
And when once you believe such within your being,
You have given an imagined reality
To that which you believe you need.
But you have also created fear,
And your own death.

Have you ever thought to yourself,
What really is this fear?
For I have said there are only two emotions,
Love and fear. (2)
And I have said love is freedom. (18)
So what is this fear, really?
FEAR IS THE FEELING YOU HAVE
WHEN YOU ANTICIPATE THE LOSS
OF SOMETHING YOU VALUE.
How, then, does one become free of fear?
'Tis simple, is it not?
Be free of your valuing.
That is all.
Let go of your values, of all that which you deem
Necessary in order for you to BE.
Let go of those values,
And you shall be free.
When you do, you shall spread your wings
And fly into the world of love,
And into the Kingdom of God.

Perhaps you feel it is so difficult
To imagine loving without valuing.
Indeed, those of you here on this earth
May find it most difficult
To imagine loving without valuing.
But I tell you, in the Kingdom of God
It is not possible to love and value at the same time.
When you value something, anything,
You have a sense of NEEDING whatever it is.
You have a sense of needing that something
To BE a certain thing, or a certain way,
In order for YOU to be
What you wish to be.
Therefore, you restrict yourself,
And put yourself in a prison.

Insofar as you EVER want another being,
Or another circumstance, to BE a certain way,
Which YOU define,
You would deny freedom to that being, or that circumstance.
And as you deny freedom to another,
You are really saying within your soul,
"I do not wish YOU to be free.
Nor do I wish for MY SELF to be free."
Imagine that God Himself,
When He made you His Son, and co-creator of All That Is—
Imagine that He said,
"I create you the Son of God, EXCEPT FOR . . . ,"
And then placed restrictions on what you could do, or be.
You would not be free.
And NEITHER WOULD GOD HIMSELF.
God, in His wisdom, knew that,
And made you free.

You are even free to imagine all of this earth,
To imagine it so real that you seem to come here
And struggle with all of its existence.
Indeed, you cannot change what you ARE.
But you are free to IMAGINE yourself
To be anything you wish.
Such is the freedom given you by God.

And I ask you now,
Do your brothers deserve any less than God has given you?
When you value,

You ultimately are saying to another being, or circumstance,
"I want you to be free, EXCEPT FOR . . . ,"
Then you place the restrictions.
Then you set up the prison bars.
And the longer the list that follows "EXCEPT FOR . . . ,"
The less love you can know.

The only way, the ONLY way
You can know and experience real love
Is to know and experience real freedom.
And the only way you can experience real freedom
Is to give absolute freedom to all beings,
WITH NO EXCEPTIONS.
And the only way you can love thusly is not to value.

The Kingdom of God is, indeed,
Likened to the playtime of little children.
For little children create with their imaginations
Anything which they wish to imagine.
They do not become attached to it,
Do not cry when their imaginings are done.
They merely let them go
And move on to another set of imaginings.
Such is the goal of God for each and all of you.

How is it that you can feel comfortable, and free,
About loving without valuing?
The answer is this—
Hear me well.
For this is what you need to know within your being.
As the Son of God, as co-creator with God,
You ALWAYS experience, in each moment,
EXACTLY what it is you choose to experience.
And whatever it is you shall imagine
Shall BE that which you experience.
And all of Creation shall celebrate it with you.

Try for a moment now,
To go beyond your thinking to experience.
Try to feel what it would be like to be so free that you KNEW
That in ANY instant of your time
You could experience EXACTLY what you chose to experience,
With no limitations and no restrictions.
What then, would be the purpose of valuing anything?

For valuing MUST be tied to your fear
That something shall pass away.

So try to realize within your being
What it would be like to know
That if you had a particular experience which delighted you,
You are free to experience it, to reexperience it,
And to reexperience it for as long as you like—
Exactly that same experience.
And nothing in all of Creation can stop you from doing that,
Or can take it away from you.

Everything you experience comes from within you.
There is no circumstance external to yourself
Which can control that which you do or feel.
And THAT is what makes you free.

So try to imagine within your being the confidence,
The freedom you would feel in knowing
That every instant you are free
To experience exactly what you choose.
If you have had an experience of love, as you call it,
Which you want to reexperience,
You can do so, anytime.
And nothing can stop you from having that experience.
Nothing, that is, except your valuing and your fear.
Even experiences on this earth, in this physical plane,
You are free to experience and to reexperience as oft as you like.
And nothing can stop you from doing so except your values
And the fear that follows from them.

An important comment now—
In your valuing, and the fear that follows from it,
You always insist on FORM.
In the world of Spirit,
Form does not exist,
Only CONTENT. (43)
But you, on this earth,
When you experience what you call physical love,
Always seem to believe that that love will be lost
Unless the FORM is maintained by the presence
Of certain bodies, the ones you have chosen.
Nothing is further from the truth,
That this should be necessary.

For the essence is the feeling, and the experience.
And to the extent that you wish to experience love,
In whatever manner you choose,
You can experience that as long as
You free yourself of the values
That demand a certain form of your choosing.

Thus we say,
Take your thoughts, relax, and let them go.
For when you let them go,
You let go your desire and demand for specific form,
As well as the values which accompany that desire.
And then the whole universe, in all its Oneness,
Shall rush in to fill your being
With whatever it is you wish to experience,
With whatever it is you can imagine.

What is the Kingdom of God, then?
It is your natural state.
It is what you are. (44)
It is your freedom, unbound and unfettered,
To experience anything you can imagine,
Anytime, and for as long as you like.

And the doorway through which
You enter the Kingdom of God,
Which you can do in an instant, if you choose,
Is the doorway at which you shed all your values,
And the fear that comes with them.

For then you pass into a world of freedom,
And a world of true love,
In which you shall give absolute freedom
To every being and circumstance in your life.
You shall therefore experience for yourself
That same absolute freedom.
And, without your values,
The whole universe shall, with great love,
Rush in to fill your being
With whatever you shall desire.

Blessings upon you all. That is all.

THE WORLD

Greetings again. I am Jeshua. I have come this day
To further, with you, my discussion of
A Course in Miracles.

Today I would speak to you of the world—
Not the Kingdom of God,
But this world, this earth,
This physical world, this solar system,
Its universe, its stars, its galaxies.

The world is not true. (45)
There is not one thing in this physical world that is true.
Hear me well.
Do not be deceived by this fact.
The world is not, and cannot ever be,
An accurate reflection of what you are as the Son of God.

The world, therefore, as I have said,
Is false perception. (46)
Perception itself is your awareness based on your thinking.
True perception is NOT of the Kingdom of God.
True perception IS possible as you walk this earth.
However, to the extent that you ever think
That even one aspect of this physical world is real,
Then you are choosing to be the victim
Of your false perception.

It is so easy for those of you who read A Course in Miracles,
Or for those of you who hear my words,
To feel that what I have just said is negative.
However, what I have just said
Is the key that shall open for you the door to freedom,
And the door to the Kingdom of God.

Remember, as I have been saying for many weeks,
Your thinking leads to your concepts of what and who you are.
Then you value those concepts.
And you create an image of what you are,

Which is nothing more than a reflection of those values.
And it MUST include the fear of death.

All of those are products of the world.
Apart from this world, I assure you,
There is no thinking.
There are no concepts based on the thoughts of who you are.
There is nothing to value.
For the issue does not even arise.
You, the essence, the Son of God,
Do not change, do not fear,
And can never die.
So there is nothing to value.
There is nothing you can ever need.

What of this world, then?
Truly, this world is but a reflection of the thought
That the Son of God could be separate from himself,
And therefore, from God.
Herein lies the fact that none of it is true.
You ARE the Holy Son of God.
You are Spirit.
You are One, within your Self,
Within all other aspects of Spirit,
And One with God.
There is nothing that can change that.
Again, over that you have no choice.
So the entire thought that you could be separate,
That you could isolate your Self, even for a moment—
All of that is nothing but vain imaginings.
Not one thing in this world is true.
Hear me well.

Does one hate the world, then?
The answer, as I shall discuss with you now is
No, indeed.
There is nothing in all of Creation to be hated or despised.
For everything, even the imaginings,
Is a reflection of the freedom of the Son of God.
So, insofar as you, all of you, as One,
Have imagined this world, literally have created this world,
To the last blade of grass,
To the last hair on your head,
To the last star in the farthest corner of the universe,

All of it reflects your thinking,
Your own perceptions,
And your own valuing.

God rejoices in your freedom, and your creativity.
God has made you free.
And free you shall always be.
You shall be free long after the word "always,"
And the time to which it refers,
Have passed away.
Nothing can ever be but your total freedom.
And the universe itself sings in joy
At the expression of your freedom,
And your creativity.
So I tell you,
The universe rejoices at what you have created here,
False though it be,
Even though it be but a vain imagining.

If you could look God in the face, and say,
"Do you care if I play with vain imaginings?"
God Himself would look you in the eye, and say,
"My Son, you are free.
And nothing shall ever infringe upon,
Or take away,
Your freedom."

What of the world, then?
How many of you can walk this world
In the awareness of your total freedom?
How many of you can walk this world
With no thought whatsoever of what others think of you,
Of how they may act out that thinking?
How many of you can walk this world,
As I suggested two thousand years ago,
With no thought of the morrow,
Knowing that you shall be clothed and fed,
Even as the lilies of the field are clothed and fed?
How many of you can walk this world
Living each instant as nothing more than the instant it is,
With no thought or concern about what you call time,
And the instants to follow?
You have already answered those questions
Within your own being.

And the answer, generically, is
Very, very few of you.

So what of the world, then?
The world is a reflection, in your mind,
Of the vain belief that you are not free.
And I tell you,
That is not true.
Anything that would ever cause you to imagine
That you might not be free
Is not true,
And cannot be real.

How many of you can walk this earth with no fear whatsoever
Of what might happen to your body?
Be it the effect that nature might have on it,
Or the effect that another "separate" brother might have on it,
Or the effect that lack of food might have on it—
The list goes on and on.
The answer is the same—
Generically, very few of you.

For your body itself is the primary expression
Of your belief that you are not free.
That is why I have said to you,
Again and again, that which IS true,
"You are NOT a body. You are free.
For you are still as God created you." (L 201)
And that you cannot change.

What, then, of the world?
The problem WITH the world, the problems IN your world,
All stem from your valuing.
Always, that which you perceive to be yourself, you value.
Then you fear its loss.
And in that fear,
YOU GIVE UP YOUR FREEDOM.
Always, your valuing of this world is a reflection of your fear.
And so it is that I have said,
Fear has made everything you think you see. (47)
Your valuing always brings with it your fear.
This shall remain true beyond your choice
For as long as you value this earth,
Or anything in it.

Once again, does this mean for you to hate this earth,
The source of your fear, and the source of your pain?
The answer is again,
No, indeed.
The universe rejoices in your vain imaginings.

What is the purpose, for you now, on this earth?
The purpose for you now
Is to walk this earth in joy and in freedom.
And all it takes to do that
Is for you to know
That this world holds nothing that you want.
All it takes to walk this earth in peace
Is for you to know that nothing here
Has any effect on the reality of what you are,
Which is the Son of God.
All it takes to walk this earth in peace
Is to know that you are, indeed, Spirit,
That Spirit is One,
That all your brothers, separate as they may seem,
Are One with you.
All it takes to walk this earth in peace
Is to know that as Spirit
You are the creative source—
And nothing can ever happen to you
That is not totally your own choice.
And all it takes to walk this earth in peace
Is to know that God, and you,
Are love,
And freedom,
And peace,
And joy.

If what you seem to experience is not of love,
Does not offer total freedom to yourself and all your brothers,
Does not bring peace,
Does not bring joy,
Then KNOW that it is not of God.
Know that it is not of the nature of what you are,
That it is based on your thinking and your valuing,
And therefore, cannot be real.
And in your knowing, beyond your thinking,
Beyond your concepts,
That such is NOT real—
In that knowing you shall be free.

Walk this earth, then, as a little child.
Walk this earth as a child so little
That he does not form attachments to any of his toys.
Walk this earth with the freedom of a child,
To literally laugh and play with that which you have created,
Even though you know it is but a daydream for you to enjoy.
For you will not find your freedom, your peace, and your joy,
Until you CAN walk this earth
Knowing it is but a dream, a dream of no consequence.
For then, in the moment of your waking,
You shall, with a chuckle,
Dismiss the dream,
And merely go on with your joy.

This world is not true.
This world is but your toy.
This world is but a dream.
As soon as you can realize,
As soon as you can come to a state half-waking enough
To know it is but a dream,
Then you shall be free to enjoy the dream
As often and as much as you wish.
And then when you no longer choose to dream it,
You shall merely let it go.
And in your waking,
You shall know it was not real.
The state of your half-waking
Will bring you to the point where you know
That when you wake and the dream is over,
It was a thing of no consequence whatsoever.

What then of the world?
The world is the product of your creative energy.
The world is a reflection of what you are as the Son of God,
Albeit THIS world is a reflection
Of the vain imagining that you can be separate,
Which you cannot.
However, the grass, the sky, the clouds, the trees,
The birds and their songs in the morning,
The chatter of the animals,
Indeed, the movements and the laughter
Of that which you call your body,
The wind upon your cheek,
The snowfall, the rain,
The Sun and its warmth—

All of it is a reflection of your creative power as the Son of God.
And the universe rejoices with you,
That this is so.

In your half-dreaming, and your half-waking,
Be free to laugh as the wind caresses your cheek,
And to joy at the songs of the birds in your mornings.
However, never lose sight of the fact
That it is but a dream.
For then you shall be free.

Should you hate this world, then?
No, indeed.
Be again like a small child.
And for as long as you choose to walk this earth,
Do it with joy.
And if it is not joy, know that you have valued something here.
Stop, pause, and do what you can
To free yourself of that value.
And then the joy will return.

What then of this earth, and the world?
There are countless upon countless brothers
Who are lost in their imagining that they are separate.
The gift you can give to them,
Which shall be your gift to yourself,
Is your own freedom.
For as you walk this earth with softness in your eyes,
A smile on your face, and peace within your heart,
Your brothers shall see that,
And in their Oneness with you shall know of their own peace,
And their own freedom.

So the greatest gift you have to give
To yourself and your brothers,
As you walk this earth,
Is your freedom, and your joy.
And that shall come to you
With the freedom from your valuing.
That shall come to you in your freedom
From imagining that any of it is real.

So I say to you this day,
Walk this earth for as long as you shall like.
Walk it in peace, and joy, and freedom.

If you do not sense those,
Know that you have valued something,
And are imprisoning yourself,
And your brothers.
Walk this earth,
Never forgetting that it is not real.

And as you do so,
As you know that it is not real,
There will be nothing you shall not forgive,
Within or without.
And in your forgiveness,
The whole world shall be a place of love and joy.
Be like children, my brothers.
Love, and go your way.
Go your way in freedom.

Blessings upon you all. That is all.

SIN AND GUILT

Greetings again. I am Jeshua. I have come this day
To further, with you, my discussion of
A Course in Miracles.

Today I wish to discuss with you
Two things which do not exist.
They are sin and guilt.
It is spoken so well, and so often,
In A Course in Miracles—
There is no sin. (13) The Son of God is sinless. (48)
There is no guilt. (14)
Guilt is simply that which you have imagined,
And as such, should not, and cannot, exist.

In the Kingdom of God,
Not only do sin and guilt not exist,
They are incomprehensible.

Sin and guilt could not even enter consciousness
In the Kingdom of God.
You would say to a being in the Kingdom of God,
"And what of sin?"
His only response could be,
"I don't understand."
For it would be a totally foreign thing to him.

That is in the same sense that God knows you
Only in your completion and your perfection.
Truly, if one would say to God,
"What of all this misery, and death,
And bodies, and fear, and sin, and guilt,
And all of that?"
God would say,
"I don't understand. My Son is perfect. My Son is free."

What then of sin and guilt?
Both are products, ultimately, of your thinking.
The thinking, as you recall, is that which generates and creates

The concepts you hold about what you are,
And what this earth is.

The initial thought that it took
To create this world of imagination
Was the thought of separation.
You, the Son of God, imagined, in a moment,
What it would be like to be separate.
In a moment, all of this was played out,
With all of its time, all of its struggle—
And in a moment, was dismissed.
To honor your creation, you imagine playing it out in time.
But all of it was created, came, went, and disappeared,
In less than an instant.
And the thought of separation
Is what created your thought of sin, and guilt itself.

First I shall speak of guilt.
For, indeed, guilt was the precursor of the thought of sin.
Normally, you might think it to be the opposite,
That one would first sin,
And then feel guilty about that sin.
However, guilt came first.
What is guilt, as I speak of it in *A Course in Miracles*,
And as it applies to your life,
To your existence here on this earth?
Guilt is the feeling you have
When you try to imagine that you are a separate, isolated being,
Apart from God,
Apart from your brothers,
And from the rest of the universe.

That is impossible.
As I have told you so often,
You are the Son of God.
You are Spirit.
You are One.
Over that you have no choice.
So when you try to imagine
That you ARE
What you ARE NOT,
What follows, without recourse, is conflict.
Trying to imagine that you are separate
When there is nothing you can do, whatsoever,

To actually BE separate,
MUST bring you conflict.
And as long as you try to maintain that illusion
That you are separate,
You will remain in conflict.

Conflict is not peace.
Conflict is not joy.
Conflict is not happiness.
Indeed, peace and joy and happiness
Cannot exist within your being
While you are, and remain,
In conflict.
And guilt, as I use the word guilt,
Simply refers to the conflict which you must feel
As you try to imagine yourself separate.

What of sin, then?
Sin does not arise until after, in your time,
You begin to imagine that you are separate.
In order to play out your fantasy of separation
You have chosen bodies,
These grand illusions which seem, in space and time,
To be separate one from another.
But of course, as you have heard so many times,
That is all this is—
One grand fantasy,
Not to be valued, but to be enjoyed,
To be played with, with laughter and a chuckle,
Nothing more.
As you play out your fantasy
That you are separate, and can be separate,
Then, in the absence of your peace,
In the absence of your joy,
In the absence of your happiness,
You tend, rather you find yourself bound,
To try to imagine the causes for their absence.

Ultimately, all of the conflict,
All of the unhappiness,
All of the absence of peace,
All of the absence of joy,
Is nothing but a reflection of the conflict I have just described.
However, were you to live on this earth, in this body,

And yet remain fully aware of the truth
That all of your conflict and misery
Was because you had chosen to imagine separation,
You would most likely, in an instant, say,
''I choose not to do this.''
And you would leave.

Thus is born the ego.
The ego is a product of your guilt.
The ego is the collection of the thoughts and concepts
You form about what and who you are.
And in order to imagine this separation
In such a form that you can tolerate being here,
You must hide from yourself
The conflict that generated all this in the first place.
Your ego is, in a measure,
The opposite of what you really are.

I speak of the ego almost as your enemy.
I say the ego would do this and that to you.
The ego would hide this and that from you.
The ego thinks thusly, and on and on.
And always, the ego is the collection of thoughts
You have formed about who you are.

And the necessity is that the ego delude you enough
To make you unaware
That the conflict at the base of all your misery
Is actually the source of your being here.
So the delusion which the ego creates
Which must keep from you the secret truth that you are God,
That you are free, and that you have created this, all of it—
In the attempt to keep from you that secret,
Your ego must make you understand
From whence comes your misery, your grief,
Your sorrow, and your fear.

You have imagined separation.
And where better to substantiate the separation
Than to build into your concept of who you are
The belief that the beings separate from you
Are the cause of your conflict and your misery.
How clever you have been in your thinking!
How clever is the ego!

And how strong it can be in its cleverness!
Do you see?
So in order for you not to realize that
YOU are the source of your own conflict,
You choose to look outside yourself,
And blame others.

So what others seem to do to you,
Which seems to create what you are,
And which substantiates your self-concept,
That is what you call sin.
For always, when you try to imagine yourself separate,
You rob yourself of your happiness,
And your peace, and your joy.
And insofar as you can believe
That SOMEONE ELSE has robbed you of your peace,
And joy, and happiness,
What better to call that than sin?
Thus sin becomes that which someone else does
To cause misery and grief in another.

To the extent that you can imagine
That another can sin against you,
Then it must be that you can sin against another.
And in your belief that you can harm another,
You then can feel, and believe in, guilt.
In your cleverness,
You have even displaced the feeling of guilt itself.
For now you see guilt as the feeling you have
When you have done something inappropriate to another,
I.e., made him unhappy.
You believe in that as your guilt,
The product of your sin.
But ultimately the guilt itself that created this world
Is your imagining that you could be separate at all.

What then do you do if it is not clear
That someone else did something to you
To cause your misery?
What then, or who then, do you blame?
Ah, yes, I am sure you see it already.
YOU BLAME GOD.
In your misery, in your lack of happiness,
In the absence of your peace and your joy,

When you cannot see your way clearly
To blame another person,
You attach personality to God, and blame Him.
And thus you become the victim of God.
How is that most commonly expressed
Here, on your earth?
With these words:
IT IS GOD'S WILL.
Is it not true,
When illness comes, when tragedy strikes,
When people die,
So commonly it is said,
"It is God's Will."
As if God would do such a thing to any being,
Much less His own Son.

And how long does it take,
After one starts to believe
That God would do such things to ANY being,
For one to become frightened of God?
And indeed, ultimately,
To hate God?

All of it follows easily and clearly.
Furthermore, it follows of some necessity.
For as soon as you came here
In the vain imagining you call separation,
And could not stay lest you hid from yourself
The separation that was the cause of it all,
You simply furthered your imaginings
To include the notion of sin,
Which allows you to blame another
For the absence of your own peace.

Of sin and guilt, then,
They are not real.
They do not exist.
'Tis absolutely certain the Son of God is sinless.
And in the absence of sin,
There is no guilt.

How then, as you walk this earth,
Do you deal with what I say to you this day?

You are sinless. You are free.
Truly, anything which you can imagine
Is your rightful inheritance,
Given you by God.
For He has created you free.
But in that freedom, in that inheritance,
Which allows you to imagine anything you will,
NOTHING YOU IMAGINE
CAN EVER DO ANYTHING TO ANOTHER.

In your freedom, as I have told you,
The entire universe celebrates with you
Whatever it is you can imagine.
The Spirit of God finds joy in your imaginings,
And presses you to imagine whatever it is
You might choose to experience.
For the flow of creation,
And the unlimited experience it brings
Is the feeling
You call love.

So first, realize as you walk this earth,
You cannot EVER do anything to another.
In your interactions,
Even your interactions among bodies which SEEM separate,
You are not separate.
And nothing you can imagine will transpire
Unless there be a part of Creation, which is but your Self,
And which agrees, out of love,
To imagine that selfsame experience with you.
And since it is always merely experience,
Of no consequence, and not even real,
There is always someone willing to be on your stage,
If you wish to think of it that way,
To help you experience whatever you would imagine.

And no matter what you choose to imagine,
It is not sin.
For you have done nothing to another
That he, in the Oneness, with you,
Did not choose to share.
And more importantly,
No one EVER does anything to you

Which you have not chosen to experience.
It cannot be otherwise.
For such is the nature of God.

You cannot sin against another.
And another can never, ever, under any circumstance,
Sin against you.
So guilt, then,
In the sense of what you call sin,
Does not exist.
There is no reason to ever feel guilty
For what you think you have done to another.
And there is no reason for another
To ever feel guilty for what you think,
Or he thinks,
He has done to you.

Herein lies the beauty to be found
In the absence of sin and guilt within your consciousness.
As soon as you no longer look outside yourself
To blame another for the absence of your peace,
As soon as you realize that guilt, in that sense, does not exist,
You will turn within.
And then you, in your time, will very, very soon
Come face to face with the real guilt
That causes the absence of your peace,
Which is your desire to be separate.
And when you look nowhere except within,
And can see that your desire for separation
Is the cause of everything you call unhappiness,
Then you shall, of your own will,
In conjunction with the Will of God,
Let it go.

Then the world shall take on new meaning.
You shall see your brothers, and all of Creation,
As One with you.
And the joy that shall well up from within your being
Will be almost greater than you can comprehend,
Almost greater than you can stand.
It shall be a happiness and a joy
Beyond what you could ever have imagined.

Hear my words today.
And remember, we are dealing not with words,
But with experience and feelings.
So as you read these words, perhaps over and over again,
Allow yourself to feel free of sin.
Allow then, your own guilt to melt away.
Allow then, any guilt you might demand of another
To melt away.
Then look within.
And you shall see shining there,
The Son of God.
And then you shall walk this earth
For as long as you choose,
In oneness,
In harmony,
And in joy.

Blessings upon you all. That is all.

THE BODY

Greetings again. I am Jeshua. I have come this day
To further, with you, my discussion of
A Course in Miracles.

I have spoken to you lately of things which do not exist.
What of the world? we asked.
The world is not so, I told you.
I spoke to you of sin and guilt, which do not exist.
Today, I would speak to you of another thing which
Truly, I tell you, does not exist.

I would speak to you today of the body,
That which you perceive so often on this earth,
To be what you are.
IT IS NOT SO.
The body is not you.
The body cannot be you.
The body, and its fate,
Whether it lives or dies,
Whether it is healthy or sick,
Whether it seems to bring you pleasure or pain,
All of this is in no way related
To what you are as the Son of God.

''The world I see holds nothing that I want.'' (L 128)
I have spoken to you of that.
And especially, the world you see includes the body,
Which, truly, holds nothing that you want—
Because none of it has any effect
On what you truly are in reality.

However, there is a point beyond that
Which needs to be made, and made again, and made again.
The world you think you see,
You see with the images within your brain.
And that brain is of the body.
The world you see,
You think you see with your eyes, your physical eyes.

And those are of the body.
The world you experience,
You think you experience through your senses,
Be it your eyes, or ears, or nose, or mouth, or touch.
And all of those are of the body.
Hear me well,
For this message is central to *A Course in Miracles*.
None of that is true.
Indeed, none of that exists.
When you see the world
Through the eyes you think your body has,
You see, in truth,
Nothing.

But indeed, you feel that you DO see the world.
How can I say to you, 'Tis nothing?
The answer lies, as always, in your valuing.
For you see that which you have accorded value.
You, in your power as the Son of God,
Have the freedom and the ability
To create whatever it is you wish to experience.

Indeed, you are not a body.
You can never, in truth, BE a body.
Over this you have no choice.
You can, however, imagine,
Just as you have done in order to come here in the first place,
That you are a body—
Or at least that you HAVE a body.
IT IS NOT SO.
The body is a veil.
The body is a shadow.
The body is a false image,
Whose purpose is to hide from you what you really are.

What really are you?
In a word, you are Spirit. (L 97)
You are Mind. (49)
You are an idea of God. (50)
And as an idea in the Mind of God,
You EXIST, and cannot change.
For God does not change His Mind
About what He has thought,
And thus created.

As an idea in the Mind of God,
You are absolute,
Untouchable,
Unchangeable.
And as an idea, you merely exist.

YOU cannot be confined to space.
Even you know, without argument,
That your own ideas, or thoughts,
Cannot be confined to one point in space.
YOU cannot be confined to time.
And you even know that as well.
Your own thoughts are independent of time.
For in a thought,
Can you not move yourself to the past,
Or the present, or the future,
Merely by thinking yourself there?
Indeed, you can.

As an idea, you are independent of time and space.
And you must remain that way.
Any false dreams you have which might seem to limit you,
Which would seem to make you less
Than an idea in the Mind of God—
Any of those false dreams cannot be true.

The primary false dream with which you live
Is your belief in the body.
You have believed that the body is finite in time,
That it is born, lives, and dies, to pass away.
However, YOU are unchangeable.
You are not born. You do not die.
And you never pass away.
You simply exist.
You have believed that the body changes,
That it ages, that it becomes infirm,
That it gradually loses strength and ability,
Until eventually it dies.
YOU, in reality, do not change.
YOU do not become weak.
YOU do not become frail.
YOU do not pass away.

You have believed that the body supplies you
With your understanding of the world,

With your awareness of what you are.
You have believed that you must be educated,
Must go to school, listen to teachers,
That you also must learn by experience,
By trial and error, if you will.
All of that is a false dream.

For an idea, which you are,
Has complete access to, and is totally part of,
Every other idea.
There is nothing in all of Creation which can keep from you
Anything that has ever been experienced,
Except for your belief that you cannot find it.
And that is the veil I have referred to as the body.

You believe your body must take time to learn,
And to experience.
It is not so.
Your body is always nothing more
Than an instrument which serves you, its master,
And which serves you absolutely perfectly.
Your body IS for you, and DOES for you,
Exactly what you imagine it to do.

Your body cannot be born lest you,
Spirit, co-creator with God,
Elect for your Self to take imagined form, and be born.
And then, indeed, you seem to be born.
You cannot learn anything,
You cannot forget anything,
You cannot comprehend, or fail to comprehend, any idea,
Without that first your Spirit, in full awareness,
At its own level of truth,
Chooses the illusion that you do, or do not, understand,
That you can, or cannot, learn.
And then your body, faithful servant that it is,
Acts out exactly what you have chosen.
You cannot ever become infirmed, become weak, become frail,
You truly, cannot even die,
Without first that it be your own choice.

And when I say, your own choice,
The word "Your" ought to be capitalized.
For it refers to your One Self,
Your Real Self,

Spirit, Mind,
The Son of God.

My brothers, learn this lesson well.
Let this lesson, let my words, flow through your being,
Time and time again,
Until you shall go past the words,
Past the thoughts within your brain,
Past even the emotions,
To experience.
And when you, at the level beyond your thinking,
EXPERIENCE what I have just said,
Then you will truly realize, perhaps even in an instant,
That you ARE but an idea, a thought,
And therefore are free to be anywhere and anywhen,
In any form you choose.
And your body will respond in perfect accordance
With whatever you wish.

Always monitor your thoughts with diligence and vigilance,
Until you look at every experience
Your body seems to bring you
With the realization that this could not be
Lest you, Spirit, Son of God,
Had first deigned that it be so,
And commanded the universe to obey.

If only you knew the power that you have as the Son of God.
I did say, "commanded the universe" that it be so.
And that is exactly what I meant.
You, as Spirit,
You, as the Son of God,
You, as co-creator of All That Is,
Need only to think, at the level of your Real Self,
And that thought becomes a command to all the universe.

And the universe is not forced to obey.
Rather, the universe rejoices.
For the universe is You, in truth,
Is You, in your Oneness.
It is part of You, and One with You.
And always, whatever your true Self thinks
Is celebrated and honored instantly,
Throughout all of Creation.

Ah, but the body.
It is so frail, and seems so weak,
Seems so beset upon by a myriad of outside influences
Which, at a whim, can change what it would experience.
The Sun comes out; you feel constrained to be warm,
Perhaps too much so.
If it snows, you feel constrained to be cold,
Perhaps too much so.
If the wind blows, you feel constrained to sense the wind.
You imagine brothers, in bodies which are illusions
As grand as the illusion you have of your own;
And you think their bodies can harm you,
Can have an effect on what your body does,
Where it might go.
And none of it,
I tell you,
Is so.

Always, your body does exactly as you bid it.
In the great Oneness of all of Creation,
The wind cannot blow without it being You.
The Sun cannot shine without it being You.
It cannot snow without it being You.
And no brother can seem to act and influence your life,
Lest it be You, and that brother be celebrating with You
The thought which has been your command to all of Creation.

What of the body, then?
You are, indeed, here on this earth,
Albeit in your imagination.
Perhaps you should kill yourself, and leave this earth.
'Tis not necessary.
It would be, perhaps, a foolish thing to do.
For usually your suicides are done
Without full intent and awareness.
Those things which you do out of pain and fear
Are simply that, creations of pain and fear.
And indeed, you shall reap that pain and fear.
For such is the power of what you are.

So, indeed, you seem to be here,
On this physical earth, in this physical body,
All of you.
What shall you do with this body,

This false dream, this grand illusion
Which seems to limit your days and nights,
And bring you frustration and pain?
Two things, I recommend to you.
As I recommend them,
Always realize that you are the Son of God,
And are totally free.
I do not say to you,
You SHOULD do this.
Always I say to you, you are free.

You are free to live here
In the fear of the Sun and the wind and the snow,
In the fear of other bodies harming your own,
In the fear of illness, and the fear of death.
You are free to live with all those fears.
However, it is not necessary.
But if you would, instead,
Choose the peace, the joy, and the love
Of which I have spoken so often,
What then of the body?

First, as I have said this day,
Always remember that the body is truly
Nothing more than an expression of that
Which you have created out of your thoughts, out of your Mind,
Out of your creative Oneness as the Son of God.
Now, given that you ARE the Son of God,
NOT a body, but free,
How then shall you walk this earth
Seemingly IN your body?
I have told you that the body, if seen and used properly,
Is nothing more than a means of communication. (25)
When I say "properly,"
I do not mean there is a right and a wrong.
I merely mean,
If you wish to escape the misery of this earth
And find peace,
Then "properly" will be thusly.

The body is nothing more than a means of communication.
Firstly, it communicates to you, in this dream,
That which you have thought in the dream.
You may always look at what the body seems to do,

What the body seems to see, what the body seems to feel,
And it will reliably tell you, it will communicate to you
That which you have thought.
If your body suffers pain and is ill,
Know that, in your thinking, you have imagined it to be ill.
If your body suffers misfortune,
Know that you have imagined, and desired,
That the misfortune befall you.
If you experience peace and joy,
Know that you have thought and imagined
Peace and joy.
So the body communicates to you, every second,
What you, in that instant, have thought and desired,
And have created in your imagination—
Constant, immediate, feedback
Of what is going on within.
So simply be aware of that,
Never forgetting that what is real
Is what goes on within,
Not the external appearance.

Secondly, your body, when used properly,
Will be a means of communication
Between you and your brothers.
For you have made up your words and your thoughts.
And always, every brother knows every thought you think,
And vice versa.
And as you know, within this dream,
That your thoughts extend to every brother,
That your words communicate to your brothers,
That your body represents that which has been created
Within your own thinking,
Then you may communicate to your brothers in that vein.

As you allow yourself to let go,
To say, "I do not know,"
Then the Holy Spirit,
Which shall be a still, small voice within you,
Shall use your body for communication.
Your thoughts, your actions, your words,
Shall always communicate oneness, cooperation, and harmony.
Your brother shall see a hand extended to help him,
Someone to walk beside him in equality and in oneness—
Not someone to lead or follow,

But someone with whom to share, equally and freely.
Your brother shall see it in you,
And you likewise shall see it in him.

Likewise, the wind, the rain, and the Sun
Shall sense the same Oneness.
And you shall feel within your being
A oneness with all of this earth,
With its grass, and its flowers,
Its clouds and its sky,
And all of its beauty.
And you shall, in experiencing that beauty,
Communicate that selfsame beauty to yourself
And to all of your brothers,
Who are indeed already your Self.

So know that your body is just
The messenger of that which is within.
As you pause, and are still, the Voice of God shall,
First, echo within your being,
And then grow until it speaks clearly.
And that Voice shall be communicated by you,
Without effort or struggle of any kind, to all of Creation.
Indeed, your BODY shall SEEM to be doing that.
And for purposes of living on this earth,
In this illusion, in this dream,
That is the dream that shall set you free.

Forgiveness, as it relates to your body,
Is the realization that it is not real,
That what happens to the body has no effect on what you are,
That your body does nothing more
Than express and communicate that which is within.

When that which is within
Becomes the awareness of love and oneness,
Then you shall communicate that to all your brothers,
And shall experience the same in return.
Then shall peace and joy and harmony
Follow you all the days of your life.
And you shall, as a psalmist said many, many years ago,
Dwell in the House of the Lord forever.

Blessings upon you all. That is all.

TRUE PERCEPTION

Greetings again. I am Jeshua. I have come this day
To further, with you, my discussion of
A Course in Miracles.

Of late, I have been speaking to you of things
Which, ultimately, do not exist, and are not real.
I have spoken to you of your body.
Truly, it is not so. It is not what you are.
And since it has nothing, really, to do
With what you are as the Son of God,
It does not exist.
I have spoken to you of sin and guilt,
Which do not even exist in the Mind of God,
And are not real.
I have spoken to you of fear which,
Other than in your imagination, does not exist.
I have spoken to you these past weeks
Of things which ARE NOT.

Today I would speak of something which IS.
In fact, for the remainder of our discussions
In this year we are sharing,
I will speak almost totally of things which do exist,
Things which ARE of the Kingdom of God.

Do not forget, however, that this world is not real.
This world, of itself, does not exist.
This world, of itself, is of no value whatsoever.
And insofar as you experience your life
Within the context of this world,
You will not be totally free.

That is why I have spoken so often of perception,
And true perception.
Perception is that which you seem to see,
And which is based on the values
You have ascribed to this world.
To the extent that your perception is based on your valuing,

It is not true,
And what you think you see
Does not exist.

There does exist, in this world, true perception.
True perception, hear me well,
Does not exist in the Kingdom of God.
For perception itself is not necessary.
Without the body, and all the illusion it engenders,
There is only knowledge,
Complete, instantaneous, full,
With nothing left behind, nothing excluded,
And nothing remaining to be needed, or wanted, in any sense.

So as long as your awareness of life
Is experienced within this world,
The best you can do is true perception.
Do not be disheartened.
It is enough.
Your true perception shall guide you
Through your walk upon this earth,
Illusion though it be,
With peace, and joy, and freedom.
And when you choose to lift your feet,
Turn them into wings and walk off this earth,
Then your true perception
Shall pass away into knowledge.
And you shall, at last,
Be completely free.

So of the things which DO exist,
I will speak to you of true perception
As a representation of reality.
Bear in mind that, in the fullness of truth,
It, too, does not exist.
But I will speak to you of true perception as something that IS
Because it touches upon the reality of what you are,
And will not distort, will not take you away from
Your awareness of your true One Self,
And the Kingdom of God.

The true perception of which I speak leads you to vision.
And vision, which is the vision of Christ,
Which is also your vision as the Son of God—

Vision IS.
Your vision you may trust, you may honor—
For it will truly lead you along the pathway of freedom.

What is this true perception of which I speak?
What is this vision of which I speak?
Both of them stem from your awareness
Of what, in truth, you are.

I have told you, these many weeks,
What you are NOT.
You are not a body.
You are not a creature of sin.
You are not a creature of guilt.
You are not a creature of this world.
You are not bound.
You are not restricted.
You are not a creature of fear.
You are not a creature of doubt.
You are not a creature of illness.
And above all, you are not a creature of death.
Of all this I have spoken these many weeks.

I have also spoken to you of that which you ARE.
You are a creature of freedom.
You are a creature of peace.
You are a creature of joy, absolute joy.
You are a creature of light.
You are a creature of the dance,
The dance of Life and the universe.
You are a creature of poetry.
You are a creature of music.
You are a creature of all of this earth.
You are a creature of the leaves.
You are a creature of the grass.
You are a creature of the wind.
You are a creature of the birds, and of the sky.
You are a creature of your brother.
And above all, you are a creature of your One Self.

And all that you need do to know yourself
As a creature of all that of which I have just spoken
Is not to value anything of this world.
Your vision, your true perception, always stems from,

And grows out of, your awareness that nothing here is to value.
Nothing here is for you to need.
Nothing here is for you to cling to.
For in so doing you create your fear.

In the absence of your values, as I have told you,
You know that any instant, within time or without,
Any place, within space or without,
Any thing, absolutely ANY thing
Which you WISH to experience
You MAY experience in absolute freedom.
And the entire universe shall rush in to celebrate with you
Whatever it is you have imagined.

None of it, therefore, is to be valued.
The loss of NO thing, ANY thing, is to be feared.
For in any instant, in a flick of your imagination,
It is yours again, and again and again,
As oft as you shall wish.

And so it is, in your vision,
You begin by knowing that whatever you see,
You see your Self.
Always, as you look out at your world with vision,
You know that, in truth, you are looking within.
Nothing can you see that seems to be without,
But is a picture of what you have chosen within.
Your vision, your true perception, begins there.
Always, always, always,
Pursue this with vigilance and joy.
ALWAYS you look upon your Self.

Secondly, your true perception, your vision,
Arises from your awareness that you are Spirit.
You are absolutely free.
You are the Son of God, co-creator of All That Is.
All of that which I said you are NOT,
Indeed, YOU ARE NOT.
And all of that which you ARE NOT, you can not SEE.
So as you seem to look without and perceive your world,
It shall be true perception insofar as,
In the moment while you yet perceive,
You are aware within
That you are seeing the face of God,
Ultimately, that you are seeing but your Self.

And all that you can ever see,
As you look without, knowing you are but seeing within,
Is the power of the child of God
To imagine whatever it is he would choose,
Moment upon moment upon moment,
Upon forever, upon the passage and the ending of time.
Know that you are always seeing, in action,
Freedom, and joy, and peace.
As you look, seemingly without, but are aware within
Of your freedom, your peace, and your joy—
As you free yourself of values and fear,
Your perception shall be true.
And your vision shall be the Vision of Christ.

How then do you look at this world you think you see,
With its misery and its fear,
That which you call crime and illness and death,
And murder and tragedy?
As you look upon that, as you see it with your physical eyes,
Remember it is not of value,
And that you are actually looking upon yourself.
Realize that, as you look out upon your world,
What you are seeing, and truly no different from,
Is a drama played upon an imaginary screen,
Just as in the moving pictures you watch for entertainment.

As you sit in a movie,
You enjoy it, you feel feelings,
You are aware, you experience it,
All the while knowing it is nothing more
Than a grand illusion you are choosing to play with
For those few moments.

In your true perception, in your vision,
You shall see all of that which seems to be your world
As nothing more than a dream
Being played out by creatures made free by God,
But of no more consequence, and no more value,
Than the moving pictures which dance across the screens
You also think you see.
Truly, as you watch one of your moving pictures,
You know full well within your mind
That the actors are but portraying roles.
You know that the reality of what they are
Has nothing to do with the roles they are playing.

So it is with the world you think you look upon with your eyes.
You see children in a dream, playing roles.
And in your vision, in your true perception,
You shall realize that the roles these actors are playing
Have nothing whatsoever to do with the real beings
Who are choosing at that moment
To play out their dreams.

Indeed, your willingness to observe the dreams of this earth
Is also your willingness to be one of the actors in this illusion,
In this film you call life.
And the freedom from your valuing
Allows you to see, even within yourself,
That the part you play, with all its intensity and caring,
Has nothing to do with what you really are.

So as you look without value,
Know it is but a dream,
A grand creation of the Son of God, masterfully done,
Yet played out on the imaginary screen you call this world.
All the actors playing their roles are completely safe.
And when the dream is over
They will take off their masks,
And with a chuckle,
Relax back into what they truly are.

In your vision, in your true perception,
You shall always see the child of God
Playing out his imagined roles
With great intensity and great joy,
Even though much of your world may call it tragedy.
You shall see the beauty, the masterfulness
Of the creative power which you are,
In your Oneness,
As the Son of God.

You shall see the sky, the trees, the birds, and the grass.
You shall feel the wind.
You shall see your brothers
Playing out their roles with all their great passion.
And you, in your true perception,
Shall know you are looking upon,
Freely and without value,
The product of your own creative power.

And in a blade of grass,
Created by you, the Son of God,
In all its complexity,
In all its cycles of growing and dying,
Nourishing itself in the sunlight and the water,
Anchoring itself in the soil—
In that blade of grass you shall SEE
The true beauty and wonder of what you are.

My brothers, hear me well.
'Tis all a dream, this world.
In the absence of your valuing,
You are free to see it as a dream.
And then you shall see beyond the roles being played
To the actors themselves,
Each of them being part of you,
Part of each other, and part of God.
You shall see all of it as One with God and all of Creation.
You shall look beyond the roles,
Beyond the dream and its content,
To an awareness of the creative beauty
Which is what you are.

And as you look upon a single flower,
Or a bird flying through the sky,
You shall, when you first learn to truly SEE,
Wish to fall to your knees in admiration and awe
Of that which has created such beauty.
Then your peace and your freedom shall come,
When you realize, within your being, beyond your thinking,
That the awe, the admiration you feel in that moment
Is due only unto your Self.
For you are One with God,
And all of Life.

Blessings upon you all. That is all.

THE CHRIST

Greetings again. I am Jeshua. I have come this day
To further, with you, my discussion of
A Course in Miracles.

As I told you last time, during the rest of our year together
We will mostly be speaking of things which ARE.
When I say things that ARE,
I mean things which EXIST in reality,
In the real world,
In truth.

As I have told you, this world is not true.
But I would speak to you this day of things which are true.
The question in your Workbook is,
"What is the Christ?" (51)
And indeed, the Christ IS.
The Christ is real.
The Christ exists, and is found in truth.
Of the Christ, I would speak with you today.

The answer to the question,
"What is the Christ?"
Is extremely simple.
The Christ is you.
That is all.
Nothing more.
The Christ is the reality of what you are as the Son of God, (52)
Free of this world, free of the illusions,
Free of your values, free of all thought of sin and guilt,
Free of all fear,
Shining and glowing and living, without time,
In innocence and joy and peace.
That is the Christ.
And that is You.
God has created You thusly.
And what God creates cannot be changed.

All of your imaginings you are free to entertain.
But they change not the reality of what you are,
Which is the Son of God.

So the Christ is, indeed, You.
Shall I speak more of what You are?
Indeed, I shall.
Above all, the Christ, as Spirit,
Is the Son of God,
The creation of God.
And God created his Son in perfect childlike innocence.
Now, hear me well.
That has never changed,
Is so this moment,
And can never change—
Childlike innocence.
Truly, when I said, two thousand years ago,
You must become like a little child
To enter the Kingdom of Heaven,
It is that of which I spoke.

In your innocence, you have no thought of past moments.
As the Christ, the moments of the past do not exist.
You have no fear.
You have no anticipation,
Even what you might call joyful anticipation,
Of the future.
Childlike innocence knows only this moment.
And this moment is a moment of joy.
For a child, so loved, so protected, and so safe
As is the child of God,
Can this moment be anything other
Than a moment of joy?
Indeed, in your reality, it cannot be otherwise.

As I told you in the Text,
If you ever find yourself experiencing
Anything other than sheer joy,
Know that it need not be so. (53)
Know that something in your imagining,
Ultimately in your valuing,
Has gone awry.
For the Christ knows not of the past,

And cannot feel guilt because of it.
The Christ knows not of the future,
And cannot understand fear of those things
Which might yet happen.
The Christ, and that IS You,
Knows only this moment.
And in this moment, that innocent child, which is the Christ,
Knows it is absolutely loved, absolutely safe, absolutely free,
That it is so protected by its Father
That there can not be ANYTHING to fear.

Take a moment now, and look within.
As I just spoke of that child,
Of how loved, how safe, how protected he, or she, was,
Did there not come
A moment of longing within you?
All of you who walk this earth
In your dream of separation and distance
Long to be so loved and so cared for.
And the purpose of *A Course in Miracles*,
The purpose of these words,
The purpose of all the other sources
Trying to accomplish the same goal,
Is to bring you to that point where,
Within your being, beyond the words, beyond the thinking,
You know that you ARE, always,
That safe, that loved, and that protected.

As the Christ, as the child of God,
You have a Father who, literally,
Is eager to grant you your every wish,
WITH NO EXCEPTIONS.
Those of you who have been parents on this earth,
Or who anticipate being parents,
Have thought of the experience of caring for a child.
And you have, or would anticipate,
Giving that child every blessing you possibly could,
However, WITH EXCEPTIONS.
And then you make decisions about what is best for your child.
And, out of love, truly,
You limit what your child can experience.
But I tell you now,
As the child of God,

Your Father has placed on you
NO LIMITATIONS OF ANY KIND.

Ah, yes, if you wish to call it a limitation,
You ARE Spirit, and you ARE totally free.
Over that you have no choice.
Yet, you still have no limitations.
For you can, indeed, just as you do now,
Imagine yourself isolated, alone, unsafe,
Limited by your bodies,
Threatened from all sides.
You can imagine that, and play it out
With all your caring and misery and fear.
And as you act out the dream,
You can, if you wish, be terrified.
You are free to experience anything you wish,
Even though, if it is not joy,
It must be but your imagination.

So once again, as the child of God
You are free to experience your every wish.
And God is eager, presses you
To experience whatever it is you can imagine.
Indeed, this sojourn upon your earth
Is just one of those imaginings.
God has left you free to imagine it with all the zest and joy
That you can choose.
And I tell you, a time will come
When you will look back upon your fear,
Your loneliness and your misery,
And see that there actually was a joy behind it all.
So even that which you experience on this earth,
Ultimately, is a joy for you,
Though that truth may seem
Hard for you to accept at this moment.
But for your valuing, and your attitude,
You would know each experience to be joy.
Of that I have spoken many times.

So it is that YOU are the Christ.
And as you look within, as you look upon your Self,
You will see the power given you by God,
The innocence give you by God.

You will see the creative ability, the laughter,
The joy, and the peace.
And then you will recognize your Self
As the Son of God.
I tell you once again,
The only thing that prevents you
From seeing yourself thusly, this moment,
Is your valuing.

As a child, free as the wind, if you but chose
To look upon your experience here on this earth
As only that, experience—
To be experienced for the purpose of joy,
And of no other consequence,
Not to be valued, only to be joyed in,
Then you would see your Self in childlike innocence.
And you would see within your Self
The face of Christ.

There is, for you, an easier way to see the Christ.
The easier way for you to see the Christ,
To see the childlike innocence,
The purity, the joy—
The easier way, I tell you,
Is to see it in your brothers.
It is that which your forgiveness shall bring you.
As you grant to your brothers
Total freedom to be what they are,
To be whatever they imagine,
In the certainty that nothing they can do
Can ever harm you in any way—
As you grant them freedom in that sense,
Then YOU shall be free.

As you see them in what seems to be
Their pain and fear and misery,
As you, with the vision of Christ,
See beyond that to the Spirit,
To the actor playing a role for the sheer joy of it—
As you know that the enactment of that role
Does not change his reality in any way,
Then, truly, you shall SEE his freedom,
And shall receive it for yourself.

So as you truly forgive your brother,
Which is to love him for the reality of what he is,
And not for the role he is currently playing
In this world of dreams—
As you see him in light and peace,
And know what he is experiencing is only his choice,
Then you shall know the same of yourself.
And as you know, beyond your words,
That everything in YOUR life IS your own choice,
Your own creation,
Then you shall BE as free as you see your brother.

And on the negative side,
If you would restrict your brother,
If you would think him to be a body,
If you would think him to be a victim of fear,
If you would think him to be ill,
If you would think him to die,
Then that shall be your own wish for yourself.
And that you shall seem to experience
While you yet remain here on this earth.

My brothers, I see you, in reality, in truth.
I see you not as a body.
I see you as a light, an energy that glows and shimmers
And shines and shines unto forever.
I am aware, within my being,
Of your joy, your peace, and your laughter,
And your inviolable freedom
That cannot be taken away.
I see you only thusly.
And thus am I the same.

So I urge you,
Out of the greatest of love,
Look upon every brother as you would look upon me.
If you can imagine me as good, and perfect, and free,
Then every brother is no less than I,
And no less than you.
Hear me well.
I am no greater than you.
I am no greater than any brother
Who walks this earth, ever has, or shall.
For we are One.

As I know myself, in truth,
So do I know you.
And I have come here to share with you,
This day and the other days,
In order that you may come to see yourself as I see you,
And that you may see all your brothers as I see them.

So as you look about you, as I said last time,
Look upon the sky and the birds,
The grass and the wind,
The trees and the flowers,
As your own creation.
Be grateful to your Self.
But more so,
As you look upon each brother,
Look past all appearances.
Look to the freedom.
Look to the hero of the dream.
For he IS the child of God.
And he IS free.
He is filled with joy and laughter.
His condition is one of absolute peace,
Forever and ever,
Until time shall no longer be.

As you see that in your brother,
You shall see, truly, the Christ, the child of God.
Then you will know that indeed,
You are looking at the mirror of your Self.
And all that peace,
And joy,
And freedom,
Shall be yours.

Blessings upon you all. That is all.

THE VOICE OF GOD

Greetings again. I am Jeshua. I have come this day
To further, with you, my discussion of
A Course in Miracles.

Last time I spoke with you of the Christ.
And I said the Christ was, indeed,
Nothing more than You.
That is exactly so.
For You, in the reality of what You are as the Son of God,
Are completely pure, completely free,
Sinless, free of guilt,
In truth, even unknown to guilt.
And in the absence of guilt, limitations, and fear,
There is only peace. There is only joy.
In that state, you are the Christ.

There is a lesson, which you may be working with this day,
Which says,
"God's healing Voice protects all things today." (L 275)
I literally suggest in that lesson
That the Spirit within, the Holy Spirit,
Will guide you to know exactly whom to speak to, and when,
What to say, where to go, what to do.
I make it sound so simple, do I not?
All you have to do is be aware of the Holy Spirit,
And everything will be given unto you.

It would seem, perhaps, a contradiction—
If I say to you,
You will know where to go, what to do,
To whom to speak, and what to say,
To the last word and last syllable—
And then I tell you, you are totally free.
That would seem to be, perhaps, a contradiction.
But, it is not.

As the Christ, as the real You, as the One Self,
Which EXISTS,

Always you know exactly what to do,
What to be, what to say, and where to go.
Do not forget, as I have told you,
That everything is One.
I am you.
You are me.
I am each brother, whom you see as separate.
You are each brother.
The separateness you think you see is not so.
All of us are One with God, and all of Creation.
And so it is that the Christ within you
Is in total harmony with everything that is.

There is nothing in all of Creation for you to fear.
There is nothing in all of Creation which could harm you.
For there is nothing in all of Creation
Which, ultimately, is not You.
All of it is but your Self.

Your illusion of not knowing
What to think, what to do, and where to go
Is a product of your illusion of separation.
Earlier we spoke, and said,
There was one problem, and one solution.
The problem was ALWAYS separation, (54)
Or your belief in separation, false though it be.
And there was one solution,
To realize that separation was not so.

You can realize, even in your thinking,
That if everything truly is One,
Then there is no doubt about what to say.
For there is no anticipation
Of whether your words or actions will be accepted.
There is no thought whatsoever of what you SHOULD do,
Based on the past, on the standards and laws
You have created to tell you what to do, and how to do it.
None of that exists.
There is only the experience of this moment.

And "this moment" is the Holy Instant
Of which I speak so often.
In that Holy Instant, as you simply EXPERIENCE,

Free of your fears of the future,
Free of anything from the past to govern you,
Or limit you, or restrict you,
Or to guide you into what you "should" be,
There is only a spontaneousness
Which simply flows out of what you are.
That spontaneousness is the essence
Of the freedom of the Son of God.
For in that instant, in that moment,
Free of the past, free of the future,
Always there comes to you an urging,
An awareness of whatever it is you would experience.

And as the Son of God, as the Christ,
That awareness, that urging,
At that level, in the Holy Instant,
Free of the past and the future—
That urging is nothing more
Than the creative power you have
As the Son of God.
And all of Creation shares it with you.

It is so difficult for those of you on this earth
To imagine letting each moment flow, in and of itself,
Free of any connection to the moments
That have come in your imagined past.
It is so difficult to let each moment flow,
Realizing that that moment will have no effect
On what you call the future.
For there is nothing in this moment which can restrict you,
Or in any way keep you from experiencing whatever you will
In what you believe is the next moment,
As you think of your time.

So, what happens, in words,
Is that you are simply aware of what you wish to experience,
And it is done.
That is all.
So simple.
In your thinking, in your awareness,
As you let go of past and future,
And the fears and guilt that come with them—
As you live in this moment, the Holy Instant,

You will simply be aware of the quiet urgings.
In your thinking, you will interpret that
As being told what to do.
It will seem to you, as you become still within your mind,
That somehow you know what to do.
Indeed, as you think about it,
That seems to be the case.

Truly, 'tis just the flow of your being,
In harmony with all of Creation,
Which you have become aware of.
Your thinking would modify that to make it seem
That someone, or something, separate from you,
Is telling you what to do,
So that you know what to do.
It is not so.
It is but your Self, in your own knowing.

For the purposes of this Course,
I speak of that often as the Holy Spirit.
For it helps you to feel
That there is a being present to guide you.
And truly there is.
However, never lose sight of the fact that
That being, the Holy Spirit,
Is, in fact, the Christ,
And is nothing more than You.
But when I say "You,"
It is not the you which deems itself separate
From the rest of Creation.
For the Christ knows no separation from anything—
Nor do you, in your reality as the Son of God.

So as you walk this earth,
It is entirely possible for you to KNOW what to do,
And what to say.
Truly, you are NOT being guided or directed
By some being external to yourself.
You are only being your Self,
The playful child of God of which we spoke last time.
And as you live within each Holy Instant,
That playful child will simply BE.
And the adult in your mind, who watches over the child,
Will think that the child is being told what to do.

It is enough for you to have that awareness for a while,
Within your time.
For as you, the adult, trapped by your thinking
Within your body and your separation—
As you look at the child who dances out of your being,
And out of your heart—
You will, as the adult, very soon know within
That you want to be like that child.

When you FEEL that,
With great urging and great power within you,
Then you shall become it.
And you shall be free.

What is it that keeps you, the adult who thinks,
From becoming that child,
Who, in truth, you wish to be?
The answer, of course, you can certainly know already—
For I have spoken of it these many weeks.
What keeps you from your childlikeness,
What traps you in your adulthood, and your thinking,
Is, of course,
Your values.
For it is the values that determine for you
What you think you are.
It is the values that make time seem real.
And with time, you can fear the future.
With time, you can believe that, somehow,
The past affects this moment.
And thus you create all of the "shoulds" in your life.

Is it not clear, now, this moment,
That without your values,
Without all the thoughts that seem to tell you
What you can, and cannot, do,
There would be no effort, and no struggle.
You would simply BE the child.
And you would be free.

Thus I have said to you,
The word of God is given you to speak. (L 276)
As you THINK about that, as you are wont to do,
Each time there is the quiet urging within you
To be, to experience, to do, or to say,

And you do not do it, out of your fear,
Pause for a moment,
And see what it is you are fearing.
Always, you are fearing some response
That you think will come from these beings
Whom you imagine to be separate from yourself.
But remember, they are not.
Always you are carrying something
From what you call the past, that says,
"No, you should not do, or should not say, that."
And that, too, is an anticipation of the future.
For the message hidden therein is,
If you act thusly, the response and consequence will be so.

So it shall be clear to you,
That whenever you hear the still, small voice within,
It is just the child within you,
Pressing you to play with him, or her.
Whenever you hear that still, small voice, your little child,
And do not honor its request,
Pause, and look within for a moment.
And you will see there
The fence around your soul
Built by your values.
Then say to yourself,
Is this what my values bring to me?
And indeed, that is exactly the gift they bring.
Then say to yourself,
Is this the world I want?
Is this what I would choose?
Or would I rather be free like the child,
With no fear, no thought of consequence,
No guilt, no past, no future—
Only each moment, each Holy Instant,
Shining in peace and love and joy,
Into the next, and into the next,
And into the next,
Until there is no time at all—
Until there is only freedom.

So for now, I urge you,
Do not feel guilty about your belief in separation.
'Tis why you have come.

But, listen within.
Always, there is the still, small Voice.
I speak of it often as the Holy Spirit,
And will continue to do so.
But really, it is your Self.
It is the Christ.
It is the Oneness.
It is the song of all of Creation,
Doing what it can to well up within your being
And bring you joy.

Do not feel guilty about each moment
In which you do not honor the Voice.
But in your time,
Where you think it takes effort
And struggle, and yes, time,
Do what you can to listen.
Be AWARE, even if you have not yet the courage
To act on the Voice for God.
Simply hear it.
Then look with diligence
At the fence that keeps you from being the child,
And from expressing your joy.
Look each time to see which value it is.
That will help you immensely in your thinking.
You will come to realize that the values are not worth it,
That they are, in fact,
The prisons I have told you they are.

Ultimately, you are free.
You are the child.
And the child always WILL play in each moment.
Your imaginings make it seem as if
There are restrictions within those moments.
But as always, 'tis just your imaginings.
So feel free, as long as it brings you joy,
To imagine yourself not free.

It is your right, your inheritance, as the Son of God,
To imagine whatever you will.
And whatsoever you shall choose to imagine,
Be it joy, or be it imprisonment,
Be it love, or be it fear—

Whatever it is you imagine,
You shall only be loved,
By God,
By myself,
By all of Creation.
That love, always,
Moment to moment to moment unto forever,
Never changes, shall never disappear,
And is only a thought away.
For you are absolutely safe,
And so, so loved,
As the Son of God.

Blessings upon you all. That is all.

THE HOLY SPIRIT

Greetings again. I am Jeshua. I have come this day
To further, with you, my discussion of
A Course in Miracles.

Last time I spoke with you of the Voice for God.
I told you that that Voice is always present,
And will, if you wish to listen,
Allow you to know what to do,
Where to go, what to say and to whom.
I also told you that that Voice, which is always there,
Is nothing more than your Self.

However, in the Text, in the Workbook, over and over again,
I speak of the Holy Spirit.
I say the Holy Spirit will mediate
Between illusions and truth. (55)
The Holy Spirit will take all your fears, all your misery,
And transform them into light and joy and peace.
All you need do is bring your cares,
Your worries, and your fears,
To the Holy Spirit.

I tell you that you, in your creative power,
Have used that power to make all this,
Illusion though it be.
The Holy Spirit will change your perception of what is,
Will transform your awareness
Into a true perception of this earth,
And eventually, when you are no longer part of this sojourn,
Into knowledge.

So I speak to you, over and over again,
And say, bring your cares to the Holy Spirit.
Come to the Holy Instant, bringing no past and no future.
Release everything to the Holy Spirit,
And all will be taken care of.
Truly, that is exactly so.

It can easily seem confusing.
It can easily seem frustrating, when you,
In your attempts to listen for the Voice of the Holy Spirit,
Don't seem to hear.
It can seem frustrating and confusing when you,
As far as you can tell, in your thinking,
Have brought your problems to the Holy Spirit,
And the solutions do not seem to be present.

So today, I would speak to you more of the Holy Spirit,
And how it is utterly true that all you need do is
Bring to the Holy Spirit
Whatever your concerns,
Whatever your fears,
Whatever your doubts—
How they will be transformed in light,
So that you will see with a true vision,
So that your perception,
False when you bring your problems thusly,
Will be changed to true perception—
How it is that fear shall be changed to love.

I have told you many times,
You do not know.
Ultimately, your leap of faith is to say, "I do not know."
I have also told you so often,
The Holy Spirit DOES, indeed, know.
The Holy Spirit knows every facet, every aspect,
Of every being in Creation,
And always will guide you to do exactly
What is in perfect harmony with All That Is.

Yet I said to you last time,
The Holy Spirit, really, is just You.
So it follows that You, your Real Self,
Already knows everything you need to know
To allow your life to blend into a total joy,
An effortless flow, a perfect harmony with All That Is.
And that is true.
I have told you, the miracles do nothing.
You need do nothing.
For indeed, you already know.
And when I say the Holy Spirit is, in fact, You,
All I am saying is that the Holy Spirit is
That part of You which does already know.

I have told you that God created the Holy Spirit
For the purpose of correcting the error you have made
In your humanness.
When God created the Holy Spirit,
All He did was to allow you,
Whether it be your will or not,
An avenue you could use
To hear that part of your Self which does know.

So it is that you, Spirit, Son of God,
Free as the wind, free as a child,
Always have access to the part of You which does know,
And which will fully guide you, in perfect harmony,
Whenever you wish.

You can imagine yourself to be separate.
But you cannot close the door
That leads to your awareness of harmony and truth.
If you feel you cannot find that avenue,
It is only illusion that blinds you to it.
So God, in the twinkling of an eye,
When He saw your error,
Made certain in His own thought
That always, within you,
Exists the pathway to truth.
And always, if you open the door,
It shall be there—
With no exception.
So it is that the Holy Spirit,
Ultimately your Self,
Does know.
And you need do nothing in order to hear.

How is it that you, indeed, DO nothing?
I have spoken of this also, many times.
The first important step you take
As you do nothing, is
DO NOT THINK.
For as we have said,
Your thoughts are meaningless.
Your thoughts are the creator of all this illusion.
Your thoughts lead to your values,
Which create your concept of what you are,
Apart from the Oneness.

Then how is it, truly, that you do not think?
You find your access to the absence of thought
In the Holy Instant.
I have also spoken, often and often again,
Of the Holy Instant.
The Holy Instant is nothing more than this—
It is a time in which you,
As you do nothing,
Do not hold yourself to the past.
For as you do nothing to hold onto the past,
It disappears.
It is a time when you do not anticipate, in any way, the future,
Or the consequence of what you would do, or think, or say.
And as you do nothing to hold onto
Your belief in cause and effect,
The imaginary effects of this moment pass away.
So as you DO nothing,
There is no past, and no future.
In that moment, almost all of your thinking has gone.
Then the door will swing open.
And that quiet urging of which I spoke last time,
The quiet knowing within you, of what to do,
Will be there.
And you will hear it.

Again, what you need NOT do
Is hold onto your belief in the past,
And your belief that somehow
It has determined what this moment is.
For it is not so.
And what you need NOT do
Is hold onto your fear of the future,
And your belief that this moment
Will affect what the future brings.
Also, it is not so.
You are free.
Over and over again, I have said to you,
You are free.

The grandest illusion of all is your time.
You ARE free of your time,
Whether you know it or not,
Whether you believe it or not.
One moment ago has nothing to do with this moment.
Any thought, any action, any word,

Which you may have imagined in your past,
Cannot possibly have any effect
On what you do, or think, or say,
In this moment—
Unless you create such as a dream,
And hold onto it by your own choice.
It, of itself, was an experience,
Was experienced, and is gone.
Nothing more.

Likewise, the future.
The future, in your grand illusion of time,
Doesn't really exist.
Each moment in your grand illusion
Is a new, complete, free beginning,
In which whatever you imagine will be.
And the moment to follow
Is just as free as the one that follows that,
And that, and that,
Unto the end of time.

The Holy Spirit knows not of time.
That is His great strength.
You believe in time,
That the past affects the present, affects the future.
And that, if you wish to call it weakness,
Is your great weakness.
Truly, it is a major stumbling block
That keeps you from the Holy Instant,
That keeps you from hearing with perfect clarity
The Holy Spirit,
Which is your One Self.

Another way to look at this,
Which I said hundreds of years ago, is
"Thou shalt not judge."
What does it mean for you to judge?
Judging means having an opinion,
Holding a belief that you can be certain what something is,
How it became that way in your time,
And what that something should do in the future.
However, there is no cause out of your past
That can affect this moment.
And this moment is not a cause for any effect of the future.

So when you judge, you believe that you know.
You feel that you, as an ego, in your separateness,
Based upon your illusions,
Know what you want to do.
And THAT is judgment.
In doing just that you create your time.
Thus you strengthen this grand illusion,
Which keeps you from opening the door to the Holy Spirit.

I said, "Do not judge, lest you be judged."
I have also told you everything is One.
Indeed, if you judge, you MUST be judged.
But it is yourself who judges you.
Hear this well.
When you make a judgment, you create the past and the future,
And the belief in cause and effect.
And when you create that illusion, then, indeed,
You are obligated to live by that selfsame illusion.
And thus you shall BE judged.

How then can you hear the Holy Spirit?
The Holy Spirit is that part of You,
Your One Self, the Christ, the Son of God,
Who, without effort of any kind,
Is in perfect harmony with all of Creation.
Always, it will act, and feel,
In perfect harmony with All That Is.
To hear the Holy Spirit, all you need do
Is let go of the barriers to its presence,
And your awareness of its presence.
That barrier is your belief in time.
That barrier is your judgment.

So I suggest to you, this day,
That you CAN always hear the Holy Spirit.
You can best do that by taking the leap of faith,
By saying, "I do not know."
And as you say, "I do not know,"
You will never impose any limitation upon another.
For you DO NOT KNOW the measure of his freedom,
And how he shall live it out.
And as you look within,
In the absence of your fear and your illusions,
You shall realize that you, yourself, do not know
Even what YOU would do in any given moment.

So as you attempt to hear the Holy Spirit,
Be aware, always, of your judgments.
Whenever you feel any apprehension about the future,
Know that you have made a decision within, a judgment,
That you are believing in cause and effect and time.
Whenever you feel the slightest guilt about the past,
And feel that guilt determining
What you would do in that moment,
Realize that you have made a judgment,
And placed a limitation upon yourself.

As you let go of your judgments,
As you let go of your guilt from the past,
Your fear of the future,
What will be left to experience?
You will find a deep quietness within you.
At first, out of that quietness
Shall come a whispering.
As you allow your mind, more and more often,
To free itself to its own stillness,
It shall move beyond a whisper to an awareness,
Even to a Voice, if you wish to call it that.
And that shall be the whispering, the awareness,
The Voice of your One Self,
And of the Holy Spirit.

Be aware of the grand illusion of time.
Be aware of your judgments which create time.
As you but let those judgments go,
And pause into the stillness of the Holy Instant,
Then rushing toward your being
Shall come the awareness of your One Self.
And in your knowing of exactly what to do,
And to be, and to say,
You shall realize that this, indeed,
Is the Holy Spirit of which I have spoken.
And the Holy Spirit,
Which is just your Self in harmony with all of Life,
Shall be at peace, shall be filled with happiness and joy,
And shall echo that happiness and joy
Throughout all of Creation.

Blessings upon you all. That is all.

THE REAL WORLD

Greetings again. I am Jeshua. I have come this day
To further, with you, my discussion of
A Course in Miracles.

The lessons you are working on at this time
May relate to the subject, the Real World.
Today, I will discuss that with you.

All of this Course is necessary because
What you think is the real world
Is not real.
The real world is different from, in fact, is the opposite from,
That which you deem to be real.
You walk through your life, this sojourn upon the earth,
Thinking that all of this here is real,
Feeling that your body is what you are,
Feeling that the physical world can dictate to you
What you are, what you become, what you need do—
Believing that you must eat, that you must stay warm,
That you must protect yourself, that you must have food,
Or have money to buy that food,
Or even to buy seeds from which to grow the food,
Believing that you must have land in order to be safe—
All of that is but distraction,
And ultimately, illusion.
It is not real.

The real world, truly, is the opposite of
The world you have made with your thinking.
The real world is of Spirit, and only Spirit.
And the fastest way for you to become aware of,
And to experience, the real world here on this earth
Is for you to come to the realization,
First in your thinking,
Then beyond the thinking with your feelings,
Then with awareness,
Then with certainty,
That EVERYTHING is of Spirit.

You are Spirit.
You are not a body.
As Spirit, you are totally free.
Nothing can bind you.
There is nothing you need to have, nothing you need to do.
You do not even need to protect, or nourish
This body you seem to have.
For I tell you,
Your body and all of this world is created by you,
And is but a reflection of the workings of your Spirit.

I have said to you, the world is not real.
I have told you the world is not so.
I have told you over and over again,
What makes it seem real is your values.
For your values, ultimately, are those thoughts
By which you define, for yourself, who and what you are.
And your creative power is such that,
As you define, within your thinking, that which you are,
Then, indeed, *that* you seem to become—
And *that* you truly believe yourself to be.
However, in the case of this world, it is not so.

I have also told you, over and over,
Your BELIEF that you are in this prison
Cannot imprison you.
It can only make it SEEM as if you are imprisoned.
The real world is the opposite of the world you think you see.

In truth, while you remain here on this earth
You are not likely to experience the real world—
Just as knowledge is not something you will advance to here.
For in your choice to imagine being here,
You have selected this illusion of a brain,
In order to create the illusion of thoughts.
And while you are here, participating in this illusion,
You will use your thoughts to experience what is here.
As you think, you limit yourself.
As you process within this brain,
You set up barriers which separate you from reality.
And insofar as you are constrained to thinking,
You cannot experience reality here.

For I have told you,
As long as you shall THINK,

You cannot KNOW.
As long as you think, you limit what you are.
As long as you shall think,
You separate yourself from ultimate reality.
For ultimate reality IS,
And is REAL.
Your thinking can never be that.
For your thoughts, as I have told you, are only of the past.
You thoughts are only reactions, images you have formed,
Based upon the illusion you call time,
And upon what seems to have happened in the past.

Very early on in the Workbook, I said
You see only the past. (L 7)
Your thoughts are always of the past.
For they are always reactions within your brain.
Even what you call creativity,
Which would seem to be new thoughts,
Is a form of reaction to something you would call the past.
For what happens in those moments of creativity is this—
You approach momentarily the real world,
Insofar as you can know it here,
And EXPERIENCE comes.
Experience is unbound and free.
BUT, the moment you experience something new,
You begin to think about it,
To form concepts and constructs and ideas.
And even though the thoughts and concepts may SEEM
To be new to your world,
They, too, are reactions and thoughts
About the reality of the experience you had.

Again, all of your thoughts are of the past.
They are reactions, in your time, to EXPERIENCE.
And as you react, you form ideas, concepts, and constructs.
Out of those you build the unreal world, and imagine it real.
And that is what separates you
From what you are as the Son of God.

Why should you even bother with trying to find the real world?
Why not just stay here in your thinking,
Stay locked in, as it were?
Really, why do this Course at all?
I have said you are free.

Hear me well.
You ARE free.
I have told you, many times,
You are totally free, as the Son of God,
To imagine yourself imprisoned, and alone,
And separate, and struggling,
Incomplete in your abilities and your knowledge.
You are free to imagine yourself victim,
And sick, and dying.
You are even free to imagine yourself dead.
And no one shall ever castigate or punish you,
In any form, for what you are imagining.

Indeed, those of you who cling to this earth
And the belief that it is real
Are doing nothing more than cherishing your own creativity,
And your ability to imagine whatever it is you will.
It is not NECESSARY that you do this Course.
It is not necessary, ever, that you do ANYTHING.
For in your sense of time,
You have forever.
You may do anything for as long as you wish.
And all that there will be from the universe is Love.
All that YOU will be is love,
And the freedom to be whatever you wish.

So, if you want to experience the real world,
Begin by knowing that you are Spirit, and are absolutely free.
'Tis what I have been telling you, these many weeks.
You are Spirit, and you are free.
Then as you sit with your thoughts,
In the belief and the understanding that you are free,
Allow yourself to ask, in your thinking,
Is this the world I want?
Do I wish to be a victim of the weather, of illness,
Of other beings separate from myself, and their actions?
Do I wish to be constrained to struggle for money, and food,
And shelter, and warmth, and clothing?
The list goes on and on.
Say to yourself,
Is this what I wish?

But as you say that, allow yourself to FEEL,
To EXPERIENCE, deep within.

And see what you find there.
Do not settle for a belief that
Your life is good, and you are content.
Look past your thoughts, deep within.
See if you find light, sheer light,
And peace, quietness and peace,
And joy, joy that wells up within your being,
And can hardly be contained.
For those are your inheritance as the Son of God.
And if you would prefer the light, the peace, and the joy,
To that which you have here in your struggles,
Then you have reason to do this Course.

But, hear me well.
If it does not bring you joy to do so,
Then just realize that you are free.
And do whatever brings you joy.

I have spoken of the real world.
I have said, the real world is the opposite
Of the world you have made.
I have said, you are Spirit, and you are free.
It is common for those of you walking this earth,
As you think about allowing the real world
To flow into your life,
To resist giving up the world you think you see.
For it SEEMS to bring you joy.
And all of you, truly all of you,
Have things of this earth which you love with great passion.
If you did not, you would not be here.
Truly, that is so.
All of you are here out of your own joy, and your own freedom.
It is only your unawareness of what you are
That keeps you here in this unreal world.

Wherein lies the attraction that keeps you here?
The attraction lies in your love of FORM.
Indeed, that is, in significant measure,
Why you have created this world in the first place.
Experience, and awareness, are of CONTENT, not form.
Love, and its freedom, are of CONTENT, not form.
You may feel and experience whatever it is you wish.
But as you think about this world, you believe
That in order for you to experience what you wish,

You need certain physical props, as it were,
To be on your stage, to act in a certain way, at a certain time,
To say certain words, to behave thus and so.
Then you perceive that as your joy.
And your insistence upon having the props, the form,
Is what keeps you here.

'Tis all well and good
That you should play out your illusion,
Albeit in your joy.
Remember, however,
All of the form shall pass away.
And in your valuing of the form,
You create, MUST create,
Your fear, and your own death.

How is it then that you can walk this earth in peace, and in joy?
You can do it by not valuing, in any sense, the form.
Do it by experiencing life moment to moment,
Knowing you are experiencing the CONTENT,
The creative joy within your Spirit.
And as the form alters and flows and changes,
Simply let it form, let it dissipate,
Let it disappear, and form again,
Without attachment,
Without values,
Without demanding how it should be.

To the extent that you would choose to walk this earth
For years to come, if you wish for lifetimes to come,
Know that you are free to do that.
But if you wish to be joyful in this earth,
Realize simply that it is but form, an illusion,
An imaginary creation of the power that is your Spirit.
Allow the form to come and go, to ebb and flow.
Love it, moment to moment.
Never insist upon it staying,
Or not changing within your time.
For the insistence upon form and its preservation
Is what causes you all your misery,
All your fear, and all your pain.

Hear me well, my brothers.
You are Spirit. You are free.

In your freedom, you have seemed to come here to this earth.
In its creation, you have created fear, your own death,
And all the miseries and struggles that follow from those.

As you let go of the valuing,
And realize that form itself is but an echo of your Spirit,
And that the reality of what you are
Is just the ebb and flow of your Spirit,
Then you can allow the form to ebb and flow in the same way.
And you shall be free.
In your freedom, you shall walk this earth in peace, and in joy,
For as long as you like.
And then when you desire to move on,
You shall lay down your body,
A thing of no measure and no consequence,
And move on to another aspect of your freedom,
Your peace, and your joy.
And always shall go with you,
Within space and within time,
Outside of space or outside time—
Always shall go with you that which you are, which is Spirit,
That which can never deprive your Self of its freedom.

For the real world,
In which you are the Son of God,
Is your Spirit, and your freedom.
And in spite of whatever you imagine,
'Tis thusly,
And shall always be so.

Blessings upon you all. That is all.

GOD'S WILL

Greetings again. I am Jeshua. I have come this day
To further, with you, my discussion of
A Course in Miracles.

During the weeks you have been studying this Course,
Many questions have arisen, I am sure.
And as you struggle to answer those questions,
One thing you always do is create another question,
And another, and another.
I am sure it seems difficult, as you proceed through this Course,
Which I have said is NOT a thing to be learned,
For me to speak of it so often as a thing you need to learn.
Always there remains, as you THINK about this,
A nagging, a doubt, deep within.
Of that I come to speak today.

Today I would speak to you of God's Will.
I have said over and over again,
There is ONLY the Will of God.
And YOUR will IS the Will of God.
Your true desire is to know, and to be one with,
The Will of God.
The goal of this Course is to help you release all the blocks
That keep you from realizing
That your will and God's Will are the same.

I speak of God's Will as some sort of absolute.
I say God's Will cannot be changed,
For God Himself does not change.
There is nothing in the universe except God.
There exists no opposite with any wish, or device,
To alter what God is.
There is ONLY the Will of God.

I keep saying your will is the same as the Will of God.
And what you will choose, in your forgiveness,
When at last your perception becomes true perception,
And then passes away—

What you will choose, then, for yourself,
Is the Will of God.

The nagging doubt of which I spoke,
The question that always arises,
Just by the fact that you ask a question, is this—
What if I don't agree with the Will of God?
What if I don't want to do what God Wills?
Am I really free, or am I not?
What if I just want to be myself?
What if I don't want to cease to exist,
And be swallowed up by this Will of God?
You understand, I am sure.

Now hear me well.
There is no separation.
There is but One Self.
And that Self is God,
Is you,
Is me,
Is every brother,
Is all of Creation.
Resistance you might feel to losing your self,
To becoming lost in the vastness of the Will of God,
Those fears are but your ego.
They are based on that tiny, insignificant
Collection of thoughts you have about who you are,
And on which you would base the belief
That somehow you are different from God.
And indeed, you are not.

I will speak with you now of God's Will.
But as I speak, have no concern
For the questions I just mentioned.
They are of no consequence.
Indeed, they do not exist.
At the level of your Real Self, they do not exist.

God's Will is not a plan.
God's Will is not a script with billions of players assigned roles,
Which they must live out,
Somehow in accordance with God's design.
God's Will is not a master guide which must be referenced
Before you would take any action,

In order to make sure that the action
Will be in harmony with that guide.
GOD'S WILL IS FREEDOM.
AND THAT IS ALL.

In creation, God expanded Itself.
God expanded awareness.
But the expansion did not cause a breaking off,
A separation from . . .
You see, on this earth,
When you think of giving birth to a child,
You think of two SEPARATE beings
Making INDIVIDUAL contributions
In such a way that this blending of two separate wills
Spins itself, randomly you believe,
Into a form different from, and separate from, your own.
This new life then enters your world
And becomes another being, separate from, and isolated from,
Even the original two.
So when you think of God giving birth, in the form of creation,
Your natural thought is to think of separation.
But it is not so.

Creation is actually beyond your comprehension.
For you to understand, within your thinking,
The true Oneness of All That Is,
Is not possible.
Your true perception of Oneness SHALL come,
But for an instant so brief
That it shall be gone as you are swept away into knowledge.
And THEN you shall understand.
But for now, creation was the expansion of God Itself,
(Himself, Herself, One Self)—
Creation was God's expansion in such a form, without form,
That there could be, and indeed is,
An infinite number of facets to Creation itself,
None of which is the least bit separate from any of the others.
And that is God's Will.

God's will is the creation of All That Is,
And the infinity of ways
In which All That Is can be experienced.
It is God's Will that, in the entire infinity of ways,
Not one is, or can ever be, apart from any of the others.

In a body, as you see yourself, and therefore limited,
It seems to you that if you were given assignments,
Things to do, or to be, by a multitude of sources,
It would not be possible to do them all simultaneously.
In fact, the physical limitations you have imagined
Make this truly impossible.

Contained within the Will of God there are NO limitations.
There is nothing to suggest that you cannot imagine
This little life of yours, played out in your belief in separation.
There is nothing to suggest that you cannot,
AT THE SAME TIME, imagine playing out a different lifetime.
There is nothing to limit any number of lifetimes
You might wish to imagine, and to live out,
ALL AT THE SAME TIME.
And there is nothing to limit any number of lifetimes
Which you might choose to imagine and live out
ALL AT DIFFERENT TIMES.

There is nothing to limit you
From imagining yourself physical in the sense of a body,
Or physical in the sense of an animal,
Or an insect, or a rock,
Or a cloud, or the wind.
There is nothing in God's Creation
To limit you from BEING the wind,
The clouds, the rock, an animal,
A person, two persons,
Thousands of persons,
All at the same time,
All at different times,
All in the same place,
All at different places,
OR ANY COMBINATION THEREOF.
There is nothing to limit you at all.

THERE IS NOTHING IN GOD'S CREATION
TO LIMIT YOU AT ALL.
Your reality is Spirit. You exist in Spirit. You are Spirit.
You experience as Spirit does.
You create as Spirit does.
There is nothing to limit you
From any experience Spirit can imagine,

While at the same time
You might be imagining those different roles of separation
I have just mentioned.
You, Spirit, Son of God, One Self,
Part of God Itself,
Have no limitations.
You could do any, or all, of that,
In any given instant.

Now, hear me well.
YOU ARE DOING JUST THAT.
There is no separation.
Every lifetime you might have imagined,
Past, this tiny present one, future,
Lifetime as animal,
Lifetime as inanimate,
Existence as Spirit,
Sojourns between lifetimes as semi-restricted spirits—
All of them, in fact,
You are doing, have done, will do.
It is all the same.
For there are NO limitations in the world of Spirit.

That is how it is that I say,
You are One.
And that is how it is that
People who speak of your Oneness say that
You are the robber;
You are the person clinging to his possessions
In fear of being robbed;
You are the prisoner; you are the gatekeeper;
You are the lover, male and female;
You are the child, product of that love;
You are the unwanted child of that love,
Aborted before a lifetime begins;
You are the old man, the old woman,
Looking back and smiling at a lifetime, enjoying memories;
You are the sunrise, the sunset,
Yesterday, and tomorrow.
All of it is nothing but You,
But the reality of what You are remains—
Spirit, creative, unlimited Spirit,
One with God.

So we speak of learning this Course, which is beyond learning—
And of moving to a point at which your will is God's Will.
Now, perhaps, you can, in your thinking,
Get a glimmer of understanding of what I have meant.
But perhaps more,
If you let your thoughts be still for a moment,
You will FEEL, at a quiet point within,
The awareness that truly you ARE your brother.

As I have said, injury is impossible. (56)
There is nothing you could do to your brother.
For it is only your Self.
There is nothing any brother can do to harm you.
For he would only harm his Self.
And that cannot be,
For there is only Spirit.
And how can thought harm thought,
Upon thought?

As you look upon events in your life,
And have trouble imagining that they are God's Will,
Realize that all of Life, as you see it,
Is one vast harmony
In which You, in your unlimited Oneness,
Are playing out these hundreds, and thousands,
Millions, and billions, indeed, trillions upon trillions
Of seemingly separate existences,
All which are, indeed, not separate at all.

So I suggest to you, this.
If you look at your body, or a circumstance in your life,
And find it to be undesirable,
Try to begin by realizing, first within your thoughts,
And then at the level of feelings,
That it is absolutely your choice,
And therefore it IS desirable.
Open to that which you desire, and celebrate it—
For only then can it bring you joy.

If that does not seem to work for you,
Look at the circumstance which you find undesirable, and say:
"I am Spirit. In reality, this that I see is thought,
Projected upon an imaginary world.

It is not myself, rather an expression of my creativeness,
Of my unlimited creativeness.
And as I seem to be imagining something undesirable,
I yet, this very instant,
Am knowing something which is desirable;
And I am yet, this very instant,
Knowing an infinite number of other experiences
Over the entire range, in between and beyond."

Thirdly, do not try to sit and figure this out.
Do not try to sit and reason it out with your thoughts.
Do not try to understand in such a way
That you could lecture your fellow men, and have them know.
For, in your thinking, you cannot know.
And further, you cannot tell another.

Merely hear the words I speak
About what you are, and the Will of God,
And allow them to BE.
Allow your mind to be as still as you can make it,
And let them be.
For in the stillness, of your own choosing,
Shall come an awareness, beyond words,
And you shall, indeed, SEE.
And that seeing shall be the Vision of Christ.

When that Vision becomes yours,
'Tis, of course, the same for all of Creation.
Even though it seems to come in pieces, at different times,
To all these imagined different beings,
That is not so.
All of it has come, and gone, shall be, and yet it is.
It matters not, although it be true,
That there is an appointed time
In which all shall move to true perception,
And past to knowledge.
All of that will come.
For, in fact, it already has.
And yet it will.

So I speak of God's Will.
God's Will is that you know, within yourself, your freedom,
Your co-creatorness with God,

And as far as you can comprehend,
For you to know the absolute unlimitedness of what you are.
For you are so free,
And so unlimited,
That, truly,
You cannot comprehend.

Blessings upon you all. That is all.

LAST JUDGMENT

Greetings again. I am Jeshua. I have come this day
To further, with you, my discussion of
A Course in Miracles.

Today I would speak to you of the end of time.
The end of time is something you may wish
To call by other names.
You may refer to it, if you wish,
As the Second Coming of Christ.
You may refer to it, if you wish, as the Last Judgment of God.
But, truly, it is nothing more than the end of time.

I have told you in previous discussions
That time is really the product of your judgment.
For you make a decision about what you would see,
About what is, about what should be,
All the while valuing,
And believing that the decision you make
Somehow determines what you are.

The decisions, the thoughts about what you are,
And what should be,
Always are based on the past.
Always they are based on what you believe to be
The things that have already happened,
Which have brought you to this point,
And which can now affect what will happen in the future.

And what is that but the belief in time?
So your own judgment is the creator of time itself.
Your own judgment, as you decide for yourself
What it is you would experience, and the form it must take—
That judgment creates your time,
Creates your values,
And therefore creates your belief in what you are.

But I tell you, once again,
The beliefs about what you are,

Which are based upon your thoughts, upon your judgments,
Upon your belief in time and the past—
Of those beliefs,
None of them are true.
You are not a creature of time.
You are not a creature of limitation,
As I told you last time.
Each moment is new and free and clear,
And has attached to it nothing whatsoever,
Except the freedom that you HAVE, and ARE,
As the child of God.

So it is that your judgments,
Moment upon moment, upon hour, upon year, upon lifetime,
Create all of this, and its time.
They create it, albeit in your imagination.
Nevertheless, create it they do.
But it is not real.

Do not forget that your judgment is born out of
Your creative power as the Son of God.
And it SEEMS as real as if God Himself had made it,
Illusion though it be.

So I would speak to you today of the end of time.
How is it that the end of time will come?
The end of time is the end of your judgments,
And your valuing.
When I speak of the Second Coming of Christ,
What I speak of is the awareness within your Self,
And within all beings who are One with you,
Of what you truly ARE as the Son of God.
This, hear me well, SHALL occur in your time.
Over this you have no choice.

You are the Son of God.
You are Spirit.
You are free.
God has made you thus,
And no power in all of Creation, including your own,
Can change that.
It MUST BE that the awareness shall come.
Hear the words of time.
The awareness SHALL COME

When you realize that you are, indeed,
Free, Spirit, the Son of God.
And that realization is it—the Second Coming of Christ.

The Christ, the real nature of what you are,
Has always been, is independent of time,
Cannot be changed,
And shall remain long after your time has passed away.
So to say the ''Second Coming of Christ'' is redundant.
For the Second Coming Is.
And the First Coming Is.
And they are the same.
For there is no separation.

The Second Coming of Christ,
Of which I have spoken in *A Course in Miracles*,
Is a phrase I use to address your thoughts and your imaginings.
Do not think it something real.
It is no more real than the sin and guilt
Which shall pass away into nothingness,
Along with this world and its bodies, its shadow, and its pain.

That inevitable awareness of Truth
Is what I call the Second Coming of Christ.
The Second Coming, then,
Is just the moment in which you realize,
Deep within your being, beyond your thoughts,
Beyond the analyzing, beyond the struggle and the thinking—
It is just the moment in which you realize,
''Ah, 'tis true. I AM the Son of God.
I AM Spirit. And I AM free.''
In the instant when that occurs,
Deep within your being, as experience—
In that instant,
Time shall end for you.

But indeed, you ARE One with all of Life, and all of Creation.
And if time ends for you,
Then it likewise ends for your brothers.
They will be free, if they wish, to imagine for a bit longer,
That time has not ended for them.
For that is their freedom.
But when time ends for you,
It likewise ends for them.

Hear me well.
Thus it is that you, in your Oneness,
Are the Saviour of the World.

The Second Coming SHALL COME.
Nothing can stave off its arrival.
However, you are the Son of God,
Albeit the Son who has chosen this earth and its illusion.
And I urge YOU to hasten its coming.
It seems perhaps a contradiction,
But it is not.
Whenever you feel a sense of contradiction,
You may rest assured that always, you are believing in time.
And remember, time is the grand illusion, and does not exist.

So it is that the Second Coming does not exist,
Is not necessary, and yet will come.
So it is also that I urge you
To open your being to the Voice for God,
That in your so doing you shall be able to HEAR.
For as you truly HEAR, your judgment shall pass away.
As you listen deep within, there will come the knowing
Of what to do, what to say, where to go, and to whom to speak.
All the details you will know.
In that knowing there will be a certainty and a quietness.
You will then find that judgment is no longer a thing of import.
And you will let it go.

So I urge you, within your illusion of time,
To be diligent, to be vigilant,
To pursue the release of your values and your judgment,
In order that you yourself may be free,
In order that you may become the Saviour of the world.
Within the illusion of time, that is totally appropriate,
Albeit that the illusion of time truly has no effect on anything.

If you wish, you may refer to the end of time
As the Last Judgment.
For I have told you, as you cease to judge,
Which means, as you cease to decide FOR YOURSELF
That which you shall experience,
All the while believing yourself to be separate—
As you cease to decide, and judge,
And therefore to value,

Time shall pass away.
And your NEED to decide shall pass away with it.

The Last Judgment is NOT the judgment of God.
Truly, there will never come a time
Of what you have often felt would be accountability.
For the judgment of God upon you
Was created initially, is now, and shall remain, this—
YOU ARE FREE.
That is all.
God's judgment upon you is His Love.
His Love is without limit.
His Love is the gift of total freedom,
And shall never change.
Total freedom cannot contain within it,
In any sense,
Punishment, accountability,
Or even the slightest reprimand.

All of this, all this world,
Its sin and its guilt,
Its pain and its imagined murder,
Its death and sickness,
Is but illusion.
And never shall God, or any aspect of the universe,
Chastise you, in any sense,
For creating and experiencing this illusion.

In the absence of time,
All of this came and went in but an instant—
A chuckle and the awareness of freedom.
And that is all.

So it is that God shall never come to judge what you are.
For what you ARE never changes.
And God shall never come to judge
What you SHOULD HAVE BEEN.
For moment upon moment upon forever,
There is no such thing as "what should have been."
And in the absence of "what should have been,"
There can never be accountability, or sin.
Therefore, guilt, as it were, cannot exist,
Except in your imagination.

The Last Judgment, therefore, is a judgment YOU shall make.
As I have said to you,
YOUR judgment is the creator of your time,
The creator of your values,
The creator of your belief in what you are,
And therefore the creator of all the limitations
You seem to experience here in this world.
The Last Judgment is yours TO make.
And the Last Judgment you SHALL make.
And when you make it,
And FEEL it,
When you know it within your being—
When you make that Last Judgment,
Time shall end for you and for your brothers.

This must be the Last Judgment you shall make,
And the Last Judgment the entire world shall receive.
And this it is—
You shall stand as the Son of God,
Upon the throne of the universe.
You shall look within, with certainty, and peace,
And yes, laughter.
You shall feel, welling up out of your being,
An openness, a lightness without limit,
Which cannot be contained.
And you shall, indeed, judge for the last time.
This you shall say,
And KNOW as you say it—
This shall be your Last Judgment, as you say,
TRULY I AM FREE. PRAISE BE TO GOD.

Blessings upon you all. That is all.

CREATION

Greetings again. I am Jeshua. I have come this day
To further, with you, my discussion of
A Course in Miracles.

These days you may be working with the subheading entitled
"What is Creation?" (57)
I would speak to you today of Creation.
Creation, really, is just thoughts.
However, Creation is the thoughts of God.
The thoughts of God are beyond personality,
Beyond time and space.
The thoughts of God are unlimited, unbound, unrestricted.
The thoughts of God apply universally and equally
To everyone and everything in Creation itself.

None of God's thoughts select any aspect of His Creation
And give it preference, in any way at all.
None of God's thoughts give preference
Of any kind, to any being.

God, the Creator, merely contemplated, thought,
AND IT WAS SO.
God, the Creator, merely thought,
And EXISTENCE, including you and me, became a reality.
Thoughts do not leave their source.
God's thoughts exist, unchanging, inviolable, beyond time,
Or, in your words, forever and ever.

God's thoughts include you and me, all brothers,
All Spirits, all of Creation.
Creation IS All That Is.
There is nothing to oppose,
Nothing to conflict with anything of Creation.
God Itself is All That Is.
There is no duality within God.
There is no conflict within God.
There is nothing TO oppose, or which CAN oppose,
The thought of God.

So it is that Creation cannot be changed.
Creation merely IS.

If God had thought of restriction, or limitation,
Or anything to bind that which He created,
Then thus it would be, forever and ever, beyond time.
But I tell you now,
That is not so.
God, in Creation, thought of the extension,
The expansion, of Himself.
He thought of it LIKE Himself,
Not to be less than, but to be One with, Himself.

So God created you, all of you.
God created me, and all other beings,
LIKE UNTO HIMSELF.
The Bible says, "God created man in His own image."
That, indeed, is what it meant.
You are the Creation of God, and therefore are like God.

However, you cannot change the thoughts of God.
God is the Creator, the Father.
And you and I, all of us, are the creations, THE Son of God,
One Son, One Spirit,
Not male or female,
But ONE Son, Spirit.
And the CREATION cannot alter the CREATOR.

However, there is no need at all
To WANT to change the Creator.
For when God thought of us
And created Life itself, like unto Himself,
He created it, you and me, all of the Oneness,
Absolutely free, unlimited, unbound, unrestricted,
JUST LIKE HIMSELF.
That is God. That is All That Is.
And that you cannot change.

You cannot change the fact that you are free.
You cannot change the fact that you harbor within your being
The creative power of God.
You cannot change the fact
That you are absolutely unlimited, and unbound,
Just as is God Itself.

If you should now choose to call that lack of freedom,
Then so be it.
But to be totally free can hardly be considered
The absence of freedom,
Even in your minds.

I speak often in the Text, in the Workbook,
Of creation, which is of God,
And which is in contrast to things which are MADE,
Which are of you, and of the ego.
Things which are of creation are KNOWN,
And can only be KNOWN.
Things that are of the ego are MADE,
And therefore are PERCEIVED.

This world, its bodies, the brain,
The thoughts which seem to come from that brain,
All of it is illusion—
Because all of it is what you have made,
Out of your Self.

The rub come here.
As you have made it,
So indeed, you have thought of it.
And your thoughts have the same creative power
As do the thoughts of God.
However, in your thoughts,
You have imagined yourself separate, which you cannot be.
You have imagined yourself limited, which is not possible.
You have imagined yourself restricted, which likewise, is not so.
And whenever your thoughts would imagine anything
Which is the opposite of God's thoughts,
Then the thoughts of yours cannot be real.

Thus we say, "Nothing unreal exists." (20)
This world does not exist.
The illusion does not exist.
Your body does not exist.
Your thoughts do not exist,
For they are incompatible with the thoughts of God.
But you HAVE made them,
And given them value with your thinking.

Within your thinking, within your imagined separation,
For each of you, the experience of your thoughts will vary

From one to another to another to another.
Thus it is that perception is of this world,
And knowledge is of the Kingdom of God.

A fundamental aspect of the nature of God
Is open communication.
Nothing is hidden.
Nothing lies apart from, outside of, or unavailable to,
Any other aspect, or part, of Creation—
Nothing whatsoever.
God Himself is totally open,
And created you in the same manner.
If you would imagine privacy of thought or experience,
It cannot be of God, and cannot be real.
For such would demand that it is not of creation.

Can you participate in creation, here?
Indeed, you can.
That is your salvation.
That is the purpose of this Course.
When you participate, with God, in creation,
What is it you do?
YOU THINK THOUGHTS YOU SHARE WITH GOD.
When your thoughts are One with what God created,
And imagine nothing opposite to God Itself,
Nothing opposite to the Will of God,
Then you are participating in creation.

What are some of the ways you can do that,
To bring it a little more "down to earth," if you will?
As you think thoughts with God,
There can be no private thoughts,
Or any desire for privacy of your thoughts.
That is the purpose of the Holy Instant.
As I said in the Text,
The Holy Instant is a time of perfect, open communication,
To give and receive. (58)
There are no thoughts you would keep hidden
From any other aspect of Creation.
But without a past,
Why is there any reason to harbor
Any thought you would have?
Without the future, or consequence of your thoughts,
Why, again, would there be any reason

To sequester from another
That which you would think?

So if you would participate in creation,
Be diligent within yourself.
Be diligent and be willing to allow all your thoughts
To be open to all of the universe.
Then you will be participating in creation.
If there is ONE OTHER BEING you would select out,
Whom you would want not to know your thoughts,
Then you are dealing in separation,
And the ego, and perception,
And fear, and values,
And death.
And that is so.
It may sound harsh.
But it is your own creation you have made.
Hear me well, that you have MADE.

So be diligent with your thinking,
That you be willing for it to be open to all beings,
With none to be selected out.
God extends and shares Himself equally with all of Creation.
And as you do the same,
You participate in creation.

That is one way to think about special relationships.
It is true, in your physical life,
That you spend more time with certain beings than others.
If you are physical, it must be so.
But when you extend love, which must come from within,
Be willing for the CONTENT of what you think
To be shared with all of your brothers.
For then, none of them are special.
And you are sharing in creation.

I did say CONTENT.
The reality of your thought is the content, not the form.
So be diligent in your awareness of
The content of your thoughts.
Be not selective—
But share openly and equally with all brothers.
You will then be thinking thoughts of God,
And participating in creation.

Blessings will then fall upon all of Creation, including yourself.
And it shall bring you joy.

In the Holy Instant there is no past, and no future.
When you would bestow the past upon a brother,
You limit him.
And in that limiting, you will always find reason to be selective,
To exclude part of what you would give to that brother.
In the Holy Instant, there is no past.
For the past is the creator of judgment.
And judgment is the selector of specialness.
Without a past, and without your judgment,
All brothers are equal.
And you will know that within your Self.

God, in His Creation, knows you NOW.
Those words contain it all.
What you would do to share with God,
Is to know each brother NOW.
You do that when there are no barriers to communication,
When there is total openness.

As you allow the Holy Spirit, the guide created by God,
To participate in, and to direct, your thinking and your acting,
That thinking shall be open.
It shall affect you as if it were knowledge.
As long as you live on this earth, it shall be true perception.
For knowledge is not possible
While you remain in physical form.
But, be not dismayed.
True perception is quite close enough.

When I say, know your brother,
I mean, perceive him truly.
That you shall do in openness, without judgment,
With no thoughts you would keep from him,
And none you would not receive from him.
The Holy Spirit shall guide the perception of both of you.
Your relationship shall be called Holy.
And you shall know one another.

I said, know your brother NOW.
NOW simply refers to this instant, the Holy Instant.
It is, indeed, a time of perfect communication,

Because it is a time when you see your brother
Without the past, without judgment,
Without anything on which to base judgment.

And in the NOW, you allow your brother total freedom.
For nothing of this moment will affect the future.
The future just falls,
Moment upon moment upon moment upon forever.
Each moment that seems to follow another is free of its past,
And the moment that preceded it.

God created you.
God knows you.
There are no secrets you have kept, or can keep, from God,
And none God has kept, or would ever keep, from you.
God knows you NOW, in freedom,
Without a past, without guilt, without sin,
Without blemishes of any kind.
God sees you in light, as the Spirit that you are.

For you to be part of creation, all that is required
Is for you to see each brother the same way that God sees you.
And as you see your brother,
With openness to give and receive,
Free of his past,
So shall you be free of your own past.
So shall you be free to give and to receive openly.
And those blessings you shall bring upon yourself.

It is your choice.
The Holy Spirit will never leave you.
Bring your willingness, your vigilance, and your diligence,
To the Holy Spirit.
You will then see each brother openly,
And allow him freedom.
And those same blessings, again, shall be yours.
And when once they become yours,
They shall never depart.
For time shall have come to an end.
And you shall be the Saviour of your Self,
And the Saviour of the world.

Blessings upon you all. That is all.

THE EGO

Greetings again. I am Jeshua. I have come this day
To further, with you, my discussion of
A Course in Miracles.

The daily lessons in your Workbook may at this time
Be under a subtitle which is
"What is the Ego?" (59)
I wish to comment about that today.
The Text, the Workbook, over and over again,
Speak of the ego almost as an enemy.
The ego seems to be a thing with existence of its own,
Whose desire is to keep you separate from the Kingdom of God.
The ego almost seems to be a thing over which
You would have no control.
Yet I speak as if, in an instant,
You can let go of all that the ego is,
And be free.

So what really is this ego of which I speak?
Ego, as I am sure you are aware, means "I."
And what does "I" mean?
"I," in definition, means separate identity.
So whenever you use the word "I,"
You are choosing separation.
Especially are you choosing separation
When you IDENTIFY with the word "I."

I use the word "I" for the purpose of communication.
But I assure you, I have long since gone
Beyond the need to believe that I am separate.
For, indeed, you and I are One.
You and I and all brothers are One.
All brothers and God are One.

It is difficult, indeed, in this world of illusion,
To imagine what Oneness can mean.
Oneness simply means this—
You are not separate.

You are not alone.
You are not isolated.
You DO not, rather CAN NOT, act and think
In a small vacuum chamber that belongs to you alone,
And which you call your life.
Rather, Life is One.

Or, if you wish, Life merely IS.
And all things are contained fully and equally within it.
So on this earth, when you say the word "I,"
Which you do dozens, perhaps hundreds, of times in a day,
You are always referring to a separate, isolated being,
Who is alone, and apart from all other brothers.
And this little, weak, frightened, isolated being is,
In the sense of the ego,
What you believe you are.

In a word, salvation is the release from that belief.
For I tell you now, as I have told you often before,
That belief that you are separate, isolated, alone,
Is false.
Not only is it false,
But truth and reality demand
That you can NEVER do, or be, anything
Which shall cause you to BE isolated, or alone.
You are not, and cannot be, separate.

I started by saying that the ego is idolatry. (60)
The ego, this "I" which you imagine,
Which you literally put upon an altar
Within the context of this illusion you call your own life—
This ego is what you worship.
For it seems to be that IT is what gives you life.
And without it, it seems, you would not exist.

This altar upon which you imagine your self to be
Is an illusion in itself.
Your life on this earth, which you feel is what you really are,
Which you feel needs preservation and defense—
All of it is the product of your imagining
That you can be separate.

The true idol you worship, which is your ego,
Is your belief that to be separate, to be alone,

Is somehow desirable.
That belief is what has caused
This entire illusion you call your world.
If you could know, within yourself, at the level of experience,
The joy, the fullness and the beauty
That comes from the Oneness we share,
Then, in an instant, in the twinkling of an eye,
Your life would be totally changed.
And you would never court this illusion of isolation again.

The grand illusion that it is desirable to be an ''I''
Is the source of all your problems.
So let us look at that one more time, perhaps in a different light.
If it is desirable to be alone,
What is it you really desire?
Ah, 'tis the desire, is it not, to feel
That ''you,'' this isolated being,
Are the creator, the controller of your own life.
'Tis the desire, is it not, to feel
That nothing can intrude upon this little shell you call yourself.

What havoc arises from that belief,
Especially as you apply it to this physical world.
For as soon as you imagine yourself separate,
You imagine separate thoughts, separate feelings
Which no one else can touch.
Indeed, you even know that to be true.
On this earth, you know that you are free to think,
To imagine anything you wish.

But beyond that, you spend your life in fear.
For you no longer imagine yourself free,
Except insofar as you can THINK whatever you wish.
You imagine this body, illusion though it be,
To be a victim of circumstance—
Weather, injury, illness, death,
Other beings who can harm you.
You imagine yourself subject to
The absence of such things as
Money, nutrition, clothing, and shelter.
You believe if you do not have those
In adequate, acceptable amount,
That you shall somehow be changed, against your own will.

So while you know that you can THINK whatever you like,
You believe that everything else in your life
Is not under your control.
And indeed, in the illusion of your life here
As a separate, isolated being,
It is not.

Sometimes, as you begin to realize the truth of this Course,
You reach a point which can easily be confusing.
For you have accepted the notion that everything is an idea,
That everything IS a product of your thoughts,
And your thinking.
Then you come to realize that the circumstances in your life,
In whatever form they appear, are of your own choosing.
And even though you often find that belief frustrating,
You begin to feel a sense of freedom.
You begin to feel that somehow
You ARE in control of your own life—
Because you can say to yourself,
"Yes, indeed, this circumstance is a product of my thoughts,
And my thinking."

As I have said, you do know
That you can think anything you wish,
And that no one, no thing, can confine your thoughts.
However, do not be deceived.
For the state of which I have just spoken,
And which seems desirable,
Can carry with it a very subtle delusion
Which has its base in separation.
For as you feel yourself to be in control of your thoughts,
And feel that your external life IS a product of your thoughts,
You can so easily end up believing that somehow
YOU, your ego, can choose the external life you wish.
And that attitude is still based on the belief
That you are separate from other beings.

You imagine that somehow you can choose not to be sick,
Even though an OTHER might expose you to an illness.
You imagine that you can choose whether or not to die,
Even though an OTHER might attack you with intent to kill.
I am sure it is clear.
This is still the belief in separation.

And still, in that belief, you cherish the altar upon which
You put your self, this ego, this belief in what you are.

Do not discredit yourself.
Do not blame yourself if you happen to be,
At this time, passing through that state.
For it is one of the many you choose
As you grow in your learning.

But what really of the ego?
The ego, as I have said,
Is the collection of thoughts you have about who you are.
That is what you place upon the altar you call your existence.
And should anything threaten those beliefs,
Or suggest that you relinquish them,
You believe you shall, at least in part, die.

Nothing can be further from the truth.
You cannot die.
You can wish and imagine that you will die.
But it has no effect on what you are.

The ego does not exist.
You are not an ego.
Hear me well.
You are not a mere collection of thoughts about what you are.
Thoughts are perceptions, subject to change, subject to whim,
As easy to toss about as a small ship
In the wind upon the ocean.
Hardly is that befitting of the Son of God, which you truly are.

You, the Son of God,
Are beyond your thoughts about what you are.
As you let go of those thoughts of what you are,
You become truly free,
Free to spread your wings and fly through time and space,
Into eternity, to joy, and peace, and love.

As you think about what you are, you create your time.
For your thoughts, as we have said,
Are always reactions to experiences
You think you have had in the past.
Your thoughts about who you are define the past,

And therefore time.
And time, the greatest limiter of what you are,
Is the grandest illusion of them all.

As you let go of the thoughts about what you are,
You let go of the ego.
And since the thoughts of what you are are not real,
As they pass away, so does the ego.
As simply as that, it is gone.

How does it pass away?
You can free yourself of the ego, which DEFINES your time,
By letting go of your time.
Simply take the steps in reverse, if you will.
As you let go of your time, and let go of the past,
You realize that this instant is all there is of time.
And, indeed, with this instant being all there is,
There is no time.

So long as you walk this earth,
You shall carry with you memory.
Memory shall allow you to function
In this playground you have created.
However, as you free yourself of time,
You enter the Holy Instant.
And there you realize full well that there is nothing,
Nothing at all, in what you perceive as the past
That has any bearing on what you ARE in this instant.
That, indeed, is the EXPERIENCE of the Holy Instant,
And your freedom from the ego.

You may carry memory for your use to walk this earth,
For your use in communication.
But do not delude yourself.
Each instant you create is absolutely free of any other.
No thought, of or from the past,
Has any effect on what this instant contains for you.

And since this instant is totally free
Of whatever you might have imagined in your past,
There is no consequence you can bring to this moment.
For such consequence does not exist.
And in the absence of consequence, what of guilt?

It is gone.
In reality, not only is it gone,
It never existed.

So the ego is your collection of thoughts about what you are.
But, more so, it is your belief that in some measure
The past is a determiner of what you are.
Indeed, if the past determines this moment,
And this moment determines the future,
Then you are trapped.
But rejoice.
For the past does NOT determine this moment;
And this moment does NOT determine the future.
You are FREE.
And because you are free, the ego does not exist.

The ego is the trap that would bind you to the past,
That would allow judgment,
That would allow you to imprison others with your judgment,
And therefore be imprisoned yourself as the jailer,
Which you become when you make judgment itself.

So to review briefly—
You are not what you think.
What you think is of the past.
But you are not of the past.
You are of this moment.
The past you can remember.
But never think for one instant
That the past determines what you are.

In the realization that the past does not determine what you are,
You are automatically totally free of guilt of any kind.
Then the future simply shines in front of you,
As moment evolves into moment, into moment,
Each one free,
Each one a blessing of experience
Which you can celebrate, and live,
In peace and joy,
Without conflict.

And THAT is what you are as the Son of God—
Not an ego, not something imprisoned by thought and time

And the imaginings that go with them,
But a being, free as the wind,
Co-creator with God,
Made to celebrate life, instant upon instant,
Independent of time and space,
Knowing nothing but freedom,
And awareness,
And peace,
And joy.
All of this is yours. For that is what you are.

And all you have to give up,
All you have to sacrifice to SEE the Son of God,
Is the belief that you are separate,
And with it, the belief that the past
Has any effect on what you are.

Blessings upon you all. That is all.

MIRACLES I

Greetings again. I am Jeshua. I have come this day
To further, with you, my discussion of
A Course in Miracles.

I entitled it all *A Course in Miracles.*
We have spoken of many things thus far,
But not yet have I spoken to you directly of miracles.
The section in your Workbook may now be entitled
"What is a Miracle?" (61)
So I would speak to you, now, seemingly at long last,
Of miracles.

Miracles, in Heaven, do not exist.
Miracles are a thing of this world.
Miracles do not exist in Heaven
Because they are totally unnecessary.
In Heaven, there is only freedom.
Everything is One.
All beings totally give love, without need,
And receive love in joy, without need to do so.
In Heaven there is total acceptance,
And the perfect absence of fear.

The only thing that makes a miracle necessary at all
Is your fear.
And fortunately for all of us, fear is not real.
Fear is a creation of this world, its separation, its time,
Its space, and its isolated bodies—
All of it is founded upon, has its structure in,
And ultimately is composed of,
Fear itself.

So, in a word,
A miracle is what you experience in the absence of fear.
Sounds simple, does it not?
However, fear is the building block of this entire world.
Fear is the building block of all the structure you see
In space and time.

Fear is the building block of your body.
Fear is the building block of your brain,
And the thoughts it seems to think.
And if, for one instant, you could merely let go of all of that,
What you would experience the world would not understand.
And the world would say,
"It's a miracle."

Miracles are what I have been speaking of
Ever since the beginning of this Course and these tapes.
I have spoken to you over and over again,
Of love, and its freedom,
The absence of guilt, the absence of sin,
And the absence of separation.
I have spoken to you of the beauty
You will discover in all of existence
When you no longer experience those things
Which are, ultimately, only fear.
Now I say to you, that is a miracle.
And that is all.

It is absolutely certain, whether you know it or not,
Or believe it or not,
That every single thing, to the last detail in your life,
Is created by you, desired by you, valued by you,
Clearly, chosen by you.
And in your freedom, when you CHOOSE to let go of fear,
Your life will truly seem to be turned upside down.
And the world will call it a miracle.

What really happens, then,
When the world perceives a miracle?
What happens is that for one Holy Instant,
And one instant is all it takes—
What happens is that for one instant you EXPERIENCE,
Throughout your being, in every aspect of your thinking,
In every hidden corner of your mind,
WHOLENESS.
This means you experience the absence of the past.
This means that, for that instant,
You stand clear and shining and pure as the Son of God,
Without sin, without guilt.
It means that for one instant you SEE yourself as Spirit,
Spirit only, freer than the wind.

And in that instant, when you truly perceive what you are,
Anything you imagine shall seem to be.
Its form shall literally appear in this world, before your eyes,
And before the eyes of others.
And the world will again say, "A miracle."

In that moment in which you truly perceive your Self,
It MUST BE, hear me well,
With no exception,
That you see all your brothers in exactly the same light.
And, truly, Light it is.
For you are beings of Light, not darkness.
As you see yourself with true perception,
You shall see ALL brothers with true perception.

In that moment, the moment of the miracle,
You will simply be AWARE,
More fully aware than you have ever been,
More fully aware than you can even now imagine.
You shall be aware of the Oneness that links you and me,
Each brother, all beings, all of Creation, and God,
Into one harmonious whole.

In that moment,
You will not be able to sit, isolated,
And to think, to decide, at the level of your brain,
What it is you wish to have happen.
Hear me well.
If you think (hear the word "think")
You shall be able to evolve, or grow to, or reach a state
In which you can imagine yourself still isolated,
And yet decide what miracles you would have—
If you imagine thusly,
You will fail.
For miracles cannot happen in that context.

I said, when I walked this earth,
"It is not I who do these works,
But the Father working through me."
And that IS the way it was.
The Father is the awareness, without fear, of God Itself,
Of the Holy Spirit, and of the Oneness we share.
And in the moment of the miracle,

You merely know what to do, what to say,
What to be, and what to feel.
Hear me well, again.
You do not decide, out of your thinking,
To perform a miracle.
For it will not happen.

Miracles arise out of letting go of your fear,
Out of releasing all the blocks
Which are really just the fear in disguise.

Do not be dismayed by my comments.
It may be difficult for you to comprehend.
You do not lose your existence
When you move to the state without fear.
Though you cannot comprehend it now,
There exists individuality and choice within creation.
But with these words,
Which are based on brains and thoughts and bodies,
Truly, I cannot explain how that shall be.
Be content, if you will, to hear the words.
And do not be dismayed.

Your surrender to Oneness with God and all of Life,
Your surrender to the absence of fear,
Is the end result that shall release you
From all that binds you to this earth.
When those bonds are released,
You will be free to walk this earth in certainty,
And in true perception.
And it shall seem that miracles, indeed, follow you.

In that one instant, and that is all it takes,
In which you are totally free of fear,
You shall be transformed, and never again be the same.
Your brothers will not be able
Not to sense that there is a truth about you.
And that truth, understood or not,
Will echo through their beings as well as your own.
You shall be, in that instant, an example to all the world.
You shall see the world differently.
And for you, the world shall BE different.
That is the manner in which you are the Saviour of the world.

Therefore, your only goal
Is to accept the atonement for yourself.
Of that we have spoken before.

We shall speak further of miracles.
But for now, hear me well.
Miracles exist in this world.
A miracle arises out of the instant
In which you simply let go of your fears.
And you let go of your fears when, with certainty,
You experience the realization that you are safe,
Totally safe, and completely free.
You are totally safe because nothing whatsoever in this world
Can effect, or change, the truth of what you are.

Miracles arise out of an instant in which you realize
That time only SEEMS to be
That which determines what you are.
It brings to you what you call the past.
But the past is not what you are,
And has not made you what you are.
In the instant when you perceive that truth,
You shall stand fresh, and clean, and alive.
Welling up within your being shall come the realization
That you are indeed safe,
And that you are indeed free.

The world shall see the glow around your being,
The light in your eyes,
And the peace that permeates all that you are.
And the world will say,
"It's a miracle."
And indeed, a miracle it will be.
For you, at last, shall be free.

Blessings upon you all. That is all.

MIRACLES II

Greetings again. I am Jeshua. I have come this day
To further, with you, my discussion of
A Course in Miracles.

We are close to the end of this year
Which you and I have devoted to God,
To our Oneness, and to peace.
I spoke to you last time, at last, of miracles.
And I said, really, the miracles are already there.
Miracles are the natural part of your life,
Except for the blocks you carry
Which keep the miracles from expressing themselves.

We started off this year by talking about your thinking,
And how it was that thinking was reaction,
That thinking was of the past,
That thinking, thoughts, and definition,
Were the things that seemed to create,
And lend reality to this world.
But really, it is illusion.
The world is not so.

Now I would speak to you again about your thinking,
But within the context of miracles.
The greatest block you have
To the expression of miracles in your life
Is, indeed, your thinking.
Miracles merely flow from deep within you.
Miracles are your heritage and your inheritance
As the Son of God.
Miracles are based on Oneness, and true perception.
They are based on the fact that there is no difference
Between you and your brothers,
Between you and any aspect of your world.
And indeed, your thoughts are the blocks
Which keep miracles separate from you.
Your thoughts are the building blocks of separation itself.
And the separation itself
Is the building block of this entire world.

So once again I would tell you,
And ask that you hear me well—
Miracles are within you.
Miracles will take place,
Here in your time and your space,
Here in your relationships,
As long as you can and will
LET THEM BE.
The miracles will stem from the Oneness that is all of us,
And is God.
They will stem from you,
As you exist in your aspect of that same Oneness.

Initially, miracles will seem to present themselves
As nothing more than a whisper.
You will get a small feeling within,
A feeling that would lend itself to an action, or a word.
And to the extent that you follow that feeling,
And that awareness,
You open yourself to a miracle.

The great block, so common in this world, and in your thinking,
Is that immediately after you have become aware
Of the whisper, as I call it,
You begin to think and to analyze—
What if I do what my being is suggesting?
What if I say those words?
What of the future?
Will there be consequences?
Will it affect my relationship?
Will it affect my job?
Will it affect WHO I AM?
And when once you begin
That process of thinking and analyzing,
And trying to decide FOR YOURSELF,
Whether the thought or action
That is trying to escape from deep within
Will change your life, or who you are, as you perceive it—
As soon as you begin all of that,
You have blocked the miracle.

We have spoken before of the Voice for God.
Indeed, the small urging from within,
This whisper, BEFORE you begin to think about it,

Is truly part of the Voice for God.
So, if you would avail yourself of miracles,
This is the place for you to start, and end.
Do your best, with vigilance,
To be AWARE,
Not of your thinking,
Not of your analyzing,
Not of your fears,
Not of your doubts,
But of the quiet, peaceful urgings that come from within.
And when you become aware,
Follow them.

In the sense of your learning,
It is quite all right to start with the very slightest urgings,
And to follow them.
When you do, you will see the slightest miracles.
And you will realize,
Indeed, IT WORKS!
And that, in the sense of your learning,
Shall give you the courage to listen to the urgings
Which might seem to carry
Slightly greater consequence in your life.
And as you follow those,
You shall become aware of a peace, and a joy,
And slightly greater miracles in your life,
And in the lives of all beings.

So you shall grow, and grow, and grow.
The ultimate miracle shall be when you go past the courage,
Past the imagined doubts about
What might happen if you act or speak—
The true miracles shall come
When you free yourself of this world enough
To follow the urgings from within,
Without regard for consequence.

When you arrive at that point,
Miracles shall precede you every step of your life.
You shall be safe. You shall be free.
For nothing of this world can touch you
While you remain free of this world.
As you follow the quiet voice within,
Without trying to bring it to this world

Via your thinking and analyzing—
As you follow that voice within,
You shall be free of this world.

Then truly, you shall know what to do,
What to say, where to go, and what to be.
There shall be no doubts.
And you shall see, as you look back at your footsteps,
The trail of miracles you have left behind.

Really then, this is the summation of *A Course in Miracles*—
Miracles are what you are.
They are your heritage and your inheritance as the Son of God.
The only thing that blocks you
From knowing and experiencing the miracles
Is that which binds you to this earth.
And that which binds you is, indeed,
Your thinking and analyzing,
Therefore your fears,
And your concept of who you are.

As you let them go, truly it shall BE a miracle.
And you shall be free.
It would seem difficult to do this in an instant.
For most of you, steeped as you are in your belief in time,
That is so.
So for those of you who feel as if time
Is something more than an illusion,
Begin to follow miracles
By being STILL.

When you are still, you are in a state
Where your mind is not chattering
With the noise of your thinking.
When the chattering is still, and your mind is still,
Then the whispers from within, the Voice for God,
Can be heard,
Indeed, can be FELT.
Very often it will not seem to be as words,
But rather an awareness.

So the second step you would take
To follow this *Course in Miracles*
Is to make every attempt you can to be still within your mind.
The whisper, the Voice for God, is always there.

In your stillness of thought you shall hear it.
And as you, in your time,
Learn more and more
To be still,
The Voice shall become louder and louder.
And it shall become more and more clear to you
What to do, what to say,
What to be, and where to go.

You are, indeed, free to let go of your belief in time,
And have the full clarity of the Voice for God
Be upon you in an instant.
Do not forget that.
Do not chastise yourself for believing in time.
But never lose sight of the realization
That in an instant, any instant you choose,
You could be totally free.
Even in your time, as you continually remind yourself of that,
Even though it be in words,
There may come to you the instant in which, suddenly,
You find yourself free.
You will know.
And you will never be the same.

There is one other thing which shall assist you immensely
In following the course, or pathway, to miracles.
And that relates to your time.
For time, as I have said, is the grandest illusion,
The greatest bond you have to this earth.
So as you, in your consciousness,
Attempt to listen, apart from the words,
To the whispers within—
As you attempt to be still,
To allow your thinking to cease,
You can further your ability to listen and to hear
If you choose to let go of the past,
If you choose to let go of your time.

Do what you can to approach every instant
As if it were all that existed of time.
Approach every instant, insofar as you can,
With the realization that you are in that instant
By your own choice,
With total freedom—
That nothing, imagined or otherwise,

Has brought you to this point.
For that can not be so.

You may wish to simply try
To keep saying that to yourself in words.
Then a time may come when you shall realize it,
And experience it within your being.

The pathway to miracles, the "Course" in miracles,
Is to be found deep within.
It is to be found by hearing the Voice for God,
Which really is just your own voice.
For you are One.
You shall hear that Voice when your mind is still,
When it does not think, and analyze, and interpret.
You may help yourself immensely
To free yourself of your thinking and analyzing
By attempting to realize that the past is not so.
There is only this instant.
You are HERE, in your freedom and your choice,
As is every other brother in Creation.

Hear me well, once again.
Miracles belong to you.
God presses miracles upon you.
God never ceases the urging that wells up within your being,
The urging that requests you to avail yourself
Of peace, and joy, and freedom.
God never ceases to urge you from within,
To let go of all your fears,
And doubts,
And uncertainties,
And miseries.
All of them shall pass away
At such time as your thinking passes away.

When that happens,
In your freedom and your peace,
You shall say, once again,
"It's a miracle."
In that moment, you shall know your Self.
And you shall know yourself to be free.

Blessings upon you all. That is all.

WHAT AM I?

Greetings again. I am Jeshua. I have come this day
To further, with you, my discussion of
A Course in Miracles.

We are drawing nigh to the end of this year
You have devoted to God, and ultimately to your Self.
Realize this shall not be an ending, but a beginning.
For what you are does not have a beginning, or an ending.
For you simply ARE.

The question in the Workbook
Which you may be addressing currently is
"What am I"? (62)
Ultimately, this is the question that has been addressed,
In many different ways, in many different forms,
Throughout this year,
Throughout the Workbook, throughout the Text.
For when once you fully realize, within your being,
What you ARE,
This Course will slip away,
And not be necessary.

Realize full well that this *Course in Miracles*,
This pathway I have described to you,
And tried to help you experience,
Is only a tool of transition.
Do not feel that what we have done here,
And what I have shared with you,
Is an end.
For there is no end.
Do not feel that this Course is an end in itself.
For nothing ever ends in itself.
Do not feel that having finished this Course,
You are finished.
For that would alter what you are.

So I would speak with you this day
Of possible answers to the question, "What am I?"
Hear me well.

You are not what you seem.
This I have been saying to you in many forms,
These many weeks.
This earth, this world, does not accurately
Tell you of what you are.
That which you see with your eyes,
Hear with your ears, and touch with your senses,
Is not a representation of YOU.
That which you perceive based on those senses
Does not tell you of what you are.

You hold an opinion, a concept of what you are.
When that concept is based on this world,
Its thoughts, its senses, its experiences,
It is incorrect.
Not only are you incorrect when you do that,
But you are looking at the opposite of the truth.
For truly, this world, as imagined by you,
In your desire to experience your freedom,
Is an upside-down mirror of your reality.
And looking in an upside-down mirror,
You cannot see at all clearly
What you are.

The world, then, when perceived truly,
Leads you to accurate glimpses of your real nature,
But really not much more than that.
Do not depend upon this world to learn what you are.

This world seems bent on answering the questions,
"What am I?" or "Who am I?"
What results from the process of answering those questions
Is your self-concept,
Your pattern of beliefs that tells you what you are.
And as you, in your time,
Have begun to believe that
Those thoughts, those concepts, are true,
So have you equated them with yourself.
And thus the thought of separation has arisen.

Everything you would do in order to form, to maintain,
And of all horrors, to DEFEND your concept of what you are—
All that serves merely to separate you from your Self,
From your brother, and from God.

Ultimately, you and your brother and God are the same.
For all of us are One.

So indeed, a major illusion of this world
Is your concept of who you are.
And once formed, it seems to you
That if that concept meets with change,
YOU, at least in part, must die.
Thus you cling to these few meaningless thoughts
About who you are,
As if to defend them with your very life.

If only you knew how absurd such behavior was—
You would laugh, take your little concept of yourself,
Toss it over your shoulder without one backward glance,
And walk away into your freedom.

What are you?
You are One.
You are One with each and every brother.
You are One with me.
You are One with God Itself.
There is nothing, and can be nothing, whatsoever,
That is outside of you, that IS NOT you.
Everything which you imagine, and which you experience,
Is ultimately your Self.
You ARE that which you experience.
To the last tiny detail of every experience,
You ARE that experience.

And all of Creation participates, with willingness,
In your desire to experience whatever it is you choose.
That is your freedom, that is your blessing,
As co-creator with God.
All that you would experience is, in fact, but your Self.

When you harbor a concept of what you are,
Then you have a concept of
WHO is experiencing your experience.
That separates you from the experience itself.
And such separation is not real.

What are you?
You are Spirit.

You might, in the sense of this world, say that you are energy,
Energy such as life is comprised of,
Energy which knows no bounds, either of time or space—
Energy which cannot be separated from itself,
Which is the sum total of all the energy of the universe.

You are Spirit.
You are part of everything that is.
You cannot not fully and wholly blend into all of Life.
Even when you imagine, as in this world,
That there is separation,
Truly there is not.
'Tis just the image you see in your upside-down mirror
That allows you to think that you might be separate.
But you are not.

You are Spirit. You are One. And you are Free.
Of your freedom I have spoken these many weeks.
You are free in an absolute sense,
Beyond what you can imagine with your thoughts,
Beyond the powers of imagination
You carry with you here in this world.
You are so free that we can only express it
By saying that every tiniest, last detail of your life
Is the product of your own choice, your own desire,
And IS, in fact, your Self.

But your freedom is of a magnitude far greater than even that.
It is of a magnitude greater than you can comprehend.
Be content to celebrate the realization that, in your freedom,
There exist NO LIMITS OF ANY KIND.
If you are able to imagine
Any limitation whatsoever, of any form,
You are incorrect.
THERE ARE NO EXCEPTIONS TO THAT FACT.
For you to even imagine the slightest limitation about your Self,
About your brother, about God Itself—
To imagine any such limitation does nothing
But create a wall, a barrier, a block,
That separates you from your awareness of what you are
As the Child of God.

You are Spirit. You are One. You are absolutely free.
There is nothing apart from You,

Outside of You, or separate from You.
Ultimately, then, YOU ARE GOD.
True, God is Creator.
And we are, as the Son of God, the creations.
But in creation, God extended Itself fully to us.
So, indeed, you ARE God.
And as God, you are free to do and to be whatever you wish,
EXCEPT to change God,
Or to change, therefore, what you are.

As God, you are creator, co-creator of All That Is.
Truly, hear me well.
It is you, your creative power, given you by God,
That has created this world,
Its time, its space, its vastness,
This earth, its Solar System and its Sun,
This galaxy, the multitude of galaxies,
The seeming infinity of space itself,
The complexity of your bodily illusion,
The interworkings of the ecology of your entire world—
All of this have you created.
Hear me well.
For this is true.

If you think for a moment about that truth,
You will know there is no conceivable way
That your mind and its thoughts could have created such.
The fact that you HAVE created this entire world
Is a measure of how unlimited you are in your creative powers.
You have created this entire universe.
And it took, on your behalf,
Essentially NO EFFORT WHATSOEVER.
This world is but the slightest measure
Of your creative power as the Son of God.

What are you?
You are a being exercising your freedom.
You have come here to walk this earth, in a game,
A game in which you imagine yourself separate,
Futile as the attempts may be.
You have come to walk this earth in a game
Where the props speak of fear,
And pain, and death, and misery,

And isolation.
None of them are true.

For, in your true nature as the Son of God,
Were they to be true for you,
THEY WOULD ALSO BE TRUE FOR GOD.
But you do not have the power to create fear within God Itself,
Or to create the death of God,
Or to cause God to be, in any sense,
Separate from His creations.

The purpose of this entire Course has been to remind you,
To show you a path you could follow
Which would guide you to freedom from your illusion,
Which would guide you to release from the choices you made,
Which would guide you to the release
From this game you play with such seriousness.
And when once you realize that truly,
It is a game,
It is a dream,
It is illusion,
It is not real,
It is not you, and cannot change what you are—
When once you realize that,
Beyond your thoughts,
And especially beyond the concept of who you are,
Then your concept of who you are shall pass away.
And you shall be free.

When your concept of who you are passes away,
You shall know of your Oneness as Spirit.
You shall know of your freedom.
And in that moment, in that Holy Instant,
You shall be filled with the full awareness of Life Itself.
You will not be able to measure it with your thinking.
You will not be able to describe it with your words.
You will not be able, accurately, to teach another what it is.
You will only be able to experience it for yourself.
But in that moment, all your brothers will know as you know.
For you are One.

In that instant, without effort,
Without struggle, without thought,

You will simply be aware of that which you desire.
And whatever it is you desire,
You shall BECOME.
And all of Creation shall celebrate that BEING with you.

You are Spirit.
You are One.
You are God.
And you are absolutely free,
Beyond any measure of your imagination.

Blessings upon you all. That is all.

FINALE

Greetings again. I am Jeshua. I have come this day
To further, with you, my discussion of
A Course in Miracles.

This past year you have chosen to devote to your Self.
This past year you have chosen to devote to God.
And whether you know it or not,
This past year you have chosen to devote to me,
And to each brother who walks this life with you.
And, hear me well, all of those are the same.
This past year you have chosen to devote
To the awareness of truth,
The truth within you that ALL IS ONE.

I have spoken to you of many things.
This day is not to review.
This day is for love, for peace, for hope, and for courage.
Henceforth, you shall move out into your world,
Through your life, as a different being.
It is not possible for you to spend one year
With this *Course in Miracles*,
With your Self, with me, and with your God,
And yet be unchanged.

You are not different from your reality.
For that does not change.
You are the Son of God, and shall remain so,
Independent of your imaginings, your illusions,
Your space, and your time.
But as a personality, as an individual human being,
You cannot be the same again,
When once you have given this year to all of us.

We have spoken this year of many things.
Behind it all is the simple goal of creation—
Peace, absolute peace,
Joy, absolute joy,

And simple, unbridled happiness.
That is God's Will for you, and for all of Creation.
That is my will for you.
That is your own will for yourself, and all your brothers.
Even if you imagine it otherwise,
It remains so.

The peace of God does not know doubt,
Does not know hesitation,
Does not know uncertainty,
Does not know fear.
Truly, the peace of God goes beyond understanding.
It is not something we can speak of in words.
It is something you experience within your being.
When that experience comes, it comes not only as your own,
But as that of each brother as well.
So be assured that as you experience the peace of God,
You extend it to your brothers.

Do not feel that you can, with your words and your thinking,
Convince another about the peace of God.
Realize that the words are but vehicles of communication,
Designed only to serve the purpose of generating experience
And awareness beyond the words themselves.
When the EXPERIENCE is there,
The words are free to pass away.
Indeed, in Heaven there are no words,
Only peace.

I have spoken to you of your thinking.
I have told you many times
Your goal is not to think,
But to go beyond your thinking,
To go beyond your analyzing and your internal debating,
To go beyond your sense, or feeling,
That you must CHOOSE what you shall do,
What you shall say, where you shall go.
For always that generates conflict.
And the peace of God is without conflict.

I have spoken to you many times of your values,
And how it is that your values
Create your belief in what you are,

Your belief in what this world is,
All of your belief in what you SHOULD do,
And therefore, your belief in choice itself.
I have told you not to value the things of this world,
For they are not a part of you.
And they do not have to do with
Your true nature as the Son of God.

Thus it is, that without your values
You do not face the dilemma of choice.
Then choice becomes nothing more than freedom.
You never have to choose between two options.
For you always have everything.
Hear me very well.
You ARE the Son of God.
God has given you Himself.
And truly, you HAVE everything.
There is nothing that is not yours,
Nothing that can be taken from you,
Nothing that can be added to you.
For you are complete.

And in your completeness, you are free.
You are so free that, truly, everything you experience
Is of your own making, and your own choice.
Rejoice to know that.
For in the awareness that everything is of your own creation
Is to be found the awareness of true freedom.

So it is I have told you
You are the Child of God, co-creator of All That Is,
Created in absolute freedom,
Always to remain absolutely free.
There is no opposite to God
Which could take away your freedom.
Above all, your imagination that you are not free
Can have no effect on the fact that you remain free, always.

Each brother is just as free as are you.
In your freedom together, you become One.
For all of your freedom, every thought, every action,
Is accepted and honored by every brother,
As being that which you desire.

Likewise, you are aware of every thought,
Every action, of every brother.
And your true nature honors and accepts
That which each brother desires.
So it is that Life is one great harmony of existence,
Grander than your mind can possibly imagine.

I have also told you that your imaginings of evil,
Of sin, and guilt, and sorrow,
And misery, and illness, and death,
Are truly but imaginings.
I have told you that in your silence,
As you let go of your thoughts,
You shall hear the Voice of God,
Which shall carry you beyond all the miseries of the world.

I have asked you to take the leap of faith.
Ultimately, the leap of faith is your advancement, your growth,
Your movement to the point at which you can say with victory,
"I do not know."
As you, with your thinking mind, say,
"I do not know,"
You open yourself to the Oneness we all share.
And then, out of the Oneness,
You SHALL know.
You shall know, without choice, and without conflict.
You shall merely LIVE your life.
You shall be blessed.
And you shall be free.

So it is that you are God, co-creator of All That Is.
You are free to do, and to be, anything that you imagine.
However, you cannot be other than what God has created.
So it is that you and your brother are One.

This world is based on the belief that beings can be separate.
The building block of this world is the fear
That comes from the belief in separation.
The separation is not so.
I have said to you, your brother is your Self.
I have said to you, everything you give is given to your Self.
Over this you have no choice.

Your brother is a pathway to your freedom, and your salvation.
For as you see your brother as your Self,
Then you allow HIM your own freedom.
You free him from your own sin.
You release him from your own guilt.
And in your awareness that he cannot die,
You find your own eternal life.
But on the other side,
When you extend anger, or your fears,
To your brother,
Truly, you bring them upon yourself.
You are God, you are free, and you ARE your brother.

I have spoken to you of the absence of time,
And the absence of space.
You are Spirit.
You are not a body.
You are not of this world.
True, you can walk this world in peace and joy,
For as long as you like, and as often as you like.
Simply never allow yourself to be trapped
By the belief that this world,
Its time and its space and its bodies, including your own,
Has anything whatsoever to do with what you are in Spirit,
As the Son of God.
The world you see holds nothing that you want.
There is nothing here to be valued,
Simply because nothing here has any effect on
What you are as the Son of God.

I have spoken to you of the absence of time, of the Holy Instant,
Which is the time in which you are totally open to receive,
And to give all that you are, to all beings, to all of Creation,
Without guilt, without sacrifice,
Without reservation, and without exception.
In the Holy Instant you know your own completion,
And your completeness.
You are free to accept any and every brother, exactly as he is,
Knowing that always you are free.

In the Holy Instant, there is no past,
And of course, then, no sin and no guilt.

There is no future,
And of course, then, no fear.

In the final lessons, I advise you to use these words
As a constant reminder to yourself—
"This Holy Instant would I give to You [God]." (L 361)
For as you allow that Holy Instant to BE,
And do not bring with you the past and its sin and guilt,
Or the future and its fear,
Then all that shall be left is the child that you are,
The child of God.
You shall live in freedom,
And in joy,
And in peace,
And in certainty.
For there shall be no doubt upon your being.

So, in your time, this year has drawn to an end.
But there are no ends, and no beginnings.
From henceforth, as you walk this earth, go in peace.
Go in the awareness that you are the Child of God.
Go in the security that you are free to be, and to experience,
Whatever you will.
Go in the awareness that your brother is your Self,
And all that is due your brother is gratitude and love.

As you go into the world, go in peace, go in freedom.
And in the Holy Instant, when you sit and are still,
Always there shall come to your mind
The awareness of what it is
That your Real Self, the Child of God,
Truly hungers for, and desires to do.
Then you may follow that path without reservation.

And I tell you this—
Never shall you go alone.
It is not possible for you to be alone.
If ever you feel alone, pause and be silent,
Letting go of the past and the future,
Dwelling, if even for a moment, in the Holy Instant.
And I shall be there.

Go then in peace,
And in love,

And in freedom,
Knowing that you shall NEVER be alone.
Truly, as I said two thousand years ago,
And which is still true today,
And which shall be true for all of your time,
''I shall not leave you comfortless.''

Blessings, blessings upon you all. That is all.

APPENDIX I

The Jeshua Tapes were received during a year in which we were doing the daily lessons of the Workbook. The Tapes appear to be designed to accompany the lessons. What I have done in this appendix is outlined a format which you may use if your choice is to use this book as an adjunct to the daily lessons.

You will note that there are only 49 chapters, while there are 52 weeks in a year. I do not have an explanation for this discrepancy. There remains, however, the fact that for four weeks of the year there will not be an accompanying chapter.

There is a close correlation to the daily lessons up to about Lesson 140. After that the correlation is not so obvious due to the emphasis on values and valuing. The chapters on valuing are of great importance, however, which would explain why Jeshua spent so much time on them. Beginning with Part II of the Workbook, the close correlation to the lessons returns, and continues throughout the book.

As always, answers are found within your own freedom. There is nothing to suggest that you "should" use this book along with the lessons. Aside from seeming somewhat repetetive in spots, the book can stand alone as a discourse on *A Course in Miracles*. You will know the way that is best for you. What follows is a suggestion only, which may assist you in using this material.

APPENDIX II
REFERENCES FROM *A COURSE IN MIRACLES*

References from *A Course in Miracles* have been done using a dual format. Many of the references are to the Daily Lesson titles, either in direct quote or in very close paraphrase. Those references are denoted with the letter L, followed by the lesson number. As an example, Daily Lesson #7, "I see only the past," would be referenced with (L 7).

Other references from the Course are accomplished using notation developed for use with the Second Edition of the Course. This will be explained using an example from both the Text and the Workbook. Using the same format, a student who owns the First Editon should be able to readily find the passage being referenced.

From the Text, the notation T-25.I. 7:7 refers to the Text, Chapter 25, Section I, Paragraph 7, Sentence 7. "What is the same cannot be different, and what is the same cannot have different parts." From the Workbook, the notation W-pI.25 2:3 refers to the Workbook, Part I, Lesson 25, Paragraph 2, Sentence 3. "This false indentification makes you incapable of understanding what anything is for."

The specific references are listed below. It has been my intent to include all the cases in which the Course is specifically mentioned, as well as other ideas which are generally understood to be primarily attributed to the Course itself. Any oversights in this endeavor are unintentional.

1	Title	13	W-pI.101. 6:7
2	T-13.V. 1:1	14	T-14.V. 1:12
3	W-pI.13. 4:7	15	W-pI.198. 1:1
4	T-25.I. 7:7	16	W-pI.78. 1:1
5	W-pI.19. 2:3	17	W-pI.79. 2:2
6	W-pI.95. 2:5	18	T-16.VI. 2:1
7	W-pI.25. 2:3	19	T-30.VI. 1:1
8	W-pI.165. 6:3	20	T-IN. 2:2–4
9	T-26.VII. 4:7	21	W-pI.93. 7:1
10	T-29.VII. 1:1	22	T-13.I. 8:1
11	W-pI.15. 2:2	23	W-pI.95. 12:1
12	W-pI.rI.57. 3:5	24	W-pI.130. 1:1-5

25 .... T-8.VIII. 7:5–6
26 .... W-pI.135. 1:4
27 .... W-pI.133. 6:1
28 .... T-1.I. 1:1
29 .... T-16.I. 3:1–2
30 .... T-24.II. 2:7
31 .... T-17.II.
32 .... W-pI.155. 1:1
33 .... T-17.III.
34 .... W-pI.161. 2:1
35 .... W-pII.IN(181–200) 3:1
36 .... T-26.VII. 8:5
37 .... W-pI.IN. 3:1
38 .... W-pII.2.
39 .... T-18.V. 2:5
40 .... T-18.VII. 5:7
41 .... T-8.IV. 6:6
42 .... T-6.IV. 2:4
43 .... T-16.V. 12:1–3
44 .... T-4.III. 1:4

45 .... W-pI.166. 2:2
46 .... W-pII.3. 1:1
47 .... W-pI.130. 4:1
48 .... W-pII.223. 2:2
49 .... W-pI.158. 1:2
50 .... T-11.I. 1:6
51 .... W-pII.6.
52 .... T-11.VIII. 9:4
53 .... T-4.IV. 2:2
54 .... W-pI.79. 1:4
55 .... W-pII.7. 1:1
56 .... W-pI.198. 1:1
57 .... W-pII.11.
58 .... T-15.IV. 6:5–6
59 .... W-pII.12.
60 .... W-pII.12. 1:1
61 .... W-pII.13.
62 .... W-pII.14.
63 .... W-pI.189.7